Cultural Critique

'99

Spring
2018

EDITORIAL STATEMENT

Cultural Critique provides a forum for creative and provocative scholarship in the theoretical humanities and humanistic social sciences. Transnational in scope and transdisciplinary in orientation, the journal strives to spark and galvanize intellectual debates as well as to attract and foster critical investigations regarding any aspect of culture as it expresses itself in words, images, and sounds, across both time and space. The journal is especially keen to support scholarship that engages the ways in which cultural production, cultural practices, and cultural forms constitute and manifest the nexus between the aesthetic, the psychic, the economic, the political, and the ethical intended in their widest senses. While informed by the diverse traditions of historical materialism as well as by the numerous critiques of such traditions from various parts of the globe, the journal welcomes contributions based on a variety of theoretical-methodological paradigms.

Cultural Critique appears four times a year. General issues, including essays, book reviews, and thematic sections, as well as entire issues devoted to special topics, are regularly published. The editors welcome the submission of freestanding essays, special issue proposals on topics of interest to the journal, as well as reviews of relevant, new, and not-so-new books.

Cultural Critique Books is the companion series of the journal. It seeks to attract work by those scholars across the humanities and social sciences who continue to draw inspiration from, and seek to contribute to, the theoretical movements and debates so long nurtured at Minnesota. Book proposals should be addressed to one of the three editors at: *Cultural Critique*, Department of Cultural Studies and Comparative Literature, 235 Nicholson Hall, 216 Pillsbury Drive S.E., University of Minnesota, Minneapolis, MN 55455-0229, U.S.A., or via email to cultcrit@umn.edu.

HISTORIOPLASTIC METAFICTION
TARANTINO, NOLAN, AND THE "RETURN TO HEGEL"

Josh Toth

But the image of Apollo must also contain that delicate line which the dream-image may not overstep if its effect is not to become pathological, so that, in the worst case, the semblance would deceive us as if it were crude reality.

—*Friedrich Nietzsche,* The Birth of Tragedy

OPENING THE WOUND OF HISTORY

Quentin Tarantino's World War II epic, *Inglourious Basterds* (2009), concludes with a striking subjective shot. The viewer is suddenly given the point of view of Nazi Colonel Hans Landa (Christoph Waltz). By this point in the film, Hitler has been shot repeatedly in the face, burned in a celluloid-fueled fire, and then absurdly obliterated (along with the bulk of the Nazi high command) in an explosion Landa helped orchestrate. Historical fact has been flagrantly effaced and a gratuitous and self-congratulatory revenge fantasy has taken its place. Yet in this final shot we are oddly and uncomfortably trapped by the camera, left to peer out helplessly through the eyes of Landa, the infamous "Jew Hunter." As we look on, the leader of the Nazi-hunting "Basterds," Aldo "The Apache" Raine (Brad Pitt), along with the last surviving Basterd—Private Smithson Utivich (B. J. Novak)—take a moment to admire the swastika Raine has just carved into Landa's forehead. Raine and Utivich gaze steadily and contentedly into the camera. The final lines of the film are Raine's: "You know somethin' Utivich? I think this just might be my masterpiece."

The self-reflexive nature of the scene is obvious, if not ostentatious. Perhaps equally obvious is the fact that this final point-of-view shot functions to implicate the audience: like Landa, we've been justifiably branded. Given our naive enjoyment of the pointless violence of the vengeful Basterds (their scalpings, their gleeful beatings, etc.), we have exposed our own Nazi-esque impulses, our own willingness to stereo-type, to refuse the possibility of complex motivations and unique situ-ations. But surely our complicity runs deeper than this? After all, it is specifically Landa with whom we are finally linked. Like Landa, we have exposed our perverse inclination to revel in and abuse the pos-sibility of rewriting history, of rewriting our very identity. Raine, we must recall, does not get the chance to "brand" Landa until Landa turns himself over to the Americans, denies his allegiance to the Nazis, and renounces the "silly" title of "Jew Hunter" as a misnomer. Raine's final act, then—his "masterpiece"—is clearly motivated by a desire to check Landa's perverse mutability, to fix the man in his truth, to anchor him to a past he can never deny. Raine explains his motivation earlier in the film, as he prepares to inflict one of his "tattoos" on a dif-ferent German soldier: "I'm gonna give you a little somethin' you can't take off." Raine assumes that, after the war, the bulk of German sol-diers will simply remove and destroy their uniforms and in turn their complicity in the horrors of Hitler's reign. Thus, at the very moment the film seems to celebrate its clever manipulation of history, Raine works to forestall the very possibility of such a manipulation.

By linking the audience to Landa, by "fixing" the audience in an overtly restricted point of view, the film undergoes a surprising dia-lectical inversion, a certain "negation of [its] negation" (Hegel 2010, 98). On the one hand, the film clearly revels in a type of perversity (in the sense that Slavoj Žižek tends to employ the term), the very perver-sity that defines Landa's villainy—the abject willingness to be what-ever the Other desires, to be whatever the audience wants to see, to be the World War II movie we wish were true. On the other hand, the film turns its ostensibly irresponsible / postmodern playfulness against both itself and its viewers, using it to stress a certain responsibility to the very thing it simultaneously identifies as utterly out of reach: the Real of any particular historical event. In this sense, the "open" wound Raine inflicts parallels (or metonymically stands in for) the film's para-doxical attitude toward mimetic closure. While Raine literally opens up a wound that (in its perpetual openness, in its anticipated persistence as scar tissue) promises to check Landa's irresponsible abuse of sym-bolic and performative mutability, the film itself opens up and exposes the inevitable antagonism between truth and appearance, historical fact and its representation. Yet the film's negation of the truth via its own abject revelry in the infinite mutability of form is itself finally negated *as a negative*, and the "screen" of its form is offered as *a form of the truth*. By inflicting a type of mimetic wound, the film exposes the irreconcilable difference between transphenomenal truth (and/as trauma) and representational play, the Real and the symbolic. At precisely the same time, the film presents this perpetual fissure, this "limit," this point of "mediation in virtue of which something and other each *both is and is not*" (Hegel 2010, 99), as the space of artistic responsibility par excellence, an always dehiscing seam that links truth and representation absolutely *even as* it precludes the ossification of truth in representation. The trauma of the open wound is presented as absolute healing—in the sense that the stitching together of form and content entails a perpetual diremption. The fluidity of the past "in-itself" can only be expressed in those forms of representation that work sincerely to apprehend it while simultaneously opening us to and forcing us to endure what is always "leftover," or in excess of a given form, what always and necessarily escapes the move toward closure.

In this sense, a film like Tarantino's *Basterds* works to overcome postmodernism's apparent fecklessness by enacting a dialectical inversion that is markedly akin to the paradoxical inversions highlighted in the recent "return to Hegel" (Žižek 1989, 7). As contemporary theorists like Žižek and Catherine Malabou have demonstrated, a careful consideration of these inversions frustrates the long tradition of reading Hegelian dialectics as a metaphysical and/or teleological system, as a series of movements effecting ever more perfect states of "synthesis." And indeed, this return to Hegel—which, perhaps, begins with Žižek's 1988 *Le plus sublime des hystériques: Hegel passe*[1]—significantly parallels the "passing of postmodernism," a passing that was ostensibly fomented by the fall of the Berlin Wall.[2] A return to Hegel allows us to overcome the exhausted efficacy of postmodern skepticism while providing a viable theoretical analogue for the growing cultural tendency (identified by Timotheus Vermeulen and Robin van den Akker in their increasingly influential "Notes on Metamodernism") to "*oscillate*[] between a 'modern enthusiasm and a postmodern irony'" (my emphasis). These "post-postmodern" oscillations can be understood as dialectical inversions, inversions that (as we see in a film like *Basterds*) expose and endorse the perpetual and essential "play" of a Hegelian middle term, "a vanishing mediator," or dehiscing seam.[3] In this play of differences, the antithetical relation "of a universal symbolic network" (Žižek 1993, 217) to the traumatic Real it negates is itself negated, emerging as the very condition of knowledge. Recent narrative forms that *play out* this inversion renew a vital sense of artistic responsibility. The films of Tarantino and Christopher Nolan are overt because popular examples. Typically viewed as postmodern—in that they employ distinctly metafictional and self-reflexive narrative devices while presenting us with "the dispersed, plural, constructed [characters] hailed by postmodern theory" (216)—the films of these two directors tend to sublate the ostensible function of their own formal attributes. By stressing the relationship between their formal play and the overtly perverse characters they depict, these films renew the possibility of aesthetic responsibility via the very devices that seem wholly antithetical to such responsibility. The burden of mimetic authenticity is sincerely endured even as the infinite "plasticity" of a given subject (if we follow Malabou)[4] is exposed and embraced. Rather than fixating on the primacy of the signifier, on exposing the graphic and/or symbolic production of reality, these metafictional films shift our attention to a plastic Real that is effaced *even as it affects* the form of its representation. If, then, Linda Hutcheon's playful coinage—"historio*graphic* metafiction"—best defines the dominant aesthetic form of the postmodern episteme, these films are examples of historio*plastic* metafiction (14). They return us to the burden of mimetic responsibility *by* exposing the infinite mutability of a paradoxically finite truth, the plasticity (in other words) of Hegel's "Spirit." As Hegel insists, "The *being* of Spirit cannot in any case be taken as something fixed and immovable" (1977, 204). For this reason, "[Spirit] wins its truth only when, in utter dismemberment, it finds itself" (19). The truth is most certainly lost the moment it appears ossified or finally grasped in its representation; yet the assumption that this fact gives us license "to add on . . . any old thing" (Derrida, 64) is indicative of a perverse/postmodern effort to escape "the labour of the Notion" (Hegel 1977, 43), the fact that the "evanescent itself must . . . be regarded as essential, not as something fixed, cut off from the True, and left lying who knows where outside it, any more than the True is to be regarded as something on the other side, positive and dead" (27).

FORMS OF MEMORY

Let's return to *Basterds*. Like all Tarantino films, *Basterds* is an ostensibly postmodern pastiche of various genres and cinematic allusions. It is also a film about film. A central plot line concerns Shosanna (Melanie Laurent), a Jewish woman who witnessed the slaughter of her family at the hands of Landa. As we eventually learn, Shosanna moved to Paris and began passing as a gentile cinema owner. When offered the opportunity to host the premiere of Goebbels's latest propaganda film (the fictional *Nation's Pride*), Shosanna devises a plan to burn her theater (and thus the Nazi high command, along with Hitler) to the ground. Since she fuels the fire with extremely volatile celluloid, Shosanna literally uses film to destroy the Nazis. The metafictional conceit is difficult to ignore. Are we not to take the burning celluloid as a commentary on film's innate power, on its ability to efface (or burn away) history's atrocities? Perhaps. After all, the drinking game that links the first portion of the film to its dramatic conclusion certainly functions as a type of *mise en abyme*, a metonymic reminder of the film's apparent willingness to revel in play and cinematic self-reflexivity. The game sees each character attempting to guess the identity they have been assigned by a fellow player (and which is obvious to everyone else via a card stuck to their head). At this point in the film, the Basterds are fully engaged in "Operation Kino," an operation that sees them working side by side with Bridget von Hammersmark (Diane Kruger), a famous German actress, and Lt. Archie Hicox (Michael Fassbender), a British film critic, to infiltrate Goebbels's premiere and assassinate the Nazi high command. That the Basterds get caught up in this identity game while planning the assignation—a plan that, in the end, will become absurdly confused with Shosanna's—only highlights the film's own problematic willingness to *play* at representing the very real trauma of Nazi occupation in France and elsewhere, the horrors of the holocaust, and the *actual* events of World War II.

Yet the identity game exposes rather than endorses the film's apparent desire to revel in the infinite mutability of an arbitrary symbolic universe—a universe in which any truth can be reformed (or re-screened) to suit our pleasure, where identity is solely contingent upon our efforts to guess what the Other sees. Such a scene, in fact, asks us to re-approach the precise function of the film's "cavalier revisionism"

(Walters, 19), revisionism that seems "morally akin to Holocaust denial" (Rosenbaum, quoted in Walters, 19). There is certainly no denying this revisionism, yet Tarantino rarely if ever allows us to enjoy the film's revisions as simple truth. At every turn, we are reminded of the film's largely futile *dis*honesty *even as* that dishonesty announces a certain underlying, inescapable (yet *plastic*) Real. For instance, in yet another overtly metafictional flourish, Tarantino presents Goebbels's film—an ostensibly true account of a single German sniper slaying several hundred American troops—as a disturbingly inverted image of his own. Like *Basterds*, *Nation's Pride* is clearly designed for the gruesome satisfaction of its audience; Private Fredrick Zoller (Daniel Brühl), who plays himself in Goebbels's film, gleefully shoots down soldier after soldier from the relative safety of a castle tower. And, at one point, he patriotically carves a swastika into the wooden floor of the tower. While his engraving links him obviously and problematically to Raine, his role as a sniper from above links him to Sgt. Donny Donowitz (Eli Roth) and Private First Class Omar Ulmer (Omar Doom), two Basterds who eventually find themselves standing on a balcony, shooting down gleefully at several hundred trapped Nazi moviegoers. Goebbels's film thus becomes yet another *mise en abyme*, carefully framed as a film in a theater (embedded in yet another film in a theater). As Ben Walters notes, "Only a thoughtless viewer will not see him or herself reflected in shots of Hitler cackling as he watches Americans being slaughtered in *Nation's Pride*" (22).

Responding to David Denby's scathing attack of Tarantino in *The New Yorker*, Joseph Natoli argues that *Basterds* somehow manages to overcome "our postmodern climate where reason is under suspicion and history itself collapses into a narrative told from a certain perspective." This is, of course, a surprising claim, given the historical revisions that define the film. Natoli's point, though, is that Tarantino's film approaches the Real trauma of the holocaust (and our present-day understanding of that event) by refusing to acquiesce to the illusion of moral clarity. The film, Natoli asserts, does not take "a moral stand but rather repeatedly, in scene after scene, lays bare what transpires to [*sic*] a moral review instead of immediately closing it down as if we were a culture that had a commonly shared moral sense, or, one that wasn't a front for our 'moral callousness,' our deeply divided moral views, or a moral apathy that is not limited to the Millennials."

We might clarify and extend Natoli's position by turning to Hegel's notion of the notion. As Hegel repeatedly insists, the notion of something *as notion* is to be endured; it is a "strenuous effort" (1977, 35). While "notion" in Hegel can be easily and accurately replaced with "concept,"[5] Hegel clearly distinguishes his use of notion from more traditional uses of concept. Concepts are typically viewed as mere containers or forms, tools that denote the essential by subtracting the particular from the common: "as mere forms, as distinct from the content, such concepts and their moments are taken in a determination that stamps them as finite and makes them unfit to hold the truth which is in itself infinite" (Hegel 2010, 18).[6] But Hegel insists that "what in ordinary reflection is . . . at first separated from the form cannot in fact be in itself formless, . . . that it rather possesses form in it; indeed that it receives soul and substance from the form" (18–19). For this reason, and while we tend to associate concepts with the mere "correctness of knowledge" (18), the Hegelian notion/concept entails a "strenuous effort" to resist the "rhetoric of trivial truths," or "ultimate truths to which no exception can be taken" (1977, 42). At the same time, the notion has nothing to do with "common vagueness [or] the inadequacy of ordinary common sense" (43). What is necessary, then, and what a film like *Basterds* ultimately seems intent on accomplishing, is to align the truth (of an event, of evil, of a historical trauma) with its notion *as* its appearance in form. At the same time, this form (and thus the truth it manifests) must not yield to a desire for absolutes, for the weak and illusive fixity of mimetic verisimilitude. And in those moments when *Basterds* actively reflects back its own playful revisionism *as revisionism*, when the perversity of the Nazis is conflated with the potential perversity of Tarantino's own audience, we find ourselves exposed to a certain yet plastic Real. This Real is presented to us as precisely that which is *not* being captured (finally), an essential excess that we must ponder, or endure in its infinite flexibility. The film exposes the residue affected by any narrative effort to "square the circle."[7]

It is in those moments when the film's amoral revisionism seems most overt—when, that is, it seems to revel ostentatiously in its formal play—that viewers are asked to face the traumatic ambiguities of the past. Consider, for instance, the introduction and depiction of Sergeant Rachtman (Richard Sammel) and Master Sergeant Wilhelm (Alexander

Fehling)—both Nazi soldiers. Rachtman is introduced and then beaten with a baseball bat in one of the most self-reflexive scenes of the film. The scene finds the Basterds loitering in the woods, trying to convince Rachtman to give up the position of his men. During his interrogation, Raine asks Rachtman if he's ever heard of Hugo Stiglitz (Til Schweiger). After Rachtman assures him that "everybody in the German army has heard of Hugo Stiglitz," the rest of the Basterds begin to laugh raucously and the scene cuts to Stiglitz. On cue with overpowering electric guitar chords, Stiglitz's name suddenly fills the screen (in giant, yellow-embossed letters). A brief montage concerning Stiglitz's defection from the Nazis ensues, absurdly narrated by Samuel L. Jackson. Our inclination to enjoy the fantastic excess of this scene is oddly countered by Rachtman's stoicism, his willingness to protect his men rather than escape Donowitz's baseball bat. The inevitable and explicit beating that concludes the scene withholds the very enjoyment such self-reflexivity typically prefaces. As Raine asserts, "Frankly, watchin' Donny beat Nazis to death is the closest we ever get to goin' to the movies." If this is indeed the case, then the scene we've just watched is in some way equivalent to (or even worse than) the beating Rachtman willingly endures. The scene is thus an excellent example of Tarantino's "new brutality," what Paul Gormley associates with cinematic "language [that] expresses something of the desire—seen for instance in *Reservoir Dogs* (Tarantino 1991)—to produce a Hollywood action-cinema that can provoke an affective, physical shock, rather than a habitually perceptive and ritualistic response generated by most blockbuster movies of the 1980s and 1990s" (155).[8]

Wilhelm's disruption of the perverse excess (or even "inertia") of the identity game functions in a similar manner. Wilhelm intrudes upon the game *as well as* the film's tendency to suggest that identity is solely a matter of performance. Motivated by an alcohol-induced plan to get his newborn son an autograph from Bridget von Hammersmark, Wilhelm's incursion as a sincerely doting and excited new father is the catalyst that finally breaks down the game, reducing it to a series of violent and ethically suspect acts. It is Wilhelm, after all, who first draws attention to the performative nature of Hicox's German accent. Such moments (in which the necessity of form is paired with the traumatically ambiguous notion of the Real) speak to the film's overall tendency toward ironic inversion. It quickly becomes clear that, for all their joyously excessive violence, the Basterds do little or nothing to prevent loss of life, or any other wartime horrors. Operation Kino is certainly successful, but it alters the war's real timeline by (at best) weeks; at worst, days. "The Americans," as Hitler (Martin Wuttke) notes midway through the narrative, "are on the beach." There is little in the way of moral certitude here. If anything, the film simply twists or inverts a seemingly playful revenge fantasy into a fairly overt commentary on America's treatment of others, and its tendency to ignore the ambiguous "details" of its past. This commentary becomes explicit when the Gestapo agent, Major Hellstrom (August Diehl), joins the Basterds' identity game. Hellstrom's card reads "King Kong," but Hellstrom quickly comes to the very logical conclusion that he must be "the story of the Negro in America." In a manner that clearly reflects the film's own relationship to the events of World War II, the absurdity of a film like *King Kong* is offered as one of the best (if not the *only*) means of approaching (via misrecognition) the subtle contours of a traumatic and traumatically plastic past.

In these ironic and dramatic moments of inversion, the film stresses the manner in which its own representation of the past—the past's appearance in form—negates itself as mere appearance; or rather, "appearance" becomes a "judgment [of the past] that suspends itself" (Hegel 1977, 209). The film continually presents us with the undecidable, "the sense of [an] infinite self-suspending judgment and of the Notion" (209). But this is not to suggest—in line with "postmodern *doxa*"—that "the symbolic debt [necessarily effected by the effort to represent the past] is constitutive and as such unredeemable . . . [that] . . . sense . . . [must always be viewed as] truncated, marked by a stain of non-sense" (Žižek 1993, 92). The sense we get is that reality can only be recovered via its symbolic representation, and thus (paradoxically) via its effacement. For "if we renounce fictions, reality itself dissolves" (91).[9] Consequently, any claim to trivial and/or absolute truths is just as problematic as postmodern relativism. The latter sees us perversely evading the historioplastic by fixating solely on the historiographic; the former, though, sees us yielding to the illusion of "a commonly shared moral sense," a moral sense that is never anything more than "a front for our 'moral callousness'" (Natoli).

THE DREAM OF REALITY

Like Tarantino's *Basterds*, Nolan's *Inception* (2010) struggles to negotiate these extremes. Concerned with the adventures of Dominic Cobb
(Leonardo DiCaprio), an "extractor" of the secrets hidden in dreams,
the film is largely *or wholly* set within the world of dreams. The film
is careful to stress the connection between cinematic constructions
and the artificial nature of a dreamscape. Early on, Cobb tells Ariadne
(Ellen Page)—his new dream "architect"—that a person "never really
remember[s] the beginning of a dream." He tells her this after an abrupt
elliptical cut to Cobb and Ariadne sitting at an outdoor café; how they
got there is not immediately clear, though we eventually learn they
are both dreaming. A similar cut occurs in the opening sequence. After
Cobb discovers that his dead wife—Mal (Marion Cotillard)—has once
again invaded one of his team's dream constructions, the film suddenly
and inexplicably cuts to Mal and Cobb talking in a hotel room. Like
the cut to the café scene, this cut exposes the dream as construct. Of
course, such cuts are employed throughout (as they are in most films).
Given their function in the dream sequences, though, even the most
mundane of cuts become problematic once the film begins to depict
Cobb's ostensible (waking) reality. In other words, the film constantly
highlights the connection between dreams and film by pointing toward
the sleight of hand that both necessarily employ. As Cobb goes on to
tell Ariadne, being a good architect means finding ways to make what
isn't real *seem* real—like, we are encouraged to assume, a Hollywood
set designer. Constructing dreams, like making movies, is—as Cobb
tells his father (Michael Caine)—"the chance to build cathedrals, entire
cities." All of this largely amounts to the fact that *Inception* is yet another
work struggling (*à la* postmodernism) to dedoxify our sense of certainty. Our reality, like the reality of dreams, like the reality of film (or
literature), is a manipulated and manipulatable construct, a product
of endless filters, ellipses, and misdirection; or, as Hutcheon assures
us, "We can only know the world through 'a network of socially established meaning systems, the discourses of our culture'" (7). The final
scene ostensibly solidifies this fact.

    After successfully entering the mind of a young business mogul
and planting the "idea" that he should break up his dead father's
empire, Cobb is finally allowed to return home to his children in

America. He is allowed to do so because the man who hired him to plant the idea expunges his criminal record, a record he received after being convicted for his wife's murder. However, we are led to believe (via Cobb's own dreams, which Ariadne invades) that Cobb's wife committed suicide so as to frame Cobb. After living a "lifetime" with Mal in dream "limbo"—after, that is, constructing a reality based on both "fantasy" and "memory"—Cobb found he was unable to convince Mal that what they had created was *not* real. He was thus forced to "plant" (via an act of "inception") the idea that their world was not real. Once that idea grew, Mal finally agreed to join him in a joint act of suicide, an act that finally woke them to the "real" world. The problem, as Cobb explains, is that "once an idea has taken hold in the brain, it's almost impossible to eradicate." Mal continued to believe her world was not real. Desperate to force Cobb to undergo another (truly final) suicide, Mal kills herself again in an effort to make his life unlivable. For this reason, Cobb is haunted by both Mal and his children. Like Mal, his children repeatedly appear whenever he is working in a dream. They always appear as he remembers seeing them last: his daughter in a pink dress; his son in a yellow plaid shirt. When he enters his home for the first time since fleeing America, he sees his children playing just outside his backdoor. As always, they are in pink and plaid, their backs to the camera. This time, though, they turn to face the camera, and as Cobb walks out to embrace them, he stops briefly to spin his totem—a spinning top he uses to determine if he is dreaming. If the top continues to spin indefinitely, he is dreaming; if it falls, he is in reality. Cobb spins the top, but he does not wait to see the result. However, as he walks off toward his children, the camera lingers on the top. It continues to spin, then it begins to wobble. But before it falls or *reasserts its spin* the camera cuts to black; the credits roll, and we are encouraged to reassess the entire film. What *is* real? Is it possible to make *any* claim about what is real and what we merely present to ourselves as reality?[10]

Like Tarantino, Nolan returns us to the very postmodern possibility that the past, because unknowable, is simply up for grabs, open to endless and infinite interpretation. Both films, after all, offer us a happy ending *as a dream*, an effect of a past that has been consciously rewritten. Yet, at the same time (and as both films certainly point to the possibility and even the necessity of such rewriting), they simultaneously negate these rewritings *as negations* (of the truth) by exposing the irresponsibility their possibility and/or necessity might in fact authorize. This critique becomes particularly overt if we compare Landa and Cobb. Both are perverts. This will make more sense if we return (again) to Hegel—this time, via Žižek's abjectly Lacanian lens.

THE PERVERT AND THE HEGELIAN

For Žižek, Hegel's "'absolute knowledge' denotes a subjective position that finally accepts 'contradiction' as an internal condition of every identity. In other words, Hegelian 'reconciliation' is not a 'panlogicist' sublation of all reality in the Concept but a final consent to the fact that the Concept itself is 'not-all' (to use this Lacanian term)" (1989, 6). In struggling "to accomplish a kind of 'return to Hegel'—to reactualize Hegelian dialectics by giving it a new reading on the basis of Lacanian psychonanlysis" (7), Žižek makes two ostensibly opposed moves. On the one hand, he works to expose the way in which Hegelian dialectics "opened up the field of a certain fissure subsequently 'sutured' by Marxism" (6); on the other, he struggles to circumnavigate "any kind of 'post-modernist' traps (such as the illusion that we live in a 'post-ideological' condition)" (7). Žižek's Hegel is no proto-postmodernist, *even if* his project ultimately refuses the most basic assumptions of the Western metaphysical tradition. While Hegel's "'absolute knowledge' itself is nothing but a name for the acknowledgment of a certain radical loss" (7), his implicit acceptance of a perpetually and necessarily (re)open(ing) wound (of identity, of ontological certainty) is in no way the same thing as the overtly skeptical and cynical insistence on "de-doxification" that ostensibly buttressed a postmodern and/or post-structuralist ethos.[11]

For Žižek, the delusive nature of postmodern thinking—the refusal to invest in or to recognize the complex relationship linking ideology and the ground it both effaces and defines—is inextricably linked to various forms of "perversion." The pervert only ever plays a role, plays at being who they *really are* for the Other. While the distinctly postmodern subject maintains "a proper distance toward the dispersed plurality of subject-positions," remaining identifiable (only) as a "dispersed, plural, constructed subject" (1993, 216), the pervert seems to do just the opposite: "a pervert knows perfectly what he is doing, what the Other wants from him, since he conceives of himself as an instrument-object of the Other's Will-to-Enjoy" (71). But the former is just as perverse as the latter. The postmodern subject truly fears to lose . . . doubt as such, the uncertainty, the open state where everything is still possible" (70); rather than act decisively, such a subject favors being perpetually "acted upon." Thus my abject deferment of a fixed identity is hardly different from my acquiescent performance of a self that is *wholly for* the Other. Both function as perverse forms of self-objectification. At either pole I risk nothing of myself or the truth.

It is in this specific sense that both Landa and Cobb are perverts. *Basterds* consistently plays with the theme of performance, ultimately critiquing the very extremes we might identity with performativity: those characters (like Landa) who only exist *in performance* and those characters (like Zoller) who imagine there is no difference between who they perform and who they are. During his conversation with the French farmer suspected of harboring Shosanna and her family—Perrier LaPadite (Denis Ménochet)—Landa explains that he is a great "Jew Hunter" because, unlike other Germans who think only as hawks, he is capable of thinking like a rat, and thus like a Jew. In a manner that makes him oddly comparable to the Minister in Poe's "The Purloined Letter"—a character "who dares all things, those unbecoming as well as those becoming a man," and who, with his "lynx eye" (251), is capable of mimicking (if not becoming) his prey[12]—Landa stresses his perverse willingness to become whatever the situation and/or the other expects or requires. In doing so, and if we employ Žižek's phrasing, Landa "literally 'steals the kernel of our being,' the *object small a*, the secret treasure, *agalma*, what we consider most precious in ourselves, denouncing it as a mere semblance" (Žižek 1993, 48). Or, as Tarantino puts it in his screenplay, "Landa's power and/or charm, depending on the side one's on, lies in his ability to convince you he's privy to your secrets" (66). In this sense, Landa confirms the Lacanian notion that "the position of the pervert is uncannily close to that of the analyst" (71). And indeed, while exploiting his "power/charm," while performing awkward French and then suddenly switching languages, while playing the sympathetic friend, Landa finally steals LaPadite's honor, "denouncing it as a mere semblance."

Yet the pervert's reckless efforts to reveal the symbolic *as symbolic*, to revel in the possibility of unchecked play, is not entirely the same as the analysts (or, if we can extend the comparison to Poe, Dupin's), for "the position of the masochist pervert is ultimately an attempt to elude . . . [the] uncertainty [which defines the subject], which is why it involves the loss of the status of the subject, i.e., a radical self-objectivization: the pervert *knows what he is for the Other*, since he posits himself as the object-instrument of the Other's *jouissance*" (Žižek 1993, 71). Certainly, Landa is no masochist—at least not in any conventional sense; yet his willingness to become whatever the other expects, wants, or needs—his willingness, for instance, to abandon his pride in the title Jew Hunter, to define himself as nothing other than a great detective, to rewrite his history and self again and again—suggests a profound irresponsibility, an irresponsibility inextricably tied to an abject refusal to grapple sincerely with the very ambiguity that defines his being. Or rather, Landa plays with, or manipulates, the other's fantasy as fantasy, yet (unlike the moral analyst) he does not do so to effect a positive traversal of that fantasy. He merely "confirms [or exacerbates] the subject's fantasy" (72), or exposes the absence it disguises as a negative and traumatic void at the heart of being. His perversity thus mirrors and finally exposes the film's own—its own overt and potentially self-satisfying rewriting of history, its apparent willingness to abandon the impossible Real, the past itself, the traumatic complexity of what *really happened*. This brings me back to the final point-of-view shot. This shot clearly challenges our own postmodern tendency toward perversion, a tendency that has been fostered (if not instilled) by the historio*graphic* metafiction that dominated the latter half of the twentieth century. It challenges our desire to abandon the traumatic impossibility of the Real and to give over uncritically to the comforting inertia of yet another symbolic trajectory. Yet Tarantino's film finally sublates this perversity by mirroring its own cinematic play in Landa's villainy. This inversion that moves us (subtly) from perversion to analysis—or from "the inadequacy of ordinary common sense" (Hegel 1977, 43) to the plastic *notion* of the past as plastic—is perhaps "managed" most clearly by the film's insistence on its very specific historical moment: the real and inevitable end of the war. Everything, the film certainly suggests, is a matter of perspective; reality is only ever a fiction. We "forever lack any measuring-rod which would guarantee our contact with the Thing itself" (Žižek 1993, 20). Yet this fact does not sanction some "delirious solipsism" (20). The film's fiction is exposed *as fiction* so as to renew the strenuous effort of sincerely traversing the void that dirempts fiction and Thing. This space of diremption is exposed as the very point of access, the space of an impossible truth that is lost in (or that necessarily exceeds) its translation.

"FACTS, NOT [DREAMS]"

To clarify, let's make our way back to Cobb in *Inception* via a look at Nolan's earlier film, *Memento* (2000). In many respects, and as Todd McGowan makes clear, Cobb is a more subtle reimaging of *Memento*'s central protagonist, Leonard Shelby (Guy Pearce).[13] When *Memento* opens, Shelby has just finished murdering a man. The scene is played out in reverse. We see Shelby holding a picture of the dead man, a picture that is slowly fading. The picture soon returns to the Polaroid camera Shelby holds; the man rises up as a bullet leaves his body and returns to Shelby's gun. At this point there is an abrupt cut, and we are offered black and white footage of Shelby in an anonymous hotel room; he is speaking in voiceover: "So where are you? You're in some motel room. You just—you just wake up, and you're in . . . in a motel room. There's the key. It feels like maybe it's the first time you've been there, but . . . perhaps you've been there for a week, three months. It's . . . it's kind of hard to say." The film then unfolds by cutting back and forth from black and white scenes of Shelby in the motel room—speaking, as we come to realize, on a phone to some unidentified man—and color scenes of Shelby attempting to locate the man who killed and raped his wife (Jorja Fox) and left Shelby with brain damage, capable of remembering everything up to the murder of his wife but unable to remember anything since for more than a few minutes. As we come to realize these apparent facts, or "truths," we also come to realize that the black and white scenes are moving forward in time while the color scenes are jumping backward in time—each scene returning to the point immediately before the last. With each jump back, we see Shelby beginning anew without any sense of what he was doing previously. As with the Polaroid in the first scene, Shelby's realizations and actions are immediately erased moments after they are learned or performed.

In order to combat this "condition," Shelby relies on a series of mnemonic devices: tattoos, Polaroid's, notes, etc. At the beginning of the film (which is, of course, the ostensible end), we see that Shelby has tattooed "the facts" on this body, including the *fact* that the man who killed his wife has the initials "J" and "G." But these recorded facts are almost immediately problematized; they've clearly been amended on one or more occasions. At one time Shelby thought that "J" stood for James, but (immediately before the murder that opens the film) he comes to the conclusion that he's looking for a "John." Quite quickly, we come to question Shelby's various assurances that memory is irrelevant "if you have the facts."

Thus, as with *Basterds* and *Inception*, *Memento* appears to be interested in exposing the inherent unknowability of any constant, of the impossibility of reality itself. In this sense, as critics like Rosalind Sibielski have suggested, the film positions Shelby (a former insurance investigator) as a person whose desperate need for facts and truth, for the rationalism of Enlightenment teleologies, leads to desperate acts of violence, acts of violence that provide some sense of temporary order in an otherwise chaotic and unfixable (or "postmodern") world.[14] Such readings suggest that the film is postmodern, not Shelby. In having the film unfold in reverse, Nolan forces the viewer to sympathize (at least initially) with Shelby's condition; like Shelby, we have no idea when a scene is beginning, where it is beginning, or why. Moreover, as the film progresses, the black and white portions begin to destabilize another apparent "fact." As he tells the man on the phone (as well as a number of other people throughout the film), Shelby investigated an insurance case that involved a man named Sammy Jankis (Stephen Tobolowsky). Jankis had lost his short-term memory in an accident, but Shelby managed to prove that Jankis's memory loss was psychological, not physical. As a result, Jankis was denied coverage. Pushed into thinking that her husband was simply faking, Jankis's diabetic wife tried to make him snap out of it by getting him to inject her with insulin every few minutes. Jankis, though, did not snap out of it, and his wife went into a coma.

But, Shelby insists that, unlike Jankis, he has "a system": "[He] know[s] who he [is]." However, as we move further back in time, we are led to believe that Jankis's story may very well be Shelby's, and that Shelby's wife survived the accident that caused Shelby's brain damage only to die because she could not trick her husband into remembering that he had already administered her insulin. As the film approaches its end/beginning, we are even given flashes of Shelby pinching his wife's thigh, preparing it for an injection. Of course, these flashes are as unreliable as anything else Shelby knows or remembers. As Sibielski puts it, "It is impossible for either Leonard within the film's narrative or the film's spectators examining it, to ever achieve a definitive accounting of Leonard's past" (99).

The film frustrates our desire for constants by inducing a type of cinematic "memory loss" while ambiguously conflating "Sammy" and "Lenny" (a nickname Shelby hates and which, as he tells people on various occasions, he associates with his wife). By buttressing its backward and "misleading" movement toward some "redemptive temporal and casual origin" with a "quasi-confessional" phone conversation, the film (as William G. Little suggests) negotiates both "the desire for, and impossibility of, perfect interpretive redress" (71). And while Leonard persists in repeating the various gestures of a traumatized man whose desire for "a new, redemptive story about himself . . . fail[s] to entertain the missing that structures traumatic experience" (83), we are encouraged to abandon our own desire for totalizing truth claims, or absolute mimetic recall. We are, rather, "[woken] up to the impossibility of a fully redemptive redress" (83). There is little doubt that Shelby's reliance on "facts," his instance that some absolute truth lurks in the redacted police "case file" he compulsively reads and re-reads (even though he may have wrote and/or redacted it himself), is ethically problematic. Seemingly unwilling to embrace doubt, or the "missing," Shelby perpetuates unjust and violent acts in the name of an illusory justice. As we learn in the end/beginning, the man we saw shot in the opening sequence—a cop Leonard initially knows as Teddy but whom he learns is really named John Gammell, or "J.G." (Joe Pantoliano)—is not the first man Leonard has killed. Shelby, we are finally *led to believe*, has no idea when his wife died, nor does he know how many people he's already identified and killed as "J.G." Finally, and perhaps most significantly, he *apparently* does not know that each of the pictures he's taken—pictures that seem to him to be mimetically accurate at any given moment—take on new meaning each time he forgets them. Because he is unaware of these facts, his various "friends" have been able to use him, shaping his perception of reality from one moment to the next. From this angle, the film clearly endorses the very thing Shelby futilely struggles to deny: a certain postmodern perversity, a type of unchecked textual play.

However, like *Basterds*, the film undergoes a subtle yet striking inversion, a certain negation of its largely overt negation of "redemptive redress." Most obviously, the film induces in the viewer a type of memory loss by moving backward in time while inexorably negating that memory loss. Shelby may not remember how he finds himself in various moments, but (eventually) the viewer always gains this information (to some extent). Our sense of certainty increases as the film unfolds. For instance, after Shelby hits Natalie (Carrie-Anne Moss)—a woman with whom he has become involved—she simply leaves him alone for a few minutes and then returns, claiming that she was struck by an associate of her boyfriend's, a man she'd like Shelby to "take care of." We come to know, too, and without doubt, that Leonard has killed at least two men in the name of revenge (Teddy in the beginning/end and the man Teddy convinces him to kill at the end/beginning). At least one *must* be the wrong man. As a consequence of our increasingly stable *notion* of Leonard's truth, we are eventually positioned to notice the manner in which Shelby abuses (and maybe even performs) his condition. He frequently neglects to make important notes about his current situation. After he beats and ties up the man Natalie sent him to find, he simply lies down to forget what he just did. His range of memory also expands and contracts in useful ways, and he frequently seems to remember more than he admits. Indeed, he knows that Polaroids can't be torn in two, that "you have to burn them." Since we are led to assume that Shelby (in the late 1990s) has come to employ a Polaroid camera because of his condition, this is a particularly telling "memory"—even more so if we note that we eventually see Shelby burning a Polaroid so as to set up a very specific narrative.

In the end/beginning, Shelby kills Natalie's drug-dealing boyfriend, "Jimmy Grantz," only to realize that Teddy has been getting him to kill all manner of men with the initials "J.G." Rather than making a note of this, Shelby simply burns the photographic evidence of his last kill, puts on Jimmy's clothes (which leads to his encounter with Natalie), and notes beneath his Polaroid of Teddy that Teddy cannot be trusted, thus willingly setting in motion the events we've already witnessed in reverse. By the end, then, we see (as do both Teddy and Natalie) that Shelby lies to himself "to be happy," that he is "blissfully ignorant," that he "can't get scared" because he refuses to accept the very possibility of "redemptive redress." And so the film finally counters its own postmodern perversity with a critique of Shelby's, negating (in turn) the very claim it simultaneously and necessarily endorses: "the *impossibility* of a fully redemptive redress" (Little, 83, my emphasis). Shelby refuses to endure any notion of the Real. He desperately wants to lose himself in the contingency of representation, in the decedent perversity of the postmodern condition. This is most obvious when Shelby hires a prostitute to perform and therefore help him to establish his memory (or, better, version) of what happened the night he and his wife were attacked. That he "wakes up" from this exercise in memory formation and systematically burns all of the items he associates with his wife (including, we can assume, her diabetes) only serves to highlight further his intense desire to exist outside the confines of any fixed reality. In stressing this aspect of Shelby, the film provides us with yet another certainty: regardless of the reason, Shelby blames himself for what happened to his wife. He'd rather engage in an endless series of revenge acts than endure the ambiguous trauma of what cannot possibly be changed (even if it can never be apprehended fully and finally either). The film therefore demands that we struggle to engage the truths at its core via the only point of access possible: fragmented and unreliable fiction(s). This demand is finally apparent in the film's critique of Shelby as a dangerous and reckless pervert, a man whose violence is tied directly to a fear of losing "doubt as such, the uncertainty, the open state where everything is still possible" (Žižek 1993, 70).

This brings me back to Cobb. Like Shelby, Cobb repeatedly claims to be interested in the truth, in reality. He also outwardly distrusts dreams, just as Shelby outwardly distrusts memories. As Shelby puts it, "Memory can change the shape of a room; it can change the color of a car. And memories can be distorted. They're just an interpretation, they're not a record, and they're irrelevant if you have the facts." *Inception*, though, is somewhat more ambiguous than *Memento*. We are never given concrete reasons to doubt Cobb's story or his memories; we are never given a Jankis-like alternative to his ostensibly self-induced master narrative. However, the film is littered with clues: the static clothing of Cobb's children; the fact that Cobb's "totem" is actually his wife's (and Ariadne is informed that a Totem will not work if is touched by another person); Mal's very direct suggestion that "[Cobb's] world is not real," that there is something obviously suspicious and fictional about his persecution, of a reality in which he is "chased around the globe by anonymous corporations and police forces." Ultimately, then, the final shot of a top that is continuing to spin *and* about to fall places us in a position comparable to the position in which we find ourselves at the end of *Basterds*. We are tempted to give in to the suggestion that, as Mal puts it, reality is merely something we "choose." Yet the film suggests *also* that to do so—to walk away (like Cobb) as if we don't care what is real and what is not—is to fall dangerously in line with Cobb's perverse refusal to endure the traumatic notion of his loss(es). We certainly cannot lay claim to the entirety of Cobb's real story, but we can be quite certain that his return home as a heroic and doting father (after a thrilling and self-gratifying adventure) is *nothing but* a dream. Like *Basterds* (like *Memento*), *Inception* thus effaces the possibility of the truth so as to expose the *notion* of the truth in its effacement.

THE (ROMANTIC) NOTION OF A CONCLUSION

For all of its skepticism and apocalyptic pronouncements on an emergent postmodern state and consumer-based cultural production, Horkeimer and Adorno's *Dialectic of Enlightenment* gestures surprisingly (if momentarily) to the revolutionary potential of representational art. During their discussion of style—and alongside their seemingly paradoxical condemnation of the realist imperative to "embod[y] style in its least fractured, most perfect form" (103)—Horkeimer and Adorno suggest that "the great artists . . . adopted style as a rigor to set against the chaotic expression of suffering, as a negative truth" (103). Their point is this:

> It is only in its struggle with tradition, a struggle precipitated in style, that art can find expression for suffering. The moment in the work of art by which it transcends reality cannot, indeed, be severed from style; that moment, however, does not consist in achieved harmony, in the questionable unity of form and content, inner and outer, individual and society,

but in those traits in which the discrepancy emerges, in the necessary
failure of the passionate striving for identity. (103)

This "discrepancy," this self-negating impulse to direct the observer to
its own "necessary failure," is the very *raison d'être* of style. The failure mirrors and exposes the truth (or *notion*) of a content that is perpetually severed from its form, a content that is (itself) defined by a
perpetual lack of unity, or mythic fixity. Any effort to erase style, to
"embod[y] style in its least fractured, most perfect form," will most certainly erase *by ossifying* the very truth such transparency aims to expose.
Yet a perverse (or postmodern) acquiescence to style *alone* is certainly
no better. As Horkeimer and Adorno put it, "The style of the culture
industry, which has no resistant material to overcome, is at the same
time the negation of style" (102).

This insistence on the "negative truth" style has the potential to
effect is implicitly Hegelian—and, I am suggesting, the defining feature of historio*plastic* metafiction. As Žižek insists, "the Hegelian subject—i.e., what Hegel designates as absolute, self-relating negativity—
is nothing but the very gap which separates phenomena from the Thing,
the abyss beyond phenomena conceived in its negative mode, i.e., the
purely negative gesture of limiting phenomena without providing any
positive content which would fill out the space beyond the limit" (1993,
21). What is particularly significant about this "self-relating negativity" is the fact that the Hegelian Absolute is "conceived also as subject" (21); it (too) is always only "that very 'nothing,' the purely formal
void which is left over after the substantial content has wholly 'passed
over' into its predicates-determinations . . . of its 'beings-for-other,' . . .
that very X, the empty form of a 'container,' which remains after all its
content has been 'subjectivized'" (21). In this sense, the Hegelian "negation of the negation" defines the very manner by which "our very
epistemological failure [which is, we might say, exposed in the 'discrepancy' between 'form and content, inner and outer, individual and
society'] . . . throws us into the 'thing itself,' since it registers an antagonism that pertains to the very kernel of the object itself" (242 n.19).
It is precisely for this reason that Žižek positions Hegel as "the most
consequential of Kantians" (21)—a thesis that Žižek finds already well
anticipated in Adorno.[15] Hegel resolves *by radicalizing* the ambiguity
inherent in Kant's tendency to "oscillate . . . between conceiving of [the

transcendental object] as a Thing and as something which is neither phenomenal nor noumenal" (18). At the heart of this oscillation is the implication, for Hegel, that the *Thing* emerges in the necessary failure of a sincere (or, perhaps, *notional*) effort to give it (form). It is what all "versions"—or stylistically inflected models—necessarily lack; yet, for this very reason, it is the very "transcendental object" of their unification.[16] The Thing *is*—but it *is* only insofar as it *is* a no-Thing: "what at first appeared to be an epistemological obstacle turns out to be the very index of the fact that we have 'touched the Truth,' we are in the heart of the 'Thing-in-itself' *by the very trait which appeared to bar access to it*. The implication, of course, is that this 'Thing-in-itself' is already mutilated, split, marked by a radical lack, structured around an antagonistic kernel" (Žižek 1989, 177).

And so there is good reason for critics like Vermeulen and van den Akker to return us to Kant in their efforts to define the emergent episteme. The problem is that Kant cannot take us far enough. Either this emergent period of cultural production returns us to the mere idealism of the transcendent and fixed Thing, or (at best) the necessity of "pretending" (Vermeulen and van den Akker) that such a Thing is not a delusion. The former returns us to the most mendacious tendencies of an "Enlightenment project," while the latter leaves us chasing our tails in the *cul-de-sac* of canonical postmodernism. If, then, we are to take seriously Vermeulen's and van den Akker's efforts to read in contemporary cultural production "an emergent neoromantic sensibility," we must resist associating romanticism (simply) with an aesthetic tradition effected by Kant; we must approach it as it is *reflected upon* by Hegel.

In the Introduction to his *Lectures on Fine Art*, Hegel outlines his triad of aesthetic modes, or stages: the symbolic, the classical, and the romantic. In symbolic or "primitive" forms, we are exposed to "the foreignness of the Idea to natural phenomena" (76). Unable to find its satisfactory articulation in any of the forms to which it is ascribed, "the Idea [comes to] exaggerate[] natural shapes and the phenomena of reality itself into indefiniteness and extravagance; it staggers round in them, it bubbles and ferments in them, does violence to them, distorts and stretches them unnaturally. . . . For the Idea is here still more or less indeterminate and unshapable" (76). Is it not possible to associate this symbolic failure with *both* the modern *and* the postmodern? The simple difference is that, in modernism, the impulse toward "distortion"—

toward streams of consciousness, cubism, primitivism, nonlinear story-telling, etc.—is still motivated by a desire to "elevate . . . phenomenal appearance to the Idea by the diffuseness, immensity, and splendor deployed" (76). In postmodernism, this "indefiniteness and extravagance" becomes mere parody (or pastiche), pessimistic extremes that function to hollow out the very possibility of an Idea, or subject; the Idea no longer "persists *sublime* above all this multiplicity of shapes which do not correspond with it" (77). That is, the difference is one of intent, of emphasis. The modern "distortions" must ultimately be viewed as an extension of (residual) nineteenth-century social realism—and thus, if we can "redeploy" and "reorder" Hegel's terms further yet, the "classical" claim to a wholly "adequate embodiment of the Idea in the shape peculiarly appropriate to the Idea itself in its essential nature" (77). But such "vision[s] of the completed Ideal," Hegel insists, finally undermine their own naive certainty, or finality, since "[in them] the spirit is at once determined as particular and human, not as purely absolute and eternal" (79). That this "defect" necessarily leads to "the dissolution of the classical art-form" (79) may very well explain both the continuity *and* the disparity of the modern and the postmodern. Cannot the postmodern be viewed as yet another period of dissolution, the period in which a realization of the "spirit" (or true) as "merely human and particular" begins to set in, or even to fester? What we see, then—in the move *out of* the ostensible reemergence of classicism in the nineteenth century—is a progressive reemergence of the sym bolic which is, ultimately and actually, a self-negating negation of the (neo)classical, and (in turn) a gradual "stage-setting" for contemporary (neo)romanticism. Indeed, if we *return to Hegel,* "The romantic form of art cancels again the completed unification of the Idea and its reality, and reverts, even in a higher way, to that difference and opposition of the two sides which in symbolic art remained unconquered" (79). In the romantic form, we might very well say that the Idea (as truth, as subject) is finally exposed *as* the failure to expose it; it *is* "the questionable unity of form and content, inner and outer, individual and society" (Horkeimer and Adorno, 103). Or as Hegel puts it, "The new content, thus won, is on this account not tied to sensuous presentation, as if that corresponded to it, but is freed from this immediate existence which must be set down as negative, overcome, and reflected into the spiritual unity" (1975, 80).

Leonard Shelby's haunting refrain in *Memento*—"The world doesn't just disappear when you close your eyes"—thus seems to echo a certain latent classicism, a classicism faced with the postmodern dissolution of its naive claims regarding the unity of form and content, experience and representation. The naïveté of the claim is repeatedly stressed by the "indefiniteness and extravagance" of the film's form, which reflects the historiographic metafiction of high postmodernism. It is also stressed via Shelby's overt tendency to behave as if the world does indeed "disappear when[ever] you close your eyes." Yet the film's critique of Shelby's abject solipsism (or willful abjuration of the "purely abstract and eternal")—the very same critique we see played out in *Inception* (with Cobb) and in *Basterds* (with Landa)—finally negates the negation effected by the violence of the form. We are, consequently, provided the renewed possibility of touching upon the Real, the Idea, the truth itself. But this possibility is no longer caught up in the illusion of unity, or of "style in its least fractured, most perfect form." It is instead offered via our exposure to "discrepancy," to "questionable unity," to discontinuity. In these works of historioplastic metafiction, we are thus asked to endure the *notion*—the notion that the world, that the Real, only appears in the failure to make it seen. Just as, then, Aldo Raine's knife opens up the wound of Landa's truth, these films (as popular representatives of a still emergent period of cultural production) effect their own mimetic diremptions, diremptions that renew the possibility of the "goal of [the spirit's] plasticity" (Hegel 1977, 39), the completion of which "will need the history of the world in its development through thousands of years" (Hegel 1975, 90).

Josh Toth is associate professor of English at MacEwan University. He is coeditor of *The Mourning After: Attending the Wake of Postmodernism* (2007) and author of *The Passing of Postmodernism: A Spectroanalysis of the Contemporary* (2010) and *Stranger America: A Narrative Ethics of Exclusion* (2018).

Notes

1. A translated portion of this dissertation—titled "The Most Sublime of Hysterics: Hegel with Lacan"—can be found in *Interrogating the Real*. While sketching out many of the ideas he unpacks more fully in *The Sublime Object of Ideology* and

Tarrying with the Negative, Žižek works to expose "the fundamental wager of the Hegelian strategy: 'inappropriateness as such' (in our case, that of opposing definitions) 'gives away the secret' ['*l'inappropriation comme telle fait tomber le secret*']— whatever presents itself initially as an obstacle becomes, in the dialectical turn, the very proof that we have made contact with the truth. We are thus thrust into the thing by that which appears to obscure it, that which suggests that 'the thing itself 'is hidden, constituted around some lack" (49–50).

2. While the exact date of "post-postmodernism's" inception remains undetermined, critics tend to agree that, as Christian Moraru puts it (in his introduction to *American Book Review*'s special issue on "Metamodernism"), "disputes around postmodernism's limitations and obsolescence started, significantly enough, at the end of the Cold War, probably with John Frow's 1990 landmark contribution 'What Was Postmodernism?' to Ian Adams and Helen Tiffin's collection *Past the Last Post: Theorizing Post-Colonialism and Post-Modernism*" (3). Or, as Irmtraud Huber suggests, "one may point . . . to the change in the political climate after the end of the Cold War, to the rise of fundamentalism, to 9 / 11 and its aftermath, to the technical advances and life-changing influences of globalisation, to a neo-liberal hypercapitalism gone rampant and the dissolution of economic optimism in the course of global financial crisis, to the spreading awareness of the finiteness of resources and the global challenge of climate change, and surmise that the circumstances under which postmodernism arose have seen quite radical change" (5). While the defining specifics of what comes after postmodern continue to be disputed—see, for instance, Josh Toth's *The Passing of Postmodernism*, Mary K. Holland's *Succeeding Postmodernism*, Jeffrey T. Nealon's *Post-Postmodernism*, Moraru's *Cosmodernism*, or Huber's *Literature After Postmodernism*—a common thread is the suggestion that recent cultural production is marked by a renewed interest in narrative efficacy and social responsibility, what Adam Kelly has termed (in light of David Foster Wallace's work) a "New Sincerity" (136).

3. Vermeulen and van den Akker embrace a specifically Kojèvian (or, perhaps, Marxist) reading of Hegel. For them, Hegel's distinctly "'positive' idealism [is defined by the] notion of history dialectically progressing toward some predetermined Telos." They thus overlook the Hegelian imperative to "[tarry] with the negative" (1977, 19) and employ (what they call) the "'negative' idealism" of Kant to explain the dynamic "oscillations" of "metamodernist" works (Vermeulen and van den Akker). Such works, they argue, expose us to the fact that humans are "not really going toward a natural but unknown goal, but they [must] *pretend* they do so that they progress morally as well as politically" (my emphasis). In light of such a claim, my point in stressing the salience of a specifically Hegelian dialectical model is this: if the move beyond postmodernism returns us, merely, to a communal willingness to "pretend," then the move has been more illusion than fact. Even Oedipa Maas—at the end of Pynchon's quintessentially postmodern novel, *The Crying of Lot 49*—finds herself awaiting the "crying" of lot 49, *pretending* (at least monetarily) that she'll finally get the answers she seeks. By embracing a "return to Hegel" (Žižek 1989, 7), though, we might begin to treat these recent "oscillations"

as sincere attempts to return to the "notion" of absolutes (insofar as access to any given absolute is necessarily contingent upon its effacement).

4. See Malabou's *The Future of Hegel*, in which she uncovers the vital theme of plasticity as it runs throughout Hegel's oeuvre. For Malabou, "Plasticity appears [in Hegel] as a process where the universal and the particular mutually inform one another" (11). Malabou thus suggests that the innate plasticity of the absolute (Thing) allows it to be given in (a plastic) form while implying the possibility and necessity of yet another (re)formation. I deploy Malabou's specific reading of Hegel's concept of plasticity in both "Healing Postmodern America: Plasticity and Renewal in Danielewski's *House of Leaves*" and "Toni Morrison's *Beloved* and the Rise of Historioplastic Metafiction." Like the films of Tarantino and Nolan, novels like *House of Leaves* and *Beloved* exemplify the characteristics of historioplastic metafiction.

5. Both "concept" and "notion" are viable translations of the German *Begriff*. A. V. Miller, of course, translates *Begriff* as Notion—with, almost invariably, a capital letter. George di Giovanni, however, uses concept (without a capital). For the sake of consistency, I use "notion" throughout; but I do not impose a capital outside direct quotations.

6. For this reason, suggests Hegel, "Healthy common sense instinctively felt that it had the upper hand . . . and it contemptuously relinquished acquaintance-ship with [concepts] to the domain of school logic and school metaphysics" (18).

7. I'm alluding here to Lacan's reference to "the inexhaustible quadrature of the ego's verifications" ("Mirror Stage" 4). Or, as Žižek puts it, "The Real is that X on whose account this 'squaring of the circle' ultimately is doomed to fail" (1993, 43).

8. Gormley goes on to discuss the ambiguous glow that emanates from the briefcase in *Pulp Fiction*. The "curiosity" this glow provokes "suggests the *possibility* of depth and meaning, as the viewer strains to see the object producing the golden light" (160). Thus "The imagined bottom of the briefcase suggests that, beyond the surface play of references to other images, lies a depth that is impossible for the viewer to see (which does not stop him or her from trying)" (160). We might very well relocate this glow in *Basterds* as the truth of World War II and the Holocaust, a glow that "breaks through" every time the film turns its overt play-fulness against itself.

9. Žižek's discussion in this section of *Tarrying* seems to evoke the section on "Force and the Understanding" in Hegel's *Phenomenology*. Here Hegel asserts that "the inner world, or supersensible beyond [of Things] . . . *come[s] into being* . . . *from* the world of appearance which has mediated it; in other words, appearance is its essence and, in fact, its filling" (89). Žižek's insistence on the primacy of the fictional—or the "world of appearance"—is clearly reflected in his style, his constant (and often bewildering) tendency to shift from concrete theoretical explication to abstract "examples" while constantly returning (from book to book) to the same arguments. Of course, this investment in shell over content (as outlined in Žižek's famous and ridiculous Kinder Surprise example [cf. *The Pervert's Guide to Cinema* and "On Resistance in the Digital Age"]) occasionally seems to effect *perversely* irresponsible (because unjustified) assertions—or rather, a tendency to

evade "the strenuous effort" of the notion. However, the matter of Žižek's potential perversity is a topic for another paper.

10. These are, of course, hackneyed questions. Todd McGowan—whose own Hegelian reading of Nolan's films predates and certainly anticipates my own—makes just this point. As McGowan puts it, while countering Robert Samuel's suggestion that *Inception* merely reflects and exasperates our contemporary "inability to differentiate between fantasy and reality" (147), Nolan's film ultimately "deceives the spectator . . . by making it seem that reality has a privileged status relative to fantasy or the dream" (151). In other words, the film encourages us to ask a question ("what is real?") that assumes a static reality anterior to the dream *as* fiction. But such a reality is always already contingent upon, and inseparable from, the dream. McGowan thus suggests that Cobb "wants the image and certainty of paternity more than he wants reality, though he believes that the latter will provide a vehicle for the former" (170). We might wonder, though, if Cobb is this naive. If he is, then he is (perhaps) simply and tragically caught up in the fantasy of reality *as* the law of the father; he does not choose this fantasy *as fantasy*. If, though, Cobb's are the intentional and irresponsible choices of a pervert, then the film's ethics become that much more profound.

11. Žižek, after all, is as anxious to liberate Lacan from the field of poststructuralism as he is to save Hegel from those commentators who might reject him as the ultimate idealist.

12. Of course, such a comparison might carry more weight if we recall, too, Lacan's seminar on Poe's story. Lacan explains that "the minister is . . . a monster, a man devoid of principles . . . [because] [h]e suspends the power conferred on him by the letter in indeterminacy, he gives it no symbolic meaning, all he plays on is the fact that this mirage, this reciprocal fascination is established between himself and the Queen" (187). In other words, the Minister refuses to acquiesce to a desire for symbolic closure. He merely prolongs the game for his own enjoyment.

13. In *Memento*, McGowan notes, Nolan "establishes Leonard as a character seemingly in pursuit of knowledge and then reveals that pursuit as disingenuous. The case is less clear with Cobb in *Inception*, but the procedure parallels that of *Memento*" (149).

14. As Sibielski notes, "Leonard's belief in his photographs as transparent signifying facts associates him with Enlightenment modernity's unconditional faith in the infallibility of scientific investigation and empirical research" (88). For this reason, "the ultimate failure of rationality as an ordering principle in the film results, at least in part, from the photos being subject to shifting interpretations which complicate any transparent or mimetic relationship between the photographs and their referents" (88). The film, in other words (in its very form as well as its content), stresses the futility of desiring "the facts"; only "strategies of discursive subversion" are effective (if, also, potentially dangerous) in our postmodern times (99). This tends to be the standard reading of the film—cf. Peter Thomas's "Victimage and Violence" and Christopher Williams's "'Factualizing the Tattoo.'" Unlike Sibielski or Thomas, though, Williams suggests that Nolan ultimately fails to destroy the

"concept of factuality" because he fails to realize that the problem of "unreliable information due to misinformation and deception . . . is not an ontological one in which the death of the real is at stake" (33). The problem with all such readings is that they assume the "intent" of the film is to endorse a certain acceptance of postmodern skepticism/perversity.

15. "Adorno," Žižek claims, "articulates in an exemplary way this move from Kant to Hegel apropos of the failed mediation between sociology and psychology" (1993, 242 n.19). See also Žižek's discussion of the negation of the negation in *The Sublime Object of Ideology*, 177ff. and (more recently) in *Less Than Nothing*, 477–80 (specifically).

16. For Žižek, of course, the other name for this "object" is the *objet petit a*, the object cause of desire.

Works Cited

Derrida, Jacques. 1981. "Plato's Pharmacy." *Dissemination*, 61–171. Trans. Barbara Johnson. Chicago: Chicago University Press.

Gormley, Paul. 2001. "Trashing Whiteness: *Pulp Fiction*, *Se7en*, *Strange Days*, and Articulating Affect." *Angelaki* 6, no. 1:155–71.

Hegel, G. W. F. 1975. *Aesthetics: Lectures on Fine Art*. Vol. 1. Trans. T. M. Knox. Oxford: Clarendon.

Hegel, G. W. F. 1977. *Phenomenology of Spirit*. Trans. A. V. Miller. Oxford: Oxford University Press.

Hegel, G. W. F. 2010. *The Science of Logic*. Trans. and ed. George di Giovanni. Cambridge: Cambridge University Press.

Holland, Mary K. 2013. *Succeeding Postmodernism: Language and Humanism in Contemporary American Literature*. New York: Bloomsbury.

Horkeimer, Max, and Theodor W. Adorno. 2002. *Dialectic of Enlightenment: Philosophical Fragments*. Ed. Gunzeiln Schmid Noerr. Trans. Edmund Jephcott. Stanford: Stanford University Press.

Huber, Irmtraud. 2014. *Literature after Postmodernism: Reconstructive Fantasies*. London: Palgrave.

Hutcheon, Linda. 2002. *The Politics of Postmodernism*. 2nd ed. New York: Routledge.

Inception. 2010. Dir. Christopher Nolan. Per. Leonardo DiCaprio, Ellen Page, Marion Cotillard. Warner Bros.

Inglourious Basterds. 2009. Dir. Quentin Tarantino. Perf. Brad Pitt, Cristoph Waltz, Diane Kruger. Weinstein Company.

Kelly, Adam. 2010. "David Foster Wallace and the New Sincerity in American Fiction." In *Consider David Foster Wallace: Critical Essays*. Ed. David Hering, 131–46. Los Angeles: Sideshow.

Lacan, Jacques. 1991. *The Seminar of Jacques Lacan, Book II: The Ego in Freud's Theory and in the Technique of Psychoanalysis, 1954–1955*. Ed. Jacques-Alain Miller. Trans. Sylvana Tomaselli. New York: Norton.

Lacan, Jacques. 1977. "The Mirror Stage as Formative of the Function of the *I* as Revealed in Psychoanalytic Experience." *Écrits: A Selection*, 1–7. Trans. Alan Sheridan. New York: Norton.

Little, William G. 2005. "Surviving *Memento*." *Narrative* 13, no. 1:67–83.

Malabou, Catherine. 2005. *The Future of Hegel: Plasticity. Temporality and Dialectic*. Trans. Lisbeth During. New York: Routledge.

McGowan, Todd. 2012. *The Fictional Christopher Nolan*. Austin: University of Texas Press.

Memento. 2000. Dir. Christopher Nolan. Per. Guy Pearce, Carrie-Anne Moss, Joe Pantoliano. Newmarket.

Moraru, Christian. 2011. *Cosmodernism: American Narrative, Late Globalization, and the New Cultural Imaginary*. Michigan: University of Michigan Press.

Moraru, Christian. 2013. "Introduction to Focus: Thirteen Ways of Passing Postmodernism." *American Book Review* 34, no. 4:3–4.

Natoli, Joseph. 2009. "The Deep Morals of *Inglourious Basterds*." *Senses of Cinema* 52: n.p. Web.

Nealon, Jeffrey T. 2012. *Post-Postmodernism, or, the Cultural Logic of Just-in-ime Capitalism*. Stanford: Stanford University Press.

Nietzsche, Friedrich. 1999. *The Birth of Tragedy and Other Writings*. Trans. Ronald Speirs. Ed. Raymond Geuss and Ronald Speirs. Cambridge: Cambridge University Press.

The Pervert's Guide to Ideology. 2013. Dir. Sophie Fiennes. Written by Slajov Žižek. Zeitgeist Films.

Poe, Edgar Allan. 1998. "The Purloined Letter." In *Selected Tales*. Ed. David Van Leer. Oxford: Oxford University Press.

Sibielski, Rosalind. 2004. "Postmodern Narrative or Narrative of the Postmodern? History, Identity, and the Failure of Rationality as an Ordering Principle in *Memento*." *Literature and Psychology* 49, no. 4:82–100.

Tarantino, Quentin. 2009. *Inglorious Basterds: A Screenplay*. New York: Little, Brown.

Thomas, Peter. 2004. "Victimage and Violence: *Memento* and Trauma Theory." *Screen* 44, no. 2:200–207.

Toth, Josh. 2010. *The Passing of Postmodernism: A Spectroanalysis of the Contemporary*. New York: State University of New York.

Toth, Josh. 2013. "Healing Postmodern America: Plasticity and Renewal in Danielewski's *House of Leaves*." *Critique* 54, no. 2:181–97.

Toth, Josh. 2017. "Toni Morrison's *Beloved* and the Rise of Historioplastic Metafiction." In *Metamodernism: Historicity, Affect, and Depth after Postmodernism*. Ed. Robin van den Akker, Alison Gibbons, and Timotheus Vermeulen, 41–53. London: Rowman & Littlefield International.

Vermeulen, Timotheus, and Robin van den Akker. 2010. "Notes on Metamodernism." *Journal of Aesthetics & Culture* 2: n.p. Web.

Walters, Ben. 2009. "Debating *Inglourious Basterds*." *Film Quarterly* 63, no. 2:19–22.

Williams, Christopher G. 2003. "Factualizing the Tattoo: Actualizing Personal History through Memory in Christopher Nolan's *Memento*." *Post-Script* 23, no. 1:27–36.

Žižek, Slavoj. 1989. *The Sublime Object of Ideology*. London: Verso.

Žižek, Slavoj. 1993. *Tarrying with the Negative: Kant, Hegel, and the Critique of Ideology*. Durham: Duke University Press.

Žižek, Slavoj. 2005. "The Most Sublime of Hysterics': Hegel with Lacan." In *Interrogating the Real*. Ed. Rex Butler and Scott Stephens, 48–70. New York: Continuum.

Žižek, Slavoj. 2011. "On Resistance in the Digital Age." In *Intermedialities: Philosophy, Arts, Politics*. Ed. Henk Oosterling and Ewa Plonowska Ziarek. 163–78. Lanham, Md.: Lexington.

Žižek, Slavoj. 2012 *Less Than Nothing: Hegel and the Shadow of Dialectical Materialism*. London: Verso.

AMERICAN DREAMS FT. DAVID LYNCH

Niels Niessen

> *We're like the dreamer who dreams and then lives inside the dream.*
> *But who is the dreamer?*
>
> —Twin Peaks: The Return *(created by Mark Frost*
> *and David Lynch, 2017, U.S.)*

"Hello, you're tuned into *Interview Project*. Today we're meeting Suzy. Suzy is Daniela's aunt. Enjoy the interview." Or: "Hello, you're tuned into *Interview Project*. Today we're meeting Darryl. Darryl is waiting to buy a ranch in Montana. Enjoy the interview." We're tuned into *Interview Project*, a web-based series of 121 video portraits directed by Austin Lynch and Jason S. The videos are about four minutes each and they were posted online every three days between June 2009 and

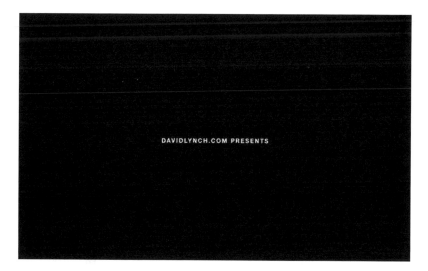

DAVIDLYNCH.COM PRESENTS

Figure 1. David Lynch presents:

Figure 2. The image scrambles while tuning in on Lynch.

Figure 3. *Welcome to Interview Project.*

May 2010. Together they document the road trip Lynch, Jason S., and their team made across a small-town United States that remains unseen by the interstate traveler. It is a portrait of a nation reminiscent of John Steinbeck (*The Grapes of Wrath*, *Travels with Charley*) as well as Walter Evans's *American Photographs* of the Great Depression, and it is in the vein of those Great-American works that *Interview Project* captures the dilapidated state of the American dream.

TUNING INTO AMERICA

Interview Project was produced by Absurda, the production company of David Lynch, Austin's father, and the project is also hosted on David Lynch's website: interviewproject.davidlynch.com. Although Lynch— David, that is—did not go along on the trip, he does introduce each of the videos, in his own Lynchian way, and above all in the *same* way each time. We press "play" and the scrambling image makes it seem like we've just powered on one of those old-school color televisions from the time color television was still a new medium. Once the image has stabilized on a close-up of his face, Lynch welcomes the viewer: "Hello, you're tuned into *Interview Project*. Today we're meeting Spira" (Figures 1–3). As always, Lynch's spirits are high. He is seated in front of a concrete wall and a yellow chest of drawers, while he's wearing a blue suit and a white, tie-less shirt that is completely buttoned up. His silver hair is combed yet messy and contrasts nicely with the wall. Cut to a medium-long, awkwardly high-angled shot that shows him sitting at a giant desk in a space that Lynch followers will recognize as his Los Angeles studio, from where for a while he also broadcast his odd daily weather reports, and which also forms the setting for the 2016 documentary *David Lynch: The Art Life* (d. Jon Nguyen, Rick Barnes, U.S./Denmark). Like so many others in this online era, Lynch has been working a lot from home lately. On his desk—messy-arranged as Lynch himself—there is an ashtray, a box of drawing utensils, a red shiny ball the size of an apple, a steaming cup of coffee (brewed, we assume, from his own signature blend), while a ray of sunlight casts all of this in a homely glow. "Spira used to dance to *The Doors* at the Whisky-a-Go-Go." Cut to the original camera position. Lynch smiles: "Enjoy the interview," upon which the intro dissolves into a disclaimer that "the views expressed in these interviews are those of the participants alone and do not necessarily reflect the views of *Interview Project* or its sponsors."

The portraits themselves are utterly sincere slices of American life. Take episode 3, which shows Kee, whom the team met in a Navajo reservation in Tuba City, Arizona (Figure 4). "Hello, my name is K, K.J., I go by K.J., but my name is Kee Jackson." Kee is framed in close-up against the backdrop of the red rocks of the Arizona desert. His mouth twitches, he seems a little nervous. A harmonica tune sets in,

Figure 4. Episode 3: Kee (Tuba City, Arizona).

a title card states Kee's name, and the now-vignetted frame offers us some *couleur locale*: a dog on a dusty road, a school bus, the city's water tower. Then Kee tells his story, which I will transcribe here with camera positions, because, as in Lynch's intros something's going on with them, even though it is hard to state in what way:

> [Long, low-angle shot of Kee, seated on the rocks] Well, I'm Virgo, and if you know anything about astrology, we are *very* wild. We are definitely naughty. [Jump cut to a close-up of Kee] Actually I grew up with a lot of friends, a lot of people that I grew up with, I was raised with. And [cut back to the long shot] because there are no jobs here in Tuba City, my parents often, you know, went out of state to provide for us, and while they did that, they put us in dormitories, which is what they call the B.I.A. [Bureau of Indian Affairs]. [Close-up] When I was in grade school, I made honors. I made great grades. I used to win spelling bees, I used to win speech contests and everything, you know, I was academically inclined in grade school. [Long shot] When I got to high school, I definitely had to deal a lot with my sexuality, where I belong, who I belong, everything, you know, just a lot of questions regarding my sexuality, and there was a time when I was depressed, because I was trying to identify who I am. [Close-up] Being raised gay, I guess, it really matters a lot when you go out there, because there is a lot of things that you're confronted with when you go out into, um, society. [Cut to a bald eagle shrieking in

the sky. The frame has been vignetted like earlier. Kee, off-screen now:] You guys are definitely seeing what God has done for me. When I was fifteen to twenty-three, I looked like a girl. [Cut to a frontal long of shot of Kee, seated silently in the vignetted frame, while we hear him in voice-over] I was wearing heels. I was, I was cross-dressing. [Close-up, sound and image still dissociated] I got to the point where you guys wouldn't've even realized that I'm a guy. You know, I was that, I was that lost. [Long shot: Kee is speaking on camera again; the frame has gone back to normal] I definitely was, and what really put me back into place was college, if, when I went back to school, that's when I learned: you can be who you wanna be without having to change yourself. [Close-up] But I'm glad that God changed me. If you guys believe in God, you'll understand what I'm talking about.

Kee's eyes light up, he smiles. Cut to the desert and a keyboard tune, and before the image fades out Kee walks back into the frame, away from the viewer, looking over his shoulder, twice, toward what must be Tuba City on the horizon.

Most interviews follow the same format as the one cited here: the interviewee introduces him- or herself, their name appears on-screen, and we hear a harmonica or piano tune of the kind so fitting for life-story portraiture that it is also somewhat cliché (and in fact some of the same tunes are heard in multiple videos). Next, with this tune as the sound bridge, we have a few vignetted mood shots: a sunset, a train, a neighborhood bar with tin ceiling and deer head, a decal "God is my co-pilot," a graffiti that reads "love," an "America" sign along the road (Figures 5–7). Many of the Americans we're introduced to are sitting in front of their houses or on their porches. Others are at their jobs, like Huey P. Long from Janesville, Wisconsin, who owns an antique store, or Kirstin from Asheville, North Carolina, who while she tells her story continues handling the dough balls spit out by a kneading machine. As in the interview with Kee, most videos at one point show the person sitting or standing silently in the vignetted frame, while their voice continues on the soundtrack, so as a voice-over now. With the interviewee speaking as if in third person, the camera just observes their mere presence, or it zooms in onto their faces, hands, and shoes, in the same intimate yet self-consciously cinematic fashion the camera at other moments gazes at the water tower, train, or decal. Through this self-reflexive cinematography, and by alternating conventional camera positions with more unusual points of view, *Interview Project* abstracts

Figures 5–7. *Interview Project* (d. Austin Lynch, Jason S., 2009–10, Absurda).

the stories from the people who live them. *Interview Project* is thus not simply the stories of 121 Americans, it also is a story of America, a *forgotten* America.

We could say, moreover, that *Interview Project* tunes into America. The act of manually tuning into a radio or television signal frequency has really disappeared from our pallet of everyday gestures. Gone is the delicate interplay between fingers and ears in order to hear what the ether has to say. Gone are the days a snowstorm made its way to our bulging screens, or one even had to climb the roof to restore reception (though soon we may talk nostalgically about spotty *wireless* fidelity during bad rainstorms). This fact that we no longer physically tune into our electronic portals as musicians tune their instrument is something to be nostalgic about. I certainly am, and so is *Interview Project*, which is an analog galore. Besides Lynch's appearance of a television announcer from the era when people still tuned into channels rather than programs, or the scrambling image at the start of each video (which in some videos returns during the actual interviews themselves, as if transmission were temporarily interrupted), there are the old media effects of the sound of a record stuck in its groove at the start of each video, the black-and-white of the interviews with Palmer Black (Blanding, Utah) and Manuel (Nashville, Tennessee), and the super-saturated 8-mm-home-video quality of the interview with T.J. from Morganton, North Carolina. In this last video the editing is also more frantic and the camera more restless, mirroring the young man's encounters with drugs: "Maybe this is just God's day, and God's night," T.J. speaks. "We get to be like souls, for like billions of years. . . . I don't understand how people can walk through their lives and not just have their minds just, completely, blown all the time, just like a baby. What do you think a baby thinks?"

To stay with the project's old media feel: in its "About" video, the sound of a reel projector accompanies a series of black-and-white samples, in which a few of the interviewed subjects repeat a question they've been asked: "How would I describe myself?" "What were my dreams as a child?" "How did I meet my wife?" "What are my plans for the future?" "What is this town like?" "How would I like to be remembered?" "When did I first experience death?" In response to this last question, Logan from Dakota, Iowa, says: "I don't know how to say this. I have died four times. . . . The fourth time was the reason why I went to the facility, because I was tired of all the pain. I was tired of all the hurt, and I ended up pouring gasoline all over my body, light myself on fire. Hour later it starts raining and I'm still standing there alive."

The questions are timeless, and they're good questions, as they allowed Angie Schmidt and Julie Pepin, who did the actual interviewing, to *tune into* and become sensitive to the stories of people whose story is not often heard in the mainstream media. In most interviews the team's perspective is edited out, by which I mean that we only hear and see the answers but not the "questions asked" (the line spoken by a sampled canned voice that the close listener is able to pick up at the start of each video). There are a few exceptions. In some videos we have a clapboard syncing sound and image, while in others we hear the interviewers' voices, as in "Can you tell us what you are doing today?" to Joyce and June while they're seated on the steps of the Methodist church in Fostoria, Ohio. Or the question is spelled out in the frame: "What do you think of America right now?" (Figure 8). Chris Swartz, from Richfield, Pennsylvania, in response to this question: "It sucks. America sucks. You know, I think we're heading into a depression. The weather is messed up. You know you got global warming going on. Makes me wonder how much the world is even going to last. . . . I used to go to church a lot, but I think this religious thing is overrated." Or Kalmar Stevenson from Anaconda, Montana: "Are you optimistic about the future?" Her response: "Well, depends on what future. This country, I don't know. Economically, I don't know, things don't look good. Look, gas just went up ten cents this week. At least here, I don't know what it's doing elsewhere. It's just terrible." But of course the questions are *always* there, if only because the participants were instructed to repeat them. "Have I lived out my dream

Figure 8. Episode 51: Chris Swartz (Richfield, Pennsylvania).

of life?," Richard from Jackson, Louisiana, asks himself. "I lived out the life that was there for me, I lived out the part of my life that I took." Or Lynn from Graham, Texas: "How would I describe myself? Broken, broken, I guess." And Jeff from Needles, California, in the very first interview: "Regrets? I have a basketful of them, but I cannot do anything about them."

Dreams and regrets is the thread that runs through *Interview Project*. Most of the persons the team met on their journey articulate modest expectations about life, such as finishing school or spending more time with their family. Some stories are little tragedies, like that of Wayne from Billings, Montana, who sees no way out of his life in a missionary shelter, or the story of Jess, who hasn't spoken to his children in twenty-five years and states to not be "proud of anything except for being alive." But there are also a few upbeat accounts, like the interview with Lauren Beach, an "earthiest" in her own words who now lives in Asheville, North Carolina, traditionally a hippie town at the

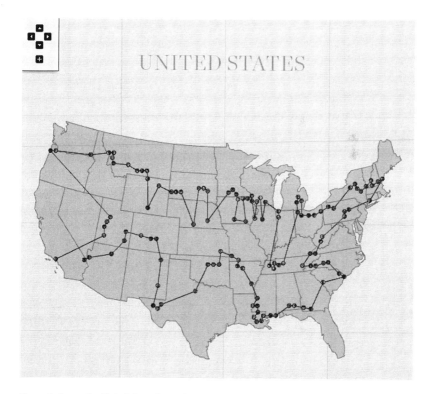

Figure 9. Across the United States bypassing interstates.

foot of the Appalachian Mountains: "I like just letting my life go. . . . I mean, living in America, and having opportunity, it's pretty nice."

In the more upbeat stories, the people interviewed often express their love for their families and children, and for God. God has been mentioned a few times now, and given the team's route (Figure 9) and the demographic of its subjects, this ubiquity of Christianity is not surprising. With exceptions including Billings, Asheville, and Nashville, all of the stops were small towns in what in terms of the U.S. political landscape we can refer to as the red parts of the nation, or now Trump country, to the extent the Republican voter base and Trump's electorate overlap. The majority of interviewees belong, moreover, to the working or lower middle classes, while like much independent cinema from the last quarter decade the project also gives face to the fact that the precarious struggle for a life story runs through traditional class divides. Moreover, like many films that can be considered part of the new realist tendency in world cinema—as far as U.S. independent cinema is concerned, one can think of *Chop Shop* (d. Ramin Bahrani, 2007), *Wendy and Lucy* (d. Kelly Reichardt, 2008), and *Rich Hill* (Tracy Droz Tragos and Andrew Droz Palermo, 2014)—*Interview Project* demonstrates a certain humanist, secular-religious outlook on people and their small worlds. This humanism is felt in the interview questions as well as in the captions that accompany the videos on the website. For example, in the caption for the video with Gordon from Moab, Utah, the team writes: "As we drove away, we all commented to each other that Gordon seemed to have found an inner peace." Or about Spira from Topanga Canyon, California: "Spira was our final interview and we think she was the perfect choice. Her spirit and beautiful outlook on life and love represents something which we hope people can take into their own lives." Directly connected to this humanist, somewhat redemptive gaze articulated by the captions, is the *instantaneous connection* to its interview subjects the team often felt. The team could *"instantly"* tell that Kee was "going to be a very special person"; they "saw Danny sitting on his porch as [they] drove past his house and *immediately* turned around to ask him for an interview"; or in the case of the seventeen-year-old Amber from Richfield, Utah, who in her interview says that she considers joining the military: "She *immediately* struck us as an interesting subject to interview" (italics in these quotations are mine).

What informed this special, immediate, and above all *human* connection the team felt so often? What informed their choice of interviewees? David Lynch's commentary on the project is not of much help here but is worth citing nonetheless. "What is *Interview Project?*" Lynch asks himself in the "About" video, while he stands against a plain black background, his shirt still fully buttoned up. I cite his answer, with a slash for each of the many cuts:

> *Interview Project* is a road trip where people have been found and interviewed. / People should watch *Interview Project*, because they're going to meet hundreds of people. / There was no plan really for *Interview Project*. / The people who were interviewed: each was different. / *Interview Project* is a 20,000 mile road trip over 70 days across and back the United States. / The team found the people driving along the roads, / going into bars, going into, you know, different locations, and there they were. / The people told their story. / It's so fascinating to look and listen to people. / What I hope people get out of *Interview Project* is a chance to meet these people. / It's, it's something that's human and you can't stay away from it.

Are the stories indeed that different from one another? Not according to Edmund Mullins, who observes a "relative sameness" of the people interviewed. "Broken dreams and missing teeth," he writes, "are the two most consistent elements that unite these individuals, making the project feel at times like a sustained exercise in poverty porn" (Mullins 2009). While I am also critical of *Interview Project*, I think Mullins is too harsh. *Interview Project* is not a freak show but a complex document of a nation in which indeed many are poor and lack access to health care. It is true, though, that the demographic of people sought out is somewhat homogenous. We mostly meet white people of fifty or above, while the project shows relatively few young people and people of color. Given the team's route, though, the project also never aimed to paint a complete, representative picture of America, or even of an *other* America, of the American 99 percent, so to speak. Whether or not we believe Lynch's claim that "there was no plan," the team stuck to less-traveled roads and smaller towns with predominantly white and older populations, while it bypassed metropolitan centers like Chicago, Baltimore, New Orleans, and thus also their large African American populations.

That inclusion would have made *Interview Project*'s chronicle of a nation even more compelling. Why, for example, didn't *Interview Project* stop by Compton, California, not that far from Lynch's home? As Dr. Dre reports on his studio album named after the city just south of LA, once Compton counted as the "black American Dream," now it's a place where crime is "as high the ghetto," while the dream that many African Americans "thought they were buying has turned sour." To stay with this African American perspective on the American dream, in *Between the World and Me* (2015), Ta-Nehisi Coates writes to his son:

> I knew that West Baltimore, where I lived; that the north side of Philadelphia, where my cousins lived; that the South Side of Chicago, where friends of my father lived, comprised a world apart. Somewhere out there beyond the firmament, past the asteroid belt, there were other worlds where children did not regularly fear for their bodies. I knew this because there was a large television resting in my living room. In the evenings I would sit before this television bearing witness to the dispatches from this other world. (Coates, 29)

Interview Project fails to incorporate this African American perspective on the American dream, as it fails to ask the question "What does it mean to be black in America today?" But like Coates, *Interview Project* also offers an outside, albeit predominantly white, outlook on an imagined other world. So how does *Interview Project* portray the America that it does? How sincere is its apparent humanism? Do we sense a tongue-in-cheek in the bright-eyed optimism of the captions? What to make of the hollowness of Lynch's "About" video? What about his smile in the intros? Is *Interview Project* playing a game with the viewer, who gets carried away by the often heartbreaking and sometimes heartwarming stories? Does the project play a game with its participants, not necessarily in the sense that it would be poking fun at them, but in that it makes them part of some ironic scheme that they've not been let into, a postmodern double layer that with stories like Kee's and T.J.'s would be nothing less than cruel? Let me be clear right away that *Interview Project* is not ironic and that its frequent invocation of a human connection actually seems heartfelt. This still leaves the question, though, of how to interpret Lynch's odd, alienating framing of the project. Lynch had no hands-on involvement in the interviews, so in that sense he's not one of *Interview Project*'s creative authors. But he's definitely the project's face. Lynch introduces each of the videos; he explains the project as a whole; and, crucially, his name is in the website's URL. In sum, Lynch's name and persona brand *Interview Project*, which I take as an invitation to consider the project in dialogue with his cinematographic oeuvre.

THE AMERICAN DREAM

When considered in the context of Lynch's oeuvre, *Interview Project* seems an odd one out, but it's not, and in fact the project gets to the core of that oeuvre's fundamentally nonironic nature. From *Eraserhead* (1977) to *Twin Peaks: The Return* (2017), the Lynchian universe is surreal, absurd, weird, and often also creepy. These adjectives even apply to *The Straight Story* (1999), which of all of Lynch's films comes closest to *Interview Project*.[1] *The Straight Story* chronicles the three-hundred-mile trip that Alvin Straight (Richard Farmsworth) makes from Laurens, Iowa, across the Mississippi River, to Mt. Zion, Wisconsin, while driving a lawnmower, in order to mend his relationship with his sick brother (Figure 10). A seventy-three-year-old World War II veteran who used to have issues with drinking, Straight is above all a quintessential Midwesterner, originally from Moorhead, Minnesota, where he and his brother grew up on a farm. Regrets? Straight has a basketful of them, to cite Jeff from *Interview Project*, but Straight has grown older and wiser. He has learned to separate "the wheat from the chaff," as he tells a hitchhiker (Anastasia Webb) whom he meets on the road. When the young woman confides her fear about her family's reaction to her pregnancy, Straight tells her a story, sitting by the

Figure 10. Alvin Straight on his lawnmower cross-fading into a snapshot of big agriculture (*The Straight Story*, dir. David Lynch, 1999).

campfire, roasting wieners: "When my kids were real little, I used to play a game with 'm. I'd give each one of 'm a stick, one for each one of 'm, and I said: 'You break that.' Of course they could, real easy. Then I said, tie them sticks in a bundle and try to break that. Of course they couldn't. Then I'd say that bundle, that's family."

As its title suggests, *The Straight Story* has a linear narrative, and at first sight it is also Lynch's most realist film. But of course the film is not realist. Take for instance those agricultural screenscapes in which John Deere vehicles, shiny as at the state fair, solemnly tend to the grain belt of America. As Todd McGowan writes in *The Impossible David Lynch* (2007):

> What appears to be an absence of fantasmatic distortion in *The Straight Story* is misleading. The deception results from the nature of the fantasy it presents—the American heartland as a site of authentic community—and the extent to which we cannot see the film as fantasmatic indicates the extent of our investment in the fantasy that it presents. The exaggerated purity of the American heartland in the film is an index of the film's fantasmatic distortion, indicating that this distortion is fully at work in *The Straight Story*. The film's central character commits himself to the logic of fantasy in a way that no character in another Lynch film does. . . . Alvin never deviates from his effort to realize this fantasy despite the trauma attached to it, and his commitment has a direct effect on the structure of the film. (McGowan, 178)

Now, as often with Lynch, the question is: Does *The Straight Story* revel in this phantasmagoric Americana, or do we also detect some irony in Lynch's audiovisual voice? For McGowan this question of whether Lynch is ironic or not is a false dilemma that says more about "our own cultural immersion in irony as spectators" than about Lynch's films themselves. McGowan observes that the urge to interpret Lynch as ironic reaches a climax with *The Straight Story*, because the only alternative would seem to interpret his vision of America as "even more mythical than the Republican National Committee" (Johnson, 138). Yet, so McGowan continues, the fantasy of *The Straight Story* differs from that of the RNC. Even though *The Straight Story* is not ironic, the film foregrounds itself as fantasmatic and in doing so exposes the phantasmagoric nature of Midwestern myths. Lynch does not necessarily deconstruct or critique that mythological understanding. "*The Straight Story* neither affirms nor undermines the image of America it proffers,"

McGowan writes. "Instead, the film illustrates precisely what it would take to construct such a mythical world" (ibid.).

The Straight Story was based on a true story (and turned into a screenplay by John Roach and Mary Sweeney). It would have also made a great story for Interview Project, which in the words of Lee Siegel "is like the elementary materials of [Lynch's] movies before they become fictions." Siegel continues:

All of Lynch's artistic creations seem to take as their starting point Norman Mailer's remark that the essence of America is the smell of gasoline and cheap perfume. For Lynch, the reality of the American dream is in marginal and vulnerable American places, where rough mobility and desperate sexuality collide and down-and-out people have no buffers between themselves and life's hard knocks. Getting knocked around is dreamlike, and Lynch always seems to be saying, through his surrealist devices, that in its hidden core, the American dream is dreamlike. (Siegel)

The American dream is indeed at the heart of Lynch's oeuvre, and in his ongoing engagement with that dream Lynch has been much more realist than his surrealism may lead one to believe. When I visited the United States for the first time, I was struck by how much diners and dive bars look like the ones I knew from Twin Peaks and one could say that what Fellini did for the spectacle that is Italy, Lynch has done for the dream that is America. It is a dream that is surreal in its reality, and it is this absurd, fundamentally ideological, dreamlike reality that Lynch keeps tuning into. As McGowan writes, Lynch reveals the oddity of the mainstream, a tactic McGowan sees reflected in Lynch's fully buttoned yet tieless shirt, an "odd appearance . . . at a time when fashion dictates an unbuttoned look" (McGowan, 13).

The American dream was originally the story of settlers and frontier towns, but it then became the story of the neighborhood. Lynch's work is all about neighborhoods. "In Lynchtown," Michel Chion writes, "everything is close and everyone knows each other," and he adds that "since Eraserhead and its next-door neighbor, the 'neighborhood' takes an almost metaphysical sense in Lynch" (Chion, 101, my translation). The quintessential Lynchtown is of course Twin Peaks, Washington, where dreams and reality flow into one another seamlessly. The television series of that name (which Lynch coauthored with Mark Frost and whose first two seasons aired on ABC in the early 1990s) sucks the viewer into the weird things that happen in this tight-knit northeastern community in the wake of Laura Palmer's murder. In charge of this murder's investigation is special agent Dale Cooper (Kyle MacLachlan), who needed some time off from the big city anyway. Whereas in American police drama, federal agents usually have a hard time winning the trust of the local authorities, Cooper blends in instantaneously. He is a community man whose heart beats faster from the smell of pine trees, doughnuts, and "a damn good cup of coffee" (Figure 11). He also meditates a lot and takes a keen interest in Tibet. In other words, he's your ideal neighbor. Other than police drama, *Twin Peaks* models itself on soap opera. The viewer is hooked by personal intrigue much like the show's characters themselves are hooked by the show-within-the-show *Invitation to Love* that is seen in each of the first season's episodes. To cite Lynch on the appeal of *Interview Project* out of context: "It's human and you can't stay away from it."

By incorporating popular television and, in his later work, plunging into a hyperbolic Hollywood (*Mulholland Dr.*, *Inland Empire*), Lynch has been postmodern in his strategies. But Lynch, so I agree with McGowan, is not ironic, at least not in a way in which irony is defined in opposition to sincerity. David Foster Wallace in his 1997 essay "David Lynch Keeps His Head" defines "*Lynchian*" as "a particular kind of irony where the very macabre and the very mundane combine in such a way as to reveal the former's perpetual containment within the latter"

Figure 11. Special agent Dale Cooper (left) lets Harry, the local sheriff of Twin Peaks, in on his little secret: "Harry, every day, once a day, give yourself a present. Don't plan it, don't wait for it, just let it happen" (*Twin Peaks*, season 1, 1990).

(Wallace, 161). Further on in this essay Wallace writes: "Nobody in Lynch's movies analyzes or metacriticizes or hermeneuticizes or anything, including Lynch himself. This set of restrictions makes Lynch's movies fundamentally unironic, and I submit that Lynch's lack of irony is the real reason some cinéastes . . . see him as naïf or a buffoon" (199). In his railing against irony, Wallace has been associated with a cultural tendency known as the "new sincerity." The term first popped up in the mid-1980s and has served as an umbrella for art, music, fiction, and cinema that seeks to reinvent a belief in speaking authentically in the wake of postmodern irony, and especially, according to Wallace, of what irony has become under the influence of television. "All U.S. irony," Wallace argues in the essay "E Unibus Pluram: Television and U.S. Fiction" (1993), "is based on an implicit 'I don't really mean what I say.' So what does irony as a cultural norm mean to say? That it's impossible to mean what you say? That maybe it's too bad it's impossible, but wake up and smell the coffee already? Most likely, I think, today's irony ends up saying: 'How very banal to ask what I mean'" (Wallace, 67–68).

Irony depends on the incongruity between a statement and its intended meaning, or in the case of situational irony, a planned and an actual course of events (not to be confounded with tough luck, which is what most situations in Alanis Morissette's song come down to). In *Postmodernism, or, the Cultural Logic of Late Capitalism* (1991), Fredric Jameson distinguishes between two modes of irony: pastiche and parody. Both forms of discourse imitate, yet with different stakes and intentions. Parody, Jameson writes, imitates with the intention of critique or laughter. Here a good example is David Byrne's 1986 film *True Stories*, in which the Talking-Heads-frontman-donned-as-Texas-cowboy addresses the viewer while he parks his convertible in a majestic parking lot. "The shopping mall has replaced the town square as the center of many American cities," so he speaks, "Shopping itself has become the activity that brings people together. . . . What time is it? No time to look back." Byrne's parody of an America that doesn't look back lines up with Jameson's analysis of postmodern society as one that has "forgotten how to think historically" (Jameson, ix). For that precise reason Jameson is critical of pastiche. Pastiche imitates, but without thinking historically, and without political motivation. Jameson writes,

> Pastiche is, like parody, the imitation of a peculiar or unique, idiosyn-
> cratic style, the wearing of a linguistic mask, speech in a dead language.
> But it is a neutral practice of such mimicry, without any of parody's ulte-
> rior motives, amputated of the satiric impulse, devoid of laughter and of
> any conviction that alongside the abnormal tongue you have momen-
> tarily borrowed, some healthy linguistic normality still exists. Pastiche is
> thus blank parody, a statue with blind eyeballs: it is to parody what that
> other interesting and historically original modern thing, the practice of
> a kind of blank irony, is to what Wayne Booth calls the "stable ironies"
> of the eighteenth century. (17)

At first sight, much of Jameson's definition of pastiche applies to Lynch, because doesn't Lynch over and again imitate the dead language of the post–World War II era American dream without positing a "healthy linguistic normality" (Jameson, 17) alongside that borrowed, abnormal tongue? The situation is more complex. Lynch does not imitate the American dream discourse, rather he speaks the language of the dream itself. Lynch's work and appearance offer no position of normality, not even *Interview Project* (to the degree, again, this is a Lynch project), whose documentation of an American Precariat seems to call for a political stance and critical distance. With Lynch we're always in the middle of the dream, even those moments when we seem to have cruelly woken up. Think of *Lost Highway* and *Mulholland Dr.*, narratives from which there is really no way out.

Lynch's discourse is thus oneiric, dreamlike, rather than ironic, and his work is an ongoing diagnosis of a dreaming America, which is why Wallace saw an ally in him. In dreams there are no incongruities, no facts and fictions, no difference between ironic and nonironic speech. Things just are, because it is not the conscious *me* who dreams, but something in me that's doing the dreaming, or as Jacques Lacan writes: the dreaming "subject does not see where [the dream] is leading, [s]he follows" (Lacan, 75). Dreaming is an activity usually done at home and it therefore would make one really uncomfortable to suspect their home was under surveillance by a stranger. One of the creepiest scenes in all of Lynch is when in *Lost Highway* (1997) Fred Madison (Bill Pullman) meets the Mystery Man (Robert Blake), and the latter claims to be at Fred's house, *right at this moment*. "Call me," the bulgy-eyed guy instructs Fred, while he hands him an early-generation mobile phone. Fred calls, and the same guy he's talking to right here at this party answers his landline: "I told you I was here." Now Fred is creeped out. "Who are you?" he asks, upon which both incarnations of the creepy guy start laughing out loud: "Give me back my phone." Just earlier that evening, Fred and his wife Renee (Patricia Arquette) were still on their couch, watching video tapings of their house anonymously left on their porch (a horror premise copied by Michael Haneke for his 2005 *Caché*, like *Lost Highway* a dream-reality Moebius strip). Understandably that night Fred and Renee don't dream that comfortable anymore.

Lost Highway, as well as *Mulholland Dr.* and *Inland Empire*, are part of a wider tendency of complex storytelling in contemporary cinema. They are films that destabilize the classical plot-story relation, because in these films elements "are not simply interwoven, but *entangled*," as Warren Buckland defines the puzzle film (Buckland, 3). But Lynch's films are not mind-game films. Mind-game films, so Thomas Elsaesser writes, are "indicative of a 'crisis' in the spectator-film relation, in the sense that the traditional 'suspension of disbelief' [is] . . . no longer deemed appropriate, compelling, or challenging enough" (Elsaesser, 16). Lynch, though, doesn't play games with the viewer. Lynch is serious, even though his smile may suggest otherwise, not deadpan serious, but serious in his surrealism and, in the case of *Mulholland Dr.* and *Inland Empire*, in his surrealist submersion in the Hollywood dream. And here it's important to emphasize that these are not Hollywood films, but films *about* Hollywood, because Lynch has always worked in the auteur tradition, the tradition of film as art.

In *Twin Peaks: The Return*, the Lynchian oneiric discourse is captured poignantly by Monica Bellucci, as she appears in a dream by FBI director Gordon Cole (acted by Lynch himself; see Figure 12): "We're like the dreamer who dreams and then lives inside the dream. But who is the dreamer?" Where the original *Twin Peaks* at least still had one unambiguous answer to this question, namely "Dale Cooper," in the show's 2017 return Cooper's character has bifurcated. While the only thing the viewer wants is to be reunited with the old Coop, there are now "two Coopers," as Cole, who is hard of hearing, yells into his smartphone. (In contrast with *Interview Project*, there's a lot of new media technology in *Twin Peaks: The Return*, from Skype and Macbooks to vlogging and texting; see Figure 13.) The two Coopers, both acted by MacLachlan, are most easily referred to as bad Coop and good Coop. Bad Coop goes back to Cooper's possession by evil, or "BOB" in the show's terminology, twenty-five years earlier at the end of season 2. Good Coop, meanwhile, is in a sleep-walker-like state and for most of the season is mistaken for Dougie Jones, an insurance agent who lives in a white-picket-fenced Las Vegas suburb with his wife Janey-E (Naomi Watts) and their son.

Twin Peaks: The Return is an absolute highlight in Lynch's oeuvre, in particular episode 8, which tells the show's origin myth. At the start

Figure 12. FBI director Gordon Cole (played by David Lynch) against the backdrop of the first nuclear bomb test in the New Mexico desert (*Twin Peaks: The Return*, 2017).

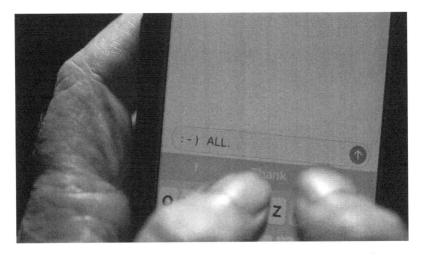

Figure 13. Bad Coop (Kyle MacLachlan) texting that the job is done.

Figure 14. Good Coop (also Kyle MacLachlan) trapped in the American dream, together with his wife Janey-E. (Naomi Watts).

of this episode we're in a car. Bad Coop is in shotgun. He has just escaped from jail and now tosses his cell phone out of the window, wary that the device might be tracked. In the next scene, he is killed, upon which he is reanimated by hobolike spirits flickering over the screen. Following an intermezzo by Nine Inch Nails in The Road House (Twin Peaks' music venue that in the last quarter century has become a stellar place to catch touring acts), the episode cuts to the first nuclear bomb test in the New Mexico desert in 1945, which coincides with the birth of BOB. The camera zooms in on the nuclear mushroom, and then *enters* it, unleashing a ten-minute avant-garde-cinema explosion: from black and white to color and at once reminiscent of Stan Brakhage and the star-gate sequence in Stanley Kubrick's *2001: A Space Odyssey* (1968). In fact, later in this crazy episode we *are* in space, from where a crystal ball containing Laura Palmer's iconic high-school image is tossed to earth to wake up Good Coop from the American dream in which he has been trapped (Figure 14). Do we read a critique of America in *Twin Peaks: The Return*, which travels from New York City to South Dakota, from Vegas to a face-off between good and bad Coop in Twin Peaks? I prefer to resist such an interpretation of *Twin Peaks* according to which the show would be an interpretation of a real dreaming America. *Twin Peaks* is a parallel reality, much like the extradimensional Black Lodge within the show's dreamworld.

As far as that American dream is concerned, its story goes back to the era that John Winthrop outlined for his Puritan audience "a city upon a hill." In his sermon on the boat to Massachusetts, Winthrop sketched a society of opportunity in which God wants that hard work shall be rewarded. The expression "American Dream" first showed up in newspapers and books in the mid- to late 1800s in reference to the ongoing stream of European settlers and the pioneers who ventured westward into the land of bounty. The myth was popularized during the Great Depression, with an important role for James Truslow Adams's *The Epic of America* (1931). Adams describes the "dream of a land in which life should be better and richer and fuller for everyone, with opportunity for each according to ability or achievement" (Adams, xvi). For the happy few, that life is the heroic journey from newspaper boy to millionaire, which on its turn is the urban adaptation of the gold rush legend, mythologized in the twentieth century by, among others, Walt Disney.

For the masses, the American dream became the middle-class ideal of a safe home, of a place for you and your family to lead a life undisturbed by outlaws and crime, a place in other words where your dreams are safe. After all, having worked all day—in the city (men) or at home (women)—in order to sustain one's dream, a good night's sleep is most welcome. Roughly speaking, this ideal of home was born in the first settlements and frontier towns. It then traveled to the small towns of Main Street, U.S.A., and from there, through time, to a neatly trimmed suburbia. Recently, the American middle classes have been moving back into the city, where the dream continues in the condo quarters that suck the life from urban centers all over America and beyond, from Seattle (Cooper's homebase) via Minneapolis to Brooklyn, Toronto, Amsterdam, and so on, because condo architecture is a transnational phenomenon.[2]

For a long time many people really believed in the American dream, and many still do, in spite of everything, like Billy in *Interview Project*:

> Hi, my name is Bill Bar; I live in Wells, Minnesota. It's a little town in Southern Minnesota, a farming community. And it's a town of about 2,400 people, and it's been hit by the agricultural revolution like most of the small towns in rural America, and the farms have all gotten bigger, and so the population has dwindled, and the main streets are being hit by the box stores and the big cities. But it's a good place to live, it's an Eden,

because we have very little crime. You can walk, jog at night, send your children out, don't have to worry about them, and people just generally look out for each other.

That America does indeed exist, but on its dark side the United States is also a country where a city like Detroit—once the cradle of the modern American dream—can go bankrupt (as if the United States is not really a union), a country chronically divided and stuck in political stalemates, of racial segregation and institutionalized police violence, a country where almost one percent of the adult population is in prison, a country where many people are sick, and where Wal-Mart encourages its underpaid "associates" to apply for food stamps. Moreover, also well before @realDonaldTrump's " Great America" show, the United States was a place where fact and fiction, reality and parody, are hard to tell apart. Who could distinguish Tina Fey from Sarah Palin? How many first-time viewers of *The Colbert Report*—in which political humorist Stephen Colbert parodied the "fair and balanced" outlook of conservative pundit programs—must have checked their remote controls to verify they had not accidentally tuned into Fox News? And which Facebook users scrolling through their timeline have never mistaken an *Onion* article for an actual news story, or vice versa? "A dream dies," *The Onion* reported in March 2011, following the news that Edward Tuffy from Pennington, Illinois, who was the last person who still believed that America is the land of boundless opportunity, "quietly let go of the dream, while watching television and eating cereal on his couch" (Figure 15).[3]

In a similar vein, *Interview Project* investigates what's left of life in small-town America after the decay of the small town, long the backbone of the American dream, now crushed by box stores, abandoned by railroads, and bypassed by interstates. Only in Disneyland, where dreams come true, has Main Street remained the thriving artery it once used to be (though truth be told, over the past few decades many small towns have adopted Main Street programs in order to preserve and revitalize traditional commercial districts).[4] But the decay of Main Street—in Disneyland only a short train ride away from Frontier Land— has not caused the fiction of America itself to disappear, a fiction that, as stated, in the second half of the twentieth century found a new home in suburbia, and in the car that gets you there. The dream became

Figure 15. March 2011: The Death of the American Dream.

an advertized life, a lifestyle, and the life that advertising sold was still a fundamentally nonironic dream. As Raymond Williams writes in "Advertising: The Magic System" (1980), modern advertising enchants the material object sold, because "if we were sensibly materialist . . . a washing-machine would be a useful machine to wash clothes, rather than an indication that we are forward-looking or an object of envy to our neighbors" (Williams, 185).

LYNCH™

A good illustration of this sincere promotion of the American way of life is found in *Mad Men* (created by Matthew Weiner, 2007–15, AMC), the story of a rookie advertising agency in 1960s New York City. In the first season's finale, titled "The Wheel," the viewer is seated front row when Don Draper (Jon Hamm) pitches his campaign for Kodak's new slide projector. Don starts by recalling the memory of an old colleague, "a Greek named Teddy," from whom he learned how to stir in his audience "a sentimental bond" with the product that goes deeper than its newness: "Nostalgia, it's delicate, but potent." On the cue of Don's "sweetheart," the only woman in the room switches on the projector, and the camera places the viewer among the men at the conference table. While the machine soothingly clicks from slide to slide,

Don continues, speaking over the frame-filling snapshots of his own seemingly perfect family life:

> Teddie told me that in Greek, nostalgia literally means the pain from an old wound. It's a twinge in your heart far more powerful than memory alone. This device isn't a spaceship; it's a time machine. It goes backwards, forwards, takes us to a place where we ache to go again. It's not called The Wheel, it's called The Carousel. It lets us travel the way a child travels, around and around, and back home again, to a place where we know we are loved.

There is no reason to believe that Don is not feeling what he's saying. He even tears up a bit. Moreover, Don is totally right that the most iconic campaigns of early post–World War II American consumer society at once tapped into and fed a collective nostalgia for a mythical, childhoodlike era in which dreams were still straightforward wish fulfillments. Similarly, *Mad Men* itself taps into the nostalgia many of us may feel for obsolete media such as slide projectors, typewriters, and Bakelite phones, and more generally for the aesthetics of the early decades of consumer culture: the fashion, the glossy household appliances, pastel-colored Chevies, habits now considered unhealthy or illicit like smoking, drinking, or having sex at work, *and* advertising. Advertising was different in the golden age, not better but different, as campaigns still sought to create the illusion to actually *believe* in the things they sold, and here it probably helped that this new car or that new laundry machine—in sum, this new *life*—was actually still "made in America."

Sincerity is more difficult to feign when the thing promoted is less a thing and above all a brand. One strategy to promote your semblance of a semblance is simply to lie that it's "the real thing," but ironically, since Coca Cola substituted sugar for high-fructose corn syrup—corn harvested from those endless Midwestern fields Alvin Straight traverses—the American consumer still in love with that old-fashioned real-sugar taste has to buy a bottle imported from Mexico, which on its turn is only a watered-down version of the Coke of the early days of Prohibition. Another strategy is to be openly ironic with your audience, like Pepsi. In his essay on television cited earlier, David Foster Wallace discusses Pepsi's famous 1980s campaign as a case in point of TV irony at work. In the ad we see a packed beach going wild at the amplified sound of a fresh can of Pepsi as it is being poured into a glass. While the voice-over calls Pepsi "the choice of a new genera-tion," a hip and hot crowd flocks toward the concession van. The ad's irony, Wallace argues (following Mark Crispin Miller), is that there is in fact little "choice" in the horde's Pavlovian reaction. It is not the revolutionary taste of the beverage itself that the ad calls to the viewer's attention, but the implied fact that Pepsi has *already* been advertised successfully. Joe Briefcase, however, who is the protagonist of Wallace's essay, is not like those will-deprived masses, and instead *gets* the ad's double layer. "The commercial invites a complicity," Wallace argues, "between its own witty irony and veteran viewer Joe's cynical, nobody's fool appreciation of that irony. It invites Joe into an in-joke that the audi-ence is the butt of. It congratulates Joe Briefcase, in other words, on transcending the very crowd that defines him" (Wallace, 60–61). That's why Joe, and with him indeed many of his generation, chooses Pepsi, and hence also the title of Wallace's essay: "E Unibus Pluram" ("From one, many"), a pun on "*E Pluribus Unum*" ("Out of many, one"), which for long was considered the de facto motto of the U.S. (until 1956 when Congress adopted "In God We Trust" as the union's official motto).

For Lynch, there are no in-jokes. His dream worlds contain a lot of pop culture, but there are no pop culture *references*, and here it's relevant to note that the 1986 film *Blue Velvet* is from well before the time that Pabst Blue Ribbon became ironic. (Moreover, Frank, played by Dennis Hopper, prefers his PBR in a glass, not in a can.) But "Lynch" definitely has become a brand. His organic Signature Cup Coffee is available at Whole Foods and online. He owns a nightclub in Paris named Silencio (after the nightclub in *Mulholland Dr.*). Lynch has taught at the European Graduate School in Switzerland. Since 2005 there is the David Lynch Foundation for Consciousness-Based Education and World Peace, which brings Transcendental Meditation—a form of mantra meditation—to "at risk populations."[5] Lynch paints, writes, and sings, often about dreams. And even though in his book *Catching the Big Fish: Meditation, Consciousness, and Creativity* (2006), he claims to be "through with film as a medium. For me, film is dead" (Lynch, 149),[6] he occasionally still does make a short on commission, includ-ing *Lady Blue Shanghai* (a 2010 Internet promotion film for Christian Dior), a music video for Nine Inch Nails ("Came Back Haunted," 2013), and in 2011 a feature-length live web broadcast of a Duran Duran con-cert, unironically sponsored by American Express (after having made commercials for Giorgio Armani, Adidas, and Sony, among others, earlier in his career). Moreover, Lynch tweets, announcing for example, in 2016, the return of *Twin Peaks*: "That gum you like is going to come back in style! #damngoodcoffee."

The element that holds this frenzy of creativity together is above all Lynch's persona, his media persona, which he himself describes nicely in his coffee web-shop: "It's all about the beans . . . and I'm just full of beans."[7] Besides loads of caffeine, the secret behind his high spirits is meditation, twice a day for twenty minutes, for over thirty years. "It was as if, as they say, I was in an elevator, and someone snipped the cables," Lynch in a television interview describes his first encounter with meditation. "Down . . . Bliss . . . The most beautiful. It was familiar and yet unique. . . . I said . . . since then, the word 'unique' should be saved for this experience."[8] As good cultural critics, we have been trained not to read the author into his work, or vice versa, but clicking through the many Lynch videos on YouTube and also following his recent appearances on both the big and the small screen, what perhaps is most striking is the consistency of Lynch's appearance across his nonscripted, "real life" performances (interviews, his lectures on meditation, the long interview with him in *The Art Life*), his creative self-performances (including the *Interview Project* intros, his daily LA weather reports, and the television episodes of *Louie* in which Lynch instructs Louis C.K. how to become a better comedian), and his acting performances, like in *Twin Peaks: The Return* and the film *Lucky* (2017, U.S.), directed by John Caroll Lynch (no family relationship), in which Lynch (David that is) plays a guy named Howard whose tortoise, "President Roosevelt," has escaped. As Howard philosophizes in a way only Lynch would be able to: "He affected me. There are some things in this universe that is bigger than all of us, and a tortoise is one of them." Though in the scripted performances like this one there is an acted absurdity absent from the nonscripted ones, there is always that familiar buttoned-up and combed-yet-wild look. And there is never any trace of irony in Lynch's voice, no double layers, no tongue-in-cheek, unlike, as for example, with Jean-Luc Godard, who always seems to be performing his media persona, also in interviews (and who, case in point, didn't show in Agnès Varda's 2017 *Visages, villages*, despite their rendez-vous, unable as he is to surrender control of the montage). Fact or fiction, Lynch's Lynchian self-presentation is always somewhat like that of a dream character with whom fiction and fact continuously blend into each other.

"Lynch" is a strong brand, but I'm not sure if it strengthens *Interview Project*. Of course, Lynch's involvement, including his name in the URL, has boosted the project's exposure and probably made it financially possible in the first place. But his presence also legitimizes us to redirect to him *Interview Project*'s guiding question, "What do you think of America right now?" Lynch in fact did answer this question in 2001, in an interview with John Powers for *LA Weekly*. Enjoy the interview:

> It's not [Powers writes] that Lynch has no idea of how he'd like the world to be. For all his dark, perverse imaginings, his social values are rooted in the sunlit credo of the American West: *Don't tread on me.* Nothing matters to him more than his freedom to do whatever he thinks up. I first saw this side of him one afternoon in 1989 when he began railing about the city government: It wouldn't let him put razor wire around his property to keep itinerants from cutting across his property. He shook his head:
>
> "You know, John, this country's in pretty bad shape when human scum can walk across your lawn, and they put *you* in jail if you shoot 'em."
>
> While Lynch doesn't seem like the sort of man who's packing heat, he was drawn to Ronald Reagan because of his "cowboy image" and laments that L.A.'s wonderland of individual freedom is being hedged in by rules and regulations. He takes building-code restrictions personally. "People," he says, "should be able to build *what* they want to build, *when* they want to build it, *how* they want to build it."
>
> · · ·
>
> Lynch's picture of the world was formed in the 1950s, and he clearly adores the mythologized version, that fabulous decade of jukeboxes and sneaky-perverse movies like *Rear Window.*
>
> "It was a feeling in the air that anything was possible. People were enthusiastically inventing things that thrilled them. And there was a happiness in the air. There was plenty going on beneath the surface, but it wasn't as dark a time because there was that other thing going along with it. The '50s was a time when people seemed to be going crazy with design. And the cars were just incredible. I mean, you look at them, and it's like you start to fall in love. That changed, you know, in the '60s and '70s. The cars were pitiful. I mean *pitiful*. It made you ashamed. You'd wanna hang your head and go in a corner. It was sickening."
>
> We're talking a couple of days before September 11, but Lynch is already gloomy about the state of the world:

"You just get the feeling that you're sort of powerless in the big picture. And it's not like 'I better get mine,' but I'm gonna burrow in and concentrate and enjoy doing that. Not try to put my head in the sand, but for my own protection let as little of that outside negativity affect me."

He lights another American Spirit. (Powers)

Now, it wouldn't be totally fair to read Lynch's crass statements about shooting people into *Interview Project*. Moreover, based on a tweet that he was feeling *the bern* (Figure 16), Lynch's political leanings may have altered since this interview. Still, *Interview Project*, in its retro-analog and naively humanist framing, unmistakably bears Lynch's outspoken and somewhat conservative stamp, thereby somewhat reducing the participants' life stories to a preconceived, mildly reactionary, and predominantly white vision on the state of the union. In other words, the "Lynch" brand imposes itself too much onto *Interview Project*. Granted, like many in this digital era I share some of Lynch's nostalgia for the design of the immediate post–World War II decades—the 1960s and '70s and also the 1980s and '90s—but it's also important to be critical of nostalgia, and to recognize one's desire for bygone times as an act of historical amnesia, to invoke Jameson's diagnosis of the postmodern condition. *Interview Project* isn't critical about its play on nostalgia, unlike *Mad Men*, which through its self-reflexive aesthetic and its exploration of the 1960s dream industry makes its viewers reflect on their own retro fetishism. *Mad Men* ends, by the way, with Don meditating, mindfully letting go of all that "outside negativity," to cite Lynch. Then, in its final moments, *Mad Men* gives us one of more proof of Don's creative genius, as a close-up of his blissful face gives way to Coca Cola's iconic 1971 hilltop commercial, bubbling up in Don's

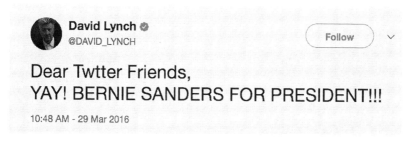

Figure 16. David Lynch feelin' the Bern.

well-rested mind. I take *Mad Men*'s finale as a reminder to not confuse meditation with politics, which is what Lynch seems to do with his Transcendental Meditation project, and as *Interview Project* does with its lovingkind outlook.

This particular brand of Lynchian humanism also inspired Austin Lynch, Jason S, and their team to take their equipment across the Atlantic for *Interview Project Germany* (2011, www.interviewproject.de). Fifty videos from all over Germany, the same introductions shot in Lynch's L.A. house ("Today we're meeting Klaus. The team found Klaus mending his neighbor's fence"), the same plan, and the same twinkle in Lynch's eyes: "There's no plan when the team sets out. They don't know who they're gonna meet. They just set out," as Lynch explains in the *Über* video. "What type of food did the team eat for *Interview Project Germany*? The team ate German food for *Interview Project Germany*." A loosely recurring theme is that of the former East-West divide. For example, Heidemarie from Nordhausen, Thüringen, born in 1944, and whose father was in the Luftwaffe, taught Russian, German, and geography. "We had to be multi-skilled in the times of the GDR," she explains in German and subtitled in English, "You had to go where you were needed." Or take Klaus Münstermann, 54, from Neubukow, Mecklenburg-Vorpommern. Klaus grew up on a farm, and he spent a year in prison, after he had been accused of "*Republikflucht*." Klaus is sitting in an electric wheelchair behind a supermarket covered in graffiti (Figure 17). Back in the day, the Stasi pressured Klaus to sign up to be an informer, but he resisted, upon which he was promised "a miserable life, that's what's taken care of." Since then, Klaus has felt like the black sheep of his community. "Here they'd like to get rid of me rather today, rather yesterday than today or tomorrow. They'd like to push me far away." How would Klaus like to be remembered? "I want to be remembered as someone who helped out, was there. . . . Who doesn't talk. Who isn't a police spy, till today. Like it's always been."

The interview with Klaus is one of the many moving portraits in what like the original *Interview Project* is a unique yet again predominantly white cross section of a population tested by life in a Western superpower. But to see Lynch struggling with the German names just makes his whole Lynchian performance a little too performed. Out of his comfort zone of the nonironic American dream discourse, Lynch's

002 KLAUS MÜNSTERMANN, NEUBUKOW (MV)   EMBED VIDEO

Figure 17. Klaus Münstermann (Neubukow, Mecklenburg-Vorpommern) in *Interview Project Germany.*

Figure 18. Billie from Wells, Minnesota, about the American dream.

"particular kind of irony" (Wallace), his particular brand of unironic irony, becomes too much of a gimmicky, hollow pastiche. Whereas the American *Interview Project* still allows us to understand Lynch's jolly and weird appearance as a sort of immanent expression of the American dream discourse, in *Interview Project Germany* the director appears as what Jameson calls "a statue with blind eyeballs."

To end on a positive note, let's look at one more American story, told by someone we've already met, namely Billy from Minnesota (the only state that, together with the District of Columbia, turned blue when Lynch's once-hero Ronald Reagan was elected president). After having eloquently praised the virtues of rural America in spite of its colonization by big agriculture, Billy, who is seated at a picnic table and who's wearing a red sweater saying "Billy's" and a purple Wildcats cap, tells the following story (Figure 18):

> A fellow during the Depression was outta work and he became a hobo. And he came into this one town, and he rapped on the door, and a gal came to the door, and he said, "I'm hungry, do you have any work for me, so I can have some food?" She said: "No, this is a house of ill repute. I have no work for you. But here's 50 cents." So he walked into town and there was a fellow sellin' bananas. And he bought 25 cents worth of bananas and ate, and then he bought some more, and he sold those bananas for 50 cents. And he started out in the American Dream. He started building a business. Pretty soon he had a stand of his own. Pretty soon he had a store of his own. Pretty soon he was a warehouse. Just was doing great. And some guy came in and said: "You know, my son just graduated from Harvard. And I'd like to buy a business for him. You have a nice, clean business. Would you like to sell?" And he says: "No, I really don't wanna sell. I'm very happy with what I'm doing." He says, "well," he says, "don't you have a price?" "No, I just don't wanna sell." He said: "I'll give you a check. You just write out what you want." And the guy says: "No, no, no, no." He says: "No, I don't want it." "Well," he said, "you could've just, you know, done anything what you wanted to. You could have gone to college and become an accountant." And he said: "If I had gone to college and become an accountant I probably would have ended up as a bookkeeper in a house of ill repute."

Billy smiles a big smile. Cut to a long shot of Billy waving presidentially from the balcony of his typically Minnesotan home, set against a joyous harmonica tune and a laugh track. Once the epitome of cheap TV, in the digital era the canned laughter makes a little nostalgic, and in doing so sums up the lure—the appeal but also the pitfall—of *Interview*

Project. Interview Project captures the current crisis of the American dream in an aesthetic framework reminiscent of the post–World War II heydays of that dream. But regardless of how much we may still be in love with that aesthetic, let's not be *too* nostalgic, lest we forget that in the United States the contradictions inherent to capitalism have always been more absurd than anywhere else.

Niels Niessen works at the University of Amsterdam. He is working on two book projects: *Miraculous Realism: The French-Walloon Cinéma du Nord* (forthcoming) and *Attention, or, What It Means to Be Present in the Internet Age* (in progress at www.attentionbook.xyz). This essay published here forms part of *Attention*, together with its "twin" essay (nonidentical), "Mad Men & Mindfulness," which is forthcoming in *Discourse*.

Notes

1. Here I should also mention *American Chronicles*, a documentary TV series produced by Lynch/Frost Productions that Lynch was sideways involved in artistically. The show aired on Fox for three months in the fall of 1990 before the network pulled it because of poor viewer ratings. It was largely the work of Mark Frost, with whom Lynch co-wrote *Twin Peaks* (that same fall in its second season on ABC). Lynch served as an uncredited Executive Producer for *American Chronicles*, and he codirected one episode, "Champions," which aired in the U.K. but not in the United States. Taking the form of montage sequences with occasional narration by Richard Dreyfuss, *American Chronicles* looks at unusual aspects of American society, including the New Orleans Mardi Gras celebrations, the Miss Texas pageant shows, Manhattan nightlife, and *Playboy*'s Hugh Hefner. See also Josh Zyber, "Auteur Theory: 'American Chronicles,'" *High-Def Digest* (September 4, 2012), http://www.highdefdigest.com/blog/american-chronicles-david-lynch/.

2. As far as Minneapolis is concerned, in a recent *Atlantic* article, "The Miracle of Minneapolis," Derek Thompson suggests substituting the question "What's wrong with American cities?" for "What's right with Minneapolis?" He observes that "no other place mixes affordability, opportunity, and wealth so well." Indeed, Minneapolis is, and historically has been, a progressive city, for a long time the Midwestern grain-exchange center, now also a center for health care and the arts. Moreover, unlike many midsize American cities, Minneapolis has a developed public infrastructure, including transit and affordable wi-fi (connected to the street-light network). On the other side, like so many U.S. cities, Minneapolis is also a place that suffers from institutionalized racism and police shootings.

3. "American Dream Declared Dead As Final Believer Gives Up" (video), *The Onion: America's Finest News Source*, http://www.theonion.com/video/amer ican-dream-declared-dead-as-final-believer-giv,19846/.

4. See http://www.preservationnation.org/main-street/about-main-street/the-programs/.

5. http://www.davidlynchfoundation.org/.

6. See also Tim Walker, "Waxing Lyrical: David Lynch on His New Passion—And Why He May Never Make Another Movie," *The Independent* (June 23, 2013), http://www.independent.co.uk/arts-entertainment/music/features/waxing -lyrical-david-lynch-on-his-new-passion—and-why-he-may-never-make-another -movie-8665457.html.

7. http://www.davidlynchcoffee.co.uk/.

8. See https://www.youtube.com/watch?v=qPsgsuSvbXo.

Works Cited

Adams, James Truslow. 2012. *The Epic of America*. Piscataway: Transaction Publishers.

Buckland, Warren. 2009. "Introduction: Puzzle Plots." In *Puzzle Films: Complex Storytelling in Contemporary Cinema*. Edited by Warren Buckland, 1–12. Chichester: Wiley-Blackwell.

Coates, Ta-Nehisi. *Between the World and Me*. New York: Spiegel & Grau.

Chion, Michel. 1992. *David Lynch*. Paris: Cahiers du cinéma.

Elsaesser, Thomas. "The Mind-Game Film." In *Puzzle Films: Complex Storytelling in Contemporary Cinema*. Edited by Warren Buckland, 13–41. Chichester: Wiley-Blackwell.

Jameson, Fredric. 1991. *Postmodernism, or, the Cultural Logic of Late Capitalism*. Durham: Duke University Press.

Johnson, Jeff. 2004. *Pervert in the Pulpit: Morality in the Works of David Lynch*. Jefferson, N.C.: MacFarland.

Lacan, Jacques. 1998. *The Four Fundamental Concepts of Psychoanalysis: The Seminar of Jacques Lacan, Book XI*. Edited by Jacques-Alain Miller. Translated by Alan Sheridan. New York: Norton.

Lynch, David. 2007. *Catching the Big Fish: Meditation, Consciousness, and Creativity*. New York: Jeremy P. Tarcher/Penguin.

McGowan, Todd. 2007. *The Impossible David Lynch*. New York: Columbia University Press.

Mullins, Edmund. 2009. "Broken Dreams, Missing Teeth: David Lynch's Interview Project." *BlackBook*, July 8, http://www.blackbookmag.com/movies/broken -dreams-missing-teeth-david-lynchs-interview-project.

Powers, John. 2001. "Getting Lost Is Beautiful." *LA Weekly*, October 17, http:// www.laweekly.com/news/getting-lost-is-beautiful-2133916.

Siegel, Lee. 2009. "David Lynch's American Dreams." *The Daily Beast*, July 20, http://www.thedailybeast.com/articles/2009/07/20/david-lynchs-american -dreams.html.

Thompson, Derek. 2015. "The Miracle of Minneapolis." *The Atlantic,* https://www
.theatlantic.com/magazine/archive/2015/03/the-miracle-of-minneapolis/
384975/.
Wallace, David Foster. 1997. *A Supposedly Fun Thing I'll Never Do Again.* New York:
Back Bay Books.
Williams, Raymond. 1980. *Problems in Materialism and Culture.* London: Verso.

THE CREATURELY MODERNISM OF AMOS TUTUOLA

Matthew Omelsky

Rarely is the work of Amos Tutuola described as modernist. In fact, his work is most often portrayed as modernism's inversion, as premodern, or "traditional." In J. M. Coetzee's *Elizabeth Costello* (2003), the character Emmanuel Egudu outlines the literary reception of the early Nigerian novelist. Africans initially rejected Tutuola's work, Egudu explains, for its "broken" English prose, for perpetuating the continent's "primitive" image. Europe, by contrast, was infatuated with the exotic imagery and language of his work. Egudu concludes that while Tutuola is an important writer, he is, ultimately, an "oral writer" whose work is "very simple" (40–51). Indeed, in Coetzee's novel we find a rendition of the all too trite appraisal of Tutuola's place in African literature. His work is often thought of as derivative of Yoruba folklore, as severed from the outside world.

Underneath this cloak of the premodern, however, lie traces of the modern. For Simon Gikandi, the apparent celebration of the premodern in much early African literature is paradoxically "a witness to its loss"—a loss that, Gikandi suggests, stems from the anxiety of the modern (2007, 12). But the modern in Amos Tutuola's work is not merely a pervasive sense of anxiety. Behind his borrowings from Yoruba oral tradition, Tutuola presents a global constellation of objects and goods— from radios to footballs to televisions—that rupture the conventional notion of an insular, primitive Africa. In Tutuola's *The Palm-Wine Drinkard* (1952) and *My Life in the Bush of Ghosts* (1954), we find figurations of capital in the many creatures and monsters that pervade his fantastical landscapes. The bodies of these curious and haunting beings are literally composed of commodities, technologies, and tropes of exchange. These creatures and their modern appendages gesture toward a vastly expanded lifeworld that extends to the farthest reaches of empire—indeed, to the farthest global reaches of capital.

Amos Tutuola's creaturely modernism, I contend, lies principally in the ontology and materiality of these creatures. Each is a freakish, worldly multitude, a melding of bacteria, television screens, maggots, and flashing lights. These creatures descend from the fantastical aesthetic tradition of West African folklore, yet the diverse objects and beings that compose their bodies mark them as part of a global system in perpetual motion. His creatures give life to the global flows of capital presupposed by their organlike commodities. Pivotal, too, is the biopolitical terrain these curious beings inhabit. They live in a world of seemingly inescapable terror, exploitation, and surveillance. The aesthetics and materiality of the creaturely body cannot be separated from the politics of modernity in which populations are controlled, ordered, and put to work. And, finally, any examination of Tutuola's modernism must attend to the question of style, to the aesthetic mode in which he articulates his creatures and their folkloric biopolitical world. His use of syntax, diction, and narrative form not only destabilizes linear time and space, but it vivifies his haunting creatures, bringing them to the fore of his fragmented episodic narratives. Amos Tutuola's creaturely modernism becomes fully apparent only when we examine the creature situated in its biopolitical environment, and when we consider the language through which this creaturely world is brought to life. To read Tutuola in such a way is meant to redirect Africanist discourse toward a more explicitly global and phenomenological conception of West African experience and aesthetics at midcentury. This notion of African modernism is not at all new; it has been in Tutuola's fantastical writing for more than half a century, shrouded under the veil of the "premodern."[1]

In the early 1950s, when Tutuola's first two novels were released, much of West Africa was embroiled in anticolonial struggle, which, in many instances, insulated these emerging nations, culturally, economically, and politically, from the rest of the world. The publication of *The Palm-Wine Drinkard* in 1952 could be said to mark the opening up of West Africa to the world at a moment when so much African cultural production and political rhetoric turned inward in search of nationhood. *Palm Wine*, in other words, was ahead of its time, espousing the global even before the collapse of colonial rule. Tutuola's use of the West African surrealist mode obfuscates allegorical readings of anticoloniality and liberation, but importantly, he retains palpable traces of a global capitalist system in which West Africa had an influential role to play. Tutuola's modernism inscribed West Africa into a *world* system, not merely an imperial system or one of national enclosure.[2]

Working through the optic of Tutuola's creatures allows us to examine a configuration of African modernism unmoored from the predictable tropes of the colonial encounter or the emergent African nation. Instead, these creatures with televisions for hands and flashing lights for eyes allow us to think of West Africa as a global nexus of consumer culture, commodity flows, and social relation. Tutuola's modernism reveals a phenomenological sense of what it means to be global, and to think globally. His Africa is a site of syncretism, a space in which airplanes, shape-shifting ghosts, photography, and palm wine merge to form a new African mode of being-in-the-world. Amos Tutuola's *sui generis* creatures open us to a global African modernism.

AFRICAN MODERNISMS

African modernism as an aesthetic category has historically been multivalent and contested. It reaches far, from figurations of subjectivity, tradition, and loss to allegories of liberation and national collapse. To be sure, Amos Tutuola is a modernist writer, but he is not one that can be read solely through these common tropes that pervade African modernist discourse. His modernism comes through the global reach of capital, not necessarily through familiar representations of the emergent nation, the individual, or postcolonial crisis. Tutuola's creaturely modernism is, however, related to that important lineage of African modernist thought.

While there may be many lenses through which to examine the modernist sensibility in African cultural production, one critical notion underlies them all. Aptly put by Okwui Enwezor, "The narratives of modernity in Africa are predicated on an encounter of antagonism" (615). This antagonism, of course, has its ostensible historical roots in the fifteenth century and the first Portuguese sea expeditions to sub-Saharan Africa. The antagonism emerged, in other words, in the rupture brought on by the European encounter and its attendant impositions of violence, capitalism, language, and social institutions. Undoubtedly, modernity is not simply synonymous with Europe, as if it brought the modern to Africa. Modernity emerged on the continent through the syntheses, mistranslations, and gaps between European and African economic and social formations. African modernity was born in the interstices of Europe and Africa. African modernism is marked by the cultural forms and tropes produced in these interstices.

Questions of liberation and nationhood are among the most frequent discursive constructs in African modernist criticism and cultural practice. The establishment and construction of the autonomous nation was a critical issue for many writers and artists of the mid-twentieth century. As Ahmadou Kourouma's *Les Soleils des indépendances* (1970) and Ngugi wa Thiong'o's *A Grain of Wheat* (1967) demonstrate, the literary text effectively inscribed itself into the political discourses of anticolonialism and nation-building. And with this comingling of the literary and the political came the fraught issue of the role of aesthetic experimentation vis-à-vis the politics of the emergent nation. The problematic concerned the extent to which experimental writers, such as the Nigerian poet Christopher Okigbo, effectively obscured a necessary sense of political engagement through oblique uses of language and form. For writers and scholars at the fore of this debate, like Wole Soyinka and Chinweizu, questions of literary form and technique were central to the role of the aesthetic in shaping the emerging nation (Quayson 2004, 826). Moreover, notions of liberation and national autonomy were also pivotal in the African visual arts, with artists in many newly independent nations, notably Senegal, establishing direct relationships with state institutions. The prominent Senegalese modernist painter Iba N'Diaye, for instance, was appointed by the Senegalese president Léopold Sédar Senghor in 1960 to direct a major section of the newly established École des Arts in Dakar, where he taught the next generation of Senegalese painters and sculptors. With the postcolonial state's enlistment of artists, a system of state patronage was formed in the interest of refashioning a sense of cultural and national autonomy to reflect the modern, independent moment. In the mid-twentieth century, African modernism was very much a nationalist undertaking, an entanglement of the aesthetic and the political.

These concerns with cultural nationalism and the new nation inform the enchantment-disenchantment dialectic of African modernism. In many African fictions, colonial modernity entails a simultaneous enchantment with the new and disenchantment with the failed promise of the new. Colonial modernity, in other words, pivots on a dialectic of loss and desire, failure and promise. The contradiction emerges when that which is considered to be "modern" is at once condemned as an alienating, repressive illusion, but also hailed as a catalyst for social and economic advancement (Olaniyan, 83). This dialectic is further complicated when we consider the linkage between this sense of disenchantment and the "metaphysics of the premodern" in African literature. Many African writers and intellectuals have looked to tradition to stave off the discontent engendered by colonial modernity. For Simon Gikandi, however, this romanticization of the premodern simply reveals what is ultimately the *loss* of the premodern. Turning to tradition as a "rescue plan from the pain of modernity" is more a symptom of the anxiety of modernity than a celebration of cultural nationalism (2007, 9–12). Instead of understanding tradition and modernity to be mutually exclusive, the two are enmeshed in modernism's anxious dialectic of loss and desire.

Inside these modernist African narratives of enchantment and disenchantment is the figure of the individual. The heightened sense of individualism, interiority, and self-reflexivity common in the work of writers such as James Joyce and Virginia Woolf finds related configurations in the work of African writers like Chinua Achebe, Kofi Awoonor, and Tayeb Salih. Predictably, this shift toward the articulation of a modernist subject has been sharply criticized as merely revealing the disintegration of African social structures, as representing a European model of the individual. But this rigidly composed binary of individualism and communalism is indeed a false one, for most African writers in fact establish a "middle space" between the two (Quayson 2004, 826–28). Gikandi illustrates this well in his discussion of Okonkwo in Achebe's *Things Fall Apart* (1958): "In spite of his [Okonkwo's] overdetermination by a communal ethos, either in support or revolt against it, Okonkwo is the classical bourgeois subject of the modern novel, a subject defined simultaneously by his alienation from his community and the charismatic hold he has on it" (2007, 5–6). The modern African subject is very much a blurring of the individual and the communal. The articulation of African modernism at the interstices of European and African cultures comes to the fore in literary figurations of the subject.

This blurring of cultures that produced African modernism shifted throughout the twentieth century, moving from tropes of nation-building at midcentury to ones of postcolonial crisis in the late century. The accompanying aesthetics of this crisis moment were, and in many cases remain, an aesthetics of fragmentation and dissonance. These aesthetics are perhaps most evident in the turn to magical realist-like writing beginning in the 1960s, in works such as Cyprian Ekwensi's *Burning Grass* (1962), Sony Labou Tansi's *La Vie et demie* (1979), and Dambudzo Marechera's *The House of Hunger* (1978). The institution of African literature itself was in crisis, having lost the claim of authority it once drew from the past (Gikandi 2007, 15). The fragmented literatures of the postcolonial moment have corresponded to society's crises of broken institutions, political instability, and fractured sense of history. Indeed, the crisis is both a product of modernity and the decay of the institutions of modernity. As Gikandi provocatively suggests, "Africa has entered its Weimar period." For him, issues of experience and truth are now inextricable from those of life and death. "What is the role of art," he asks, "when its condition of possibility is one of unprecedented crisis?" (14–18). The collapse of the euphoria of independence and the postcolony's subsequent atrophy are some of the more recent tropes of African modernism. An aesthetics of crisis has emerged in a deeply uncertain historical moment.[3]

Sarah Lincoln has recently given close attention to this period of crisis aesthetics, isolating a particular modernist mode in Nigerian magical realism. Reading Ben Okri's collection *Stars of the New Curfew* (1988), she develops the useful term "inflationary modernism" to characterize the way Okri's nonrealist aesthetics coincide with Nigeria's "oil boom" and "inflationary bust" of the 1970s and 1980s. She explains how oil wealth produced a social and political culture of excess and spectacular opulence that concealed pervasive state corruption, producing a "simulacral symbolic economy" in which the commodity became severed from the fantastic superstructure it generated. "Okri's magical realist vision [is] an attempt to bear witness to the oil economy's radical disruption of the bond holding signifier to signified, representation to reality, and the signs of value to its substance"

(250). For Lincoln, Okri's modernist aesthetics seeks to "memorialize the wasted bodies, social relations, landscapes, and dreams" rendered invisible by this break between the production of oil and the inflationary spectacle.

Another scholar to carve out new terrain in discussions of African modernism in the last few years is Tsitsi Jaji with her notion of "stereomodernism." If global circulation is implicit in Lincoln's concept of inflationary modernism, Jaji brings circulation to the fore in her examination of the ways African diasporic music circulates throughout African texts from the late nineteenth century to the present. Jaji focuses on the "symbolic roles of diasporic music in pan-African writing and film, and . . . how music informed what it meant to be 'modern' in the context of globally interconnected, mutable, and mutually constituted black identities" (2). Stereomodernism, for Jaji, is this global circulation of sound, but it is also a metaphor for the subtle (sonic and cultural) differences of sound as it circulates, akin to the notion of stereophonic surround sound wherein two separate signals produce "slight temporal differences which the ear interprets psycho-acoustically as information about spatial orientation" (13). Jaji's modernism is thus a theory of black solidarity-in-difference as it takes shape in the reverberating global circulations of diasporic music.

Both Jaji and Lincoln reread important works of twentieth-century African cultural production in order to articulate modernist modes that move beyond dominant African modernist tropes. In Amos Tutuola's modernism we can see the elements of circulation and global capital that underwrite Lincoln's and Jaji's formulations far more than the well-worn categories of the nation or the subject. In *Palm Wine* and *Bush of Ghosts*, there is no clear colony or nation to speak of. One could imagine allegorical readings in these novels—allegories of the nation, the collapse of tradition, or even postcolonial crisis. But the structures of fragmentation, wandering subjectivity, and alterity that could be read as modernist allegories could just as easily be traced back to borrowings from Yoruba oral tradition. Before we isolate Tutuola's modernist sensibility, the writer needs to be situated among his literary precursors and his audience. In doing so, it will become clear just how uncommon it is to refer to Tutuola as a modernist. Indeed, Tutuola has effectively been discarded from African modernist discourse, buried in the annals of African literature's premodernity.

OF LINEAGES AND RECEPTIONS

This ascription of the premodern is largely based on an association between the many folkloric traditions in West Africa and the narrative form, fantastical elements, and use of proverbs in Tutuola's first two novels. While most of his works follow similar patterns of narrative development, *The Palm-Wine Drinkard* and *My Life in the Bush of Ghosts* are particularly well suited to a dialogical reading. Each is an episodic journey featuring a shape-shifting picaresque hero who sets out in search of something that he ultimately attains. Both heroes travel through unfamiliar realms, encountering monsters and ghosts that violently beat them, threaten to enslave them, and some who help them attain their objectives. *Palm Wine* features a gluttonous young man in search of his palm wine tapster after the tapster fell to his death while extracting wine from a tree. The protagonist uses his "native juju" to transform himself into many different beings and nonbeings, including a bird, a lizard, a canoe, and even air, so as to evade the many "terrible and wonderful creatures" he encounters during his quest to find his tapster. *Bush of Ghosts* features a boy who walks into the "Bush of Ghosts" to elude the slave traders chasing him near his family home. The novel catalogues the events in the life of this boy in the bush, notably his encounters with various smelly, colorful, and fire-emitting creature-ghosts, as he attempts to reenter the human world and return to his family.

Since the publication of these first works, Amos Tutuola has undergone one of the most fraught receptions in African literary history. V. S. Pritchett's 1954 review of *The Palm-Wine Drinkard* in *The New Statesman and Nation* encapsulates well the exhilarating exoticism Europe and America saw in his work: "Tutuola's voice is like the beginning of man on earth, man emerging, wounded, and growing" (23). Tutuola's work was initially received as infantile and primitive in the United States and Europe, feeding established tropes of African otherness, darkness, and simplicity. While some West African readers saw the merit of Tutuola's work, many were incensed by the image of the continent depicted in his novels. As one reader, I. Adeagbo Akinjogbin, writes in a 1954 issue of the magazine *West Africa*, "Most Englishmen . . . are pleased to believe all sorts of fantastic tales about Africa, a continent about which they are profoundly ignorant. The 'extraordinary books' of Mr. Tutuola . . . will just suit the temper of his European readers as they seem to confirm their concepts of Africa" (41).

In addition to reviews in various magazines, the most prominent scholarly examinations of Tutuola's work have focused on the influence of Yoruba oral tradition.[4] The style, episodic structure, and frequent cautionary nature of Tutuola's work have been unequivocally linked to the oral tradition in several rigorous studies. In his pioneering work on the Nigerian writer, Bernth Lindfors demonstrates the clear parallels between sequences in Tutuola's first novels and Yoruba oral culture, including the episode of the "Beautiful Complete Gentleman" in *Palm Wine* in which a man lures a woman into the deep forest while returning his rented body parts to their various owners (316). Importantly, however, Ato Quayson argues that Tutuola does not merely reproduce tales from the Yoruba tradition, but instead, "brings together a whole range of oral genres such as riddles, proverbs and etymological tales so that his narratives become concatenations of several elements from Yoruba storytelling traditions" (*Strategic Transformations*, 46). For Quayson and Lindfors, Tutuola is not a novelist, nor is he simply a transcriber of tales. He's a writer who assembles and remixes oral traditions.

Intriguingly, the many creatures in *Palm Wine* and *Bush of Ghosts* appear to have been influenced by disparate sources aside from West African oral tradition. For one, the morphologies of Tutuola's monsters seem akin to those of figures in Bunyan's *Pilgrim's Progress* (1678), which Tutuola is known to have read while in school. Where Tutuola's creatures have "uncountable" fingers, wings, and eyes, the figure of Appolyon in *Pilgrim's Progress* has fishlike scales, dragonlike wings, and feet like a bear. Tutuola's creatures also share much with the creepy beings in the work of Daniel Fagunwa, the prominent Yoruba-language novelist, in whose midcentury novels we find a giant snake with the head of a man and a spirit with sixteen eyes (Lindfors, 324–29). Tutuola's monsters are composite formations derived from disparate cultural locations. Curiously, however, in the now large body of Tutuolan criticism, rarely are his creatures referred to as modern. His beings always seem to be understood as recastings of prior creaturely forms.

Indeed, discussions of modernity are scarce in Tutuolan studies. When the modern is broached, it's mentioned in passing without sufficient depth. Take, for instance, Gikandi's brief examination of the modern in *Palm Wine*. Rightly, he emphasizes, "Tutuola's fable is constantly haunted by the claims of the modern it seeks to foreclose." Despite the novel's folkloric packaging and its attendant connotations of the premodern, traces of modern life emerge throughout the text. For Gikandi, these are the traces of capitalism that pervade the Tutuolan landscape. The protagonist's concern for wealth makes him a "consummate capitalist," he says, and therefore a figure of modernity (2007, 1–2). This claim may be indisputable, but Gikandi's examination of the formations of capital in the text ends here, merely gesturing toward capital's saturation of Tutuola's surreal world. Gikandi's insight must be opened up to bring Tutuola's modernist sensibility into view.

FLOWS, COMMODITIES, AND CREATURES

Uncovering Amos Tutuola's creaturely modernism requires a new series of African modernist tropes. It calls for tropes that configure Africa as a locus of flows of capital, not merely a geography peripheral to capital's putative "center" in Europe. The theory needed to speak to Tutuola's modernism is not the overworked narrative of capital's homogenization of global cultures. It is one in which the flux of our late-capitalist moment produces an endless series of interchanges, differences, and mistranslations. The points of origin and ending of a given commodity as it circulates throughout the globe do not matter so much as the reconfigurations the object undergoes en route. Tutuola's modernism emerges when we pay attention to his commodities, when we give life to the flows of the objects embodied by his creatures.

Indeed, Sarah Lincoln's "inflationary modernism" and Tsitsi Jaji's "stereomodernism" are important catalysts for working through these elements of Tutuola's modernism. Following Lincoln, reading for the commodity form allows us to see Tutuola's midcentury aesthetic as a prefiguration of the central place of oil in Okri's modernist aesthetic: "Okri reminds us repeatedly that, underlying this entire economic and psychic complex, flows the liquid commodity on which all depends" (Lincoln, 257). And this "flow" in Lincoln's theory is crucial, in a different form, in Jaji's account of how "black diasporic music travels and circulates in cultural contexts of continental Africa," following the global circuits of capital to shape a distinct form of the pan-African modern (2). There is a phenomenological structure of global movement undergirding Jaji's and Lincoln's modernist accounts—albeit more explicitly in the former—that will be crucial to articulating Tutuola's creaturely modernism. Moreover, Jaji's insight of sonic and cultural difference in her metaphor of the stereo gestures toward the differences in shape and significance of Tutuola's creatural commodities as they move through capital's global circuits. The particularities of Jaji's and Lincoln's recent theories of African modernism may not be enough to articulate the full range of Tutuola's modernism, but they introduce us to several crucial categories through which to work out Tutuola's sprawling, global aesthetic.

Moving then toward a theory of African modernism as global flow, Stuart Hall provides a crucial next move. "With the modern . . . condition," Hall suggests, "the process of *cultural translation* means that cultural languages are not closed; they are constantly transformed from both inside and outside, continuously learning from other languages and traditions, drawing them in and producing something which is irreducible to either of the cultural elements which constituted it in the first place. . . . The West is an absolutely pivotal, powerful, hegemonic force, but is no longer the only force within which creative energies, cultural flows and new ideas can be concerted" ("Museums of Modern Art"). Hall's model is one in which the "West" remains dominant, but the center-periphery framework becomes obsolete. Commodities and technologies are certainly included in his "cultural languages" that move in flows, mutating as they wander through disparate world geographies.

The hands of the "Television-handed Ghostess" in Tutuola's *Bush of Ghosts* are part of a global circulation, and West Africa is a location in which these televisions are inserted into the body of the creature and transformed into a singular instance of the modern. Through *literal appendages*, in which commodities are actual component parts of the body, and *figurative prosthetics*, in which commodities are embodied via the comparative figure of the simile, Tutuola creates a network of global consumer culture and technology with its nexus in the creature's body. It is Tutuola's experimental use of figures of speech, syntax, and form that brings these creatures to life. His global modernism may emerge from the body of the creature, but it's his often-unexpected use of language that enables us to see the phenomenology of the creaturely body.

The notion of the creaturely, of course, is not unique to the work of Amos Tutuola. As Eric Santner's influential work *On Creaturely Life* (2006) makes clear, Tutuola's creaturely shares much with other representations in world literature. Santner suggests that the figure of the creature emerged in the German-Jewish literary tradition as a symptom of European modernity and biopolitics. "Creaturely life," he contends, "is a product . . . of [the human's] exposure to a traumatic dimension of political power and social bonds whose structures have undergone radical transformations in modernity" (12). Creaturely life, in this particular literary tradition, surfaces at the "threshold of law and nonlaw" (15). It signifies bare life: life expelled by juridical law, from juridical law, into a Schmittian state of exception. It is the deformed, excessive, less-than-human life abandoned to that "paradoxical domain in which law has been suspended in the name of preserving law" (22). Santner isolates Kafka's particular version of the creature as marked by a "chronic state of agitation and disorientation, a perpetual state of exception/emergency in which the boundaries of the law become undecidable" (21). In Kafka's world, the human-as-creature is subjected "to an agency, a master's discourse, that has been attenuated and dispersed across a field of relays and points of contact that no longer cohere, even in fantasy, as a consistent 'other' of possible address and redress" (22). The ubiquity of the modern biopolitical order renders the human a creature, relegating it to this suspended space of nonlaw, nonlife.

Indeed one might argue that the creaturely formations of the German-Jewish tradition have little in common with those of West African folklore, that there remains a kind of experiential, if not historical, incommensurability between the two. I want to suggest that Tutuola's creaturely life has more in common with the German-Jewish tradition than one might initially expect, but that, of course, Tutuola's creaturely biopolitics is in many ways distinct. Similar to Santner's exposition of Kafka's world, when the protagonist in *My Life in the Bush of Ghosts* walks into the bush, life and death, law and nonlaw become indistinguishable. There is no singularly identifiable sovereign power. Power is distributed, and violence comes from everywhere and nowhere. Achille Mbembe reads Tutuola's first two novels through this biopolitical lens, examining in these works the "forms of social existence in which vast populations are subjected to conditions of life that confer upon them the status of living dead" (1). Like Santner's study of German-Jewish writers, Mbembe studies the "threshold experiences" in Tutuola's work that render life perpetually spied upon, haunted, and unlivable. Mbembe does not use the term "modern" to describe Tutuola's creaturely world, but he does relate it to the corruption and violence that plagues "the contemporary African context." Here, of course, Mbembe alludes to the African postcolony and the violent colonial inheritance that crippled much of the continent at the onset of formal independence from Europe in the mid twentieth century. In a way, then, Santner and Mbembe speak of two sides of the same global structure of biopolitical violence that emerged in the late eighteenth century. The biopolitical structure that Santner suggests transformed the human into creature in the German-Jewish tradition must indeed be thought of as integrally related to the biopolitical structure of violent colonial incursions, racial classification and separation, and the commodification of human beings on the African continent.[5]

The biopolitical violence that shaped the modern world pervades Amos Tutuola's fiction, but he provides his own articulation of it using the fantastical logic of Yoruba storytelling. In his work, protagonists transform from human to snake to airplane, and bacteria-infested monsters are didactic storytellers. Tutuola's space of exception is one in which the folkoric and the biopolitical merge, generating an episodic series of hauntings, hallucinations, and contorted logics. Whereas Santner's creatures are still human, though perhaps *less* human, Tutuola's creaturely ontologies are nonhuman multitudes, simultaneously robot, ghost, animal, virus, and plant. They reside in their own world parallel to the human world, in this space, as Mbembe puts it, where "there is no life but a life that is fractured and mutilated" (6). And like Santner's notion of the "traumatic exposure" that renders the human a creature, Mbembe explains that in Tutuola's fiction, "[we] penetrate into the world of ghosts by means of tragedy" (8). Protagonists stumble into the exceptional space because they seek their dead tapster, or they have taken flight from slave traders: "After I had travelled sixteen miles and was still running further for the fearful noises, I did not know the time that I entered into a dreadful bush which is called the 'Bush of Ghosts'" (22). The *Bush of Ghosts* protagonist passes the threshold into the zone of folkloric terror where he encounters ghosts covered in colorful lights, excrement, and festering wounds. This is the West African iteration of biopolitics, a kind of African surrealist biopolitics. In Tutuola's world, Auschwitz blurs into a space of ghosts and the afterlife, of shape-shifting beings, tricksters, and cautionary proverbs.

I raise the question of biopolitics in Tutuola's fiction to address the world his fantastical creatures inhabit. If the ontology of Tutuola's creatures is the core of the Nigerian writer's modernist aesthetic, this ontology cannot be isolated from the modern biopolitical structure that engendered it. His creatures are of this surreal biopolitics, simultaneously victims and perpetrators of it. The bodies of these creatures through which we read histories of capital and the modern world emerge from this fantastical, worldly space. If the resonance between Tutuola's surreal biopolitical landscape and Santner's account of creaturely biopolitics in the German-Jewish tradition tells us anything, it is that Tutuola's West Africa is indisputably of the modern world, situated among the disparate forms of power and capital that gave rise to what we call modernity.

Moving from the Tutuolan biopolitical terrain to the creatures themselves, Santner's *On Creaturely Life* again provides a crucial point of entry. He begins the text with a discussion of Rilke's *Duino Elegies* particularly apt to Tutuolan creaturely forms, concerning himself not with the creaturely human, but with Rilke's animalistic conception of the creature, and the poet's corresponding notion of "the Open." For Rilke, *das Offene* is the "sphere of the creature," the space to which the animal directs its gaze. The human's gaze is inward, overwhelmingly dominated by representations and distractions; plants, animals, and insects, by contrast, see the pure phenomena of the world before them, such as the motion of a blossoming flower, or trees bending in the wind. The creature sees the subtle, hidden movements that make up its world.[6] Rilke makes it clear that the creature is also unequivocally a figure of alterity, a being that exists as the human's Other (1–5). Later in his discussion of Joseph K. in Kafka's *The Trial*, Santner turns to Emmanuel Levinas to articulate how the creature—here, the human abandoned to the juridical state of exception—feels shame both in its sense of uncanny intimacy and its sense of foreignness to itself. The creature is a figure of alterity, in other words, in relation to others, but also to itself (22–23).

These notions of alterity and "the Open" illuminate important features of Tutuola's nonhuman life forms. The freakish alterity of the creatures in *Palm Wine* and *Bush of Ghosts*—their foreignness to others and their foreignness to themselves—reveals a phenomenological sense of the world. If Tutuola's creatures are multitudes, made up of West African insects and dirt, of bacteria and viruses, of commodities and technologies that have circulated the globe, then these strangely disparate component parts have histories and relations to other commodities and viruses that span the world. Through the body of the Tutuolan creature we literally see "the Open" that is the modern world, with its global trade routes, intercontinent-traveling viruses, and histories of invention and capitalist production. In the morphology of these creatures we find Amos Tutuola's insertion of West Africa into a system of global capitalism and cultural influence. Indeed, the trope that best enables an examination of these notions of "multitude" and "the worldly Open" in Tutuola's work is the commodity form. For the worldliness and the freakishness of the Tutuolan creature derive largely from that object which Karl Marx famously characterized as "mysterious" and "metaphysical."

For Marx, the commodity is inherently a representation of something beyond itself, of the labor and social relations that produced the object. But his formulation also presupposes the commodity's proximity to a network of related circulating objects. For him, of course, the relation among commodities finds its source in the social relations among laborers. In the section on "The Fetishism of Commodities" in *Capital I*, Marx writes of the "metaphysical subtleties" that lay beyond the ostensible "thingness" of the commodity (303–29). The commodity is never a single construct—it is always already in excess of itself. It is this notion of existing *in excess* that opens us to Amos Tutuola's modernism. The footballs, radios, and photographs in his novels are all commodities that represent social relations and modes of production beyond their immediate materiality.

In *Specters of Marx*, Derrida expands on this notion of the commodity's "excess," pushing us to think of the commodity itself as a ghostly creature. Working with the tropes of the theater and the table, Derrida writes that the table becomes a commodity "when the curtain goes up on the market and the table plays actor and character at the same time." Derrida identifies the commodity as "spectral," troping on Marx's language of the commodity's "metaphysical and theological niceties." The many faces and relations behind the commodity's surface "haunt" the object in its use-value. On the stage, the commodity "stands up and addresses itself . . . to other commodities, its fellow beings in phantomality." The commodity qua specter is social, Derrida suggests, standing before its others as a "strange creature," which is at once "Life, Thing, Beast, Object, Commodity, Automaton." In its creaturely multitude, the commodity embodies a lineage of "fantastic creatures," of other beings and objects, a "lineage of a progeniture that no longer resembles it, inventions far more bizarre and marvelous." Commodities are embedded in a history of commodities that are also freakishly "many" in their own being. Commodities relate to other commodities, to workers and to nonworkers, and to the genealogies of objects and social relations that have allowed them to come into being. This, for Derrida, is the spectral "dance" of the commodity (187–97).

Tutuola's "Television-handed Ghostess" in *My Life in the Bush of Ghosts* represents this spectral dance on a global scale. This creature literally has a television embedded in each of its two palms. If Derrida refers to the commodity as a "strange creature," Tutuola's Ghostess is indeed a *hyper*-strange creature.[7] The televisions in her hands may be as strange as any commodity, but when situated in the context of the Ghostess's morphology, strangeness becomes an understatement. It is during the final stage of the unnamed protagonist's journey through the bush of ghosts that the protagonist encounters the Television-handed Ghostess. The Ghostess is more than two hundred years old, entirely bald, covered in sores and maggots, and has "uncountable" short fingers. Bizarrely, the Ghostess requests that he lick the sores on her body every day for ten years, since only that will cure her wounds. She then turns over her hand for the protagonist to see: "When she told me to look at her palm and opened it nearly to touch my face, it was exactly as a television" (161–62). The television, as commodity, is itself an object of multiplicity, but so too is the creature's body even before we consider the TV.[8] Between the embodied televisions and the living beings covering her body, Derrida's ontological description of the creaturely commodity seems astonishingly apt to Tutuola's creature: "Life, Thing, Beast, Object, Commodity, Automaton."

Derrida's specter is literalized in Tutuola's TV Ghostess. Not only is the creature itself is a specter, but it embodies the spectral commodity. That which lay beyond the TV's ontic materiality are flows of global capital and histories of social relations. The TV is composed of raw materials that have been extracted from the earth. It's an assemblage of experiments in electricity and circuitry. It embodies a lineage of prior forms of communication technology such as Morse code, the radio, and the telephone. The TV is part of a global social history in which technologies disseminated through the pathways, classes, and historical stages of empire, moving from the sitting rooms of the metropolitan privileged to those of the metropolitan working classes, the colonial administrators posted in British West Africa, the indigenous colonial elite, and on to the middle- and working-class families of postcolonial West Africa. And, of course, the television is a commodity produced by factory workers and the social relations that made their labor possible. It is situated among many other televisions of different types, sizes, ages, and weights. The televisions of the TV Ghostess are commodities formed from a global constellation of relations.

The television, understood as a singularly modern technology, is inherently in excess of itself. The television connects worlds, it links immediacies unlike any other prior technology. The Ghostess shows the wandering protagonist her television hands, in which he sees and hears his family relaxing at home. This is the location he has sought to return to for years. Still pressed by the Ghostess to cure her sores, the protagonist asks to view the television again:

> My people appeared again at the same time and as I was looking at them and also hearing what they were talking about me which I ought to answer if I was with them, luckily, a woman brought her baby who had a sore on its foot to my mother at that time to tell her the kind of leaf which could heal the sore. . . . She cut many leaves on a kind of plant and gave them to this woman, after that she told her that she must warm the leaves in hot water before using it for the sore. But as I was looking at them on the television I knew the kind of leaf and also heard the direction how to use it. (164–65)

The wanderer concocts a medication according to his mother's direction, treats the sores of the Ghostess, and within a week the sores disappear. Here, the television embodied by the creature becomes a site of sociality, of communication, and of knowledge production. Tutuola literalizes the notion of linkage inherent in the technology when the Ghostess ushers the wanderer into the image, effectively enabling him to teleport through the TV. The novel ends when the protagonist finds himself physically in the same location he had just viewed on the screen.

The Ghostess becomes a kind of surreal biopolitical gatekeeper, a haunting figure that controls the movement of populations, and determines whether one lives by passing into the world of the living. The protagonist's experience is mediated and facilitated by the television, but the Ghostess-creature reveals in her hands the Rilkean creaturely "Open" that she possesses. She gazes at the phenomena and events denied to human perception.

The Television-handed Ghostess enables the wanderer to see, and ultimately, to live the life of the image. Moments before he sees the TV hands for the first time, the Ghostess tells the wanderer, "You are seeing the way every day and you do not know it, because every earthly person gets eyes but cannot see" (162). The television, and in turn, the creaturely body, permits the protagonist to see in a way he could not otherwise, given momentary access to the creaturely Open. The TV reveals the world to him. In an insightful and very much related discussion on television, spectatorship, and social space, Raymond Williams writes of the TV viewer's need "to watch what is happening, as we say, 'out there': not out there in a specific street or a specific community but in a complex and otherwise unfocused and unfocusable national and international life, where our area of concern . . . is unprecedentedly wide" (14). Indeed, this "unprecedentedly wide" area of concern is the optic of modernity that television enacts. The TV connects disparate global geographies, reaching beyond the confines of the nation and the colony. Tutuola's television provides a similarly expansive view of the globe, one that allows us to watch and listen to what is "out there." Tutuola's TV hands perhaps reach even further than Williams's model, for Tutuola expands the protagonist's *Weltanschauung* not merely to other nations and colonies, but to another world, to the human world outside the nonhuman bush of ghosts. By connecting people, commodities, and histories on a global and even otherworldly scale, the Television-handed Ghostess is unequivocally a figure of modernity.

But this creature, certainly, is not a modernist figure merely in her worldliness or spectrality; it is undoubtedly Tutuola's particular use of language that makes these qualities possible. Consider this initial description of the Ghostess: "I noticed carefully that she was almost covered with sores, even there was no single hair on her head, except sores with uncountable maggots which were dashing here and there on her body. Both her arms were more than one and an half foot [*sic*], it had uncountable short fingers" (161). In this brief passage we find the sort of syntax and diction characteristic of Tutuola's prose. There is a staggered, jolted flow to his writing. The second clause—"even there was no single hair on her head"—at first seems out of place next to the description of sores, but he then returns to the sores only to move immediately on to "maggots." The adjective "uncountable" appears dozens of times throughout the novel, and twice in these two sentences. It is a curious word, one that Tutuola uses to describe a quantity at once excessive and indeterminate. The "uncountable maggots" and "uncountable short fingers" enact a certain revulsion in the reader, as if Tutuola were describing a threateningly alien mass, something writhing, uncontainable. And Tutuola also curiously refers to the Ghostess as both "she" and "it." He modulates its gender from feminine to neuter, perhaps even merging the two, effectively inscribing the ghostly creature outside any readily identifiable gender position. The Television-handed Ghostess herself is a beastly, multispecies creature, one that acts as the gatekeeper to the worldly Open, but it is Tutuola's language that brings this creature to life. This description, like so many in his novels, is almost sculptural. With stuttering language, he crafts the image of a horrifying, bald-headed ghost, covered with festering sores and crawling maggots. His singular use of syntax, diction, and grammar constructs the creature as something vivid, material, and fantastical. The TV Ghostess is a quintessential example of his creaturely modernism, and this is made possible by the language Tutuola uses to bring that modernism to life.

Another archetypal modernist creature in Tutuola's oeuvre is the "White Tree" creature in *The Palm-Wine Drinkard*. During the palm-wine drinkard's episodic journey to find his palm-wine tapster, the drinkard and his wife encounter a monstrous creature that is at once tree, mobile being, automaton, and a dwelling for other creatures. The tree is "about one thousand and fifty feet high in length and about two hundred feet in diameter." Its trunk, limbs, and branches are all white "as if it was painted everyday with white paint." While passing the tree, the drinkard and his wife see something "focusing" on them like a camera. Terrified, the two begin to run, but the "focusing gaze" follows them until two hands emerge from the tree, pulling them into a large door that opens on the side of the tree. Inside, they meet the

"Faithful Mother" who hosts their stay in this city-inside-a-tree. For the next year, the drinkard and his wife dance in the tree's technicolor nightclub, eat food prepared by the Faithful Mother's 340 cooks, lose all their money gambling, and are even treated for hair loss in the tree's hospital (246–52). So much happens to the couple in this episode that it is easy to forget it all takes place inside the body of a tree creature— literally inside a living, moving thing. Capital saturates this episode in the tree. The tree's colorful lights, cameras, and photographs serve as metonyms for global capitalism, some as literal appendages, others as figurative prostheses. If the Television-handed Ghostess is a multitudinous being, this tree is a super multitude in its many valences of embodied capital.

The camera is the first form of capital we encounter in this creature. The device surfaces in the figure of speech of the simile as a sort of creaturely mode of surveillance: "Somebody peeped out and was focusing us as if a photographer was focusing somebody." This does not initially appear to be an actual camera, but the comparative reference augments the sense of anxiety and invasiveness that this "focusing" instills in the couple. As the drinkard and his wife enter the dance hall inside the tree, however, they see photographs of themselves displayed on the wall:

> But our own images that we saw there resembled us too much and were also white colour, but we were very surprised to see our images there, perhaps somebody who was focusing us as a photographer at the first time before the hands drew us inside the white tree had made them, we could not say. (248)

What is initially a figurative simile—"as if a photographer was focusing"—becomes literalized in these photographs. The tree-creature is a kind of biopolitical apparatus, tracking and recording individuals passing by. If this mode of surveillance did not already feel surreal, it certainly does when the images are found to be partly obscured, turned "white colour" like the tree itself. The bleached-out photographs symbolically subsume the protagonists into the creaturely tree, increasing its multitude, collapsing them into its field of absurdist control. And the fractured language—the consecutive "but" conjunctions, the excessive stretching out of the sentence—only serves to heighten the couple's apparent baffled terror.

The curious absurdity continues inside the White Tree's technicolor dance hall, which bears its own kind of modernist lineage. With characteristic Tutuolan peculiarity, the hall is a cacophonous assemblage of sound, color, and movement:

> Over twenty stages were in that hall with uncountable orchestras, musicians, dancers and tappers. The orchestras were all busy. The children . . . were always dancing, tapping on the stage with melodious songs and they were also singing with warm tones with non-stop till morning. There we saw that all the lights in this hall were in technicolours and they were changing colours at five minutes intervals. (249)

Given the historical moment in which Tutuola writes, the aura and aesthetic of this space recalls performances only a few decades removed from Josephine Baker's *La Revue Nègre* in 1920s Paris, Duke Ellington's orchestra at Harlem's Cotton Club, and the Highlife clubs in Nigeria and Ghana in the first decades of the twentieth century. Tutuola takes a modern social space that existed throughout the world in the first half of the twentieth century and inserts it into his fantastical aesthetic, that is, into the body of a folkoric creature.

Beyond these clear manifestations of modernity in the White Tree, however, is an intriguing veiled critique of the capitalist system. This critique commences when the drinkard and his wife enter the tree: "We had 'sold our death' to somebody at the door for the sum of £70: 18: 6d and 'lent our fear' to somebody at the door as well on interest of £3: 10: 0d per month" (247). In short, the drinkard and his wife have been commodified. Consequently the two "did not care about death or fear again" while in the tree. Life becomes worry-free, they all but forget about the outside world. While living worry- and death-free, the drinkard and his wife are in awe of the opulence inside the tree. The Faithful Mother is essentially seated on a throne, "a chair in a big parlour which was decorated with costly things" (247). The walls of the dance hall are literally covered in money, "with about one million pounds (£)." The situation becomes satirical when the drinkard loses all his money—effectively everything he received when they entered the creature—while gambling inside the tree. "I had forgotten," he says, "that one day, we should leave there and need money to spend" (250). Penniless but enjoying the Faithful Mother's luxuries, the two are reluctant to leave, having become dependent on what they receive in the tree. When the Faithful Mother expels the drinkard and his wife from the tree after more than a year, the buyer of their death refuses to re-sell their death, but they regain their fear along with the final install-ment of interest. So the drinkard and his wife recommence their journey to find their palm wine tapster, but now with only their fear and no death. This is in a way a Tutuolan reconfiguration of Foucault's notion of biopower as the power to "make live and let die." The White Tree exerts its power over the drinkard by, as Foucault would put it, "inter-vening to make live"—ensuring that the drinkard not only stays alive, but, in effect, is unable to die at all (Foucault, 239–48). Tutuola's folk-loric biopower takes Foucault's notion to a fantastical extreme of pop-ulation control and regulation.

Like an individual conscripted by the capitalist system, the palm wine drinkard has no choice but to become a commodity and partake in the White Tree's system. He is forced into the tree by the giant hands, required to sell his death and lease his fear. In a surprising literaliza-tion of Adam Smith's notion of the "invisible hand," the protagonist feels that he has benefited from the tree's luxury, when in fact he's simply contributing to its parasitic internal structure. In the drinkard's gambling match, the tree regains the amount it paid for the drinkard's death. The tree has crippled him financially, yet his dependence quells his desire to escape. Living in a state of perpetual fear with no recourse to death is akin to the suffocating grip of a subsistence wage in which the capitalist system relentlessly crushes the worker, giving her just enough money to survive and continue to work. Tutuola presents a scathing critique of the capitalist system that, quite astoundingly, takes place in the body of a surreal West African creature.

Aside from the critique and figurations of capital that we find in the White Tree and the TV Ghostess, a crucial component to Tutuola's modernism is his use of the simile. The White Tree introduced us to this figure of speech in the "focusing photographer." Similes of technology and global consumer culture pervade Tutuola's *Palm Wine* and *Bush of Ghosts*. In most instances, these similes are clearly figurative compari-sons meant to vivify the creature described. Yet the disorientation pro-duced by Tutuola's incongruous juxtapositions of the literal and the figurative seems to heighten the prominence of the figurative, as if the figurative were made literal. Here, again, Tutuola's idiosyncratic, even experimental, use of language brings the figure of the creature to the fore, heightening its prominence by disrupting the distinction between literal and figurative. Take, for instance, the episode in *Bush of Ghosts* when the protagonist, still attempting to return to his family in the human world, is trapped in a room. He begins to morph into another being, his neck grows three feet and his head inflates. Tutuola uses the simile to accentuate the change in the protagonist's eyes: "Eyes which were as big and round as a football formed and appeared on this head" (68). Tutuola references a commodity from a starkly differ- ent social and cultural context (*seemingly* different, anyway). Certainly, the simile clarifies how big and shapely the creature's eyes have become. But more than actual eyes, Tutuola invites us to imagine life-size foot- balls on this creature's head—literal soccer balls as prosthetic eyeballs. The commodity at the center of the world's most popular sport has been inserted into the body of this unearthly folkloric creature. These prosthetic eyes mark this creature's body as a global relation of capital and empire.

These types of incongruous similes are scattered throughout Tutu- ola's first two novels. In *Palm Wine*, a "half-bodied baby" rises from the ashes of a burned building, "talking with a lower voice like a tele- phone" (218). When the protagonist of *Bush of Ghosts* is trapped inside a piece of "dead wood," his cry for help is overheard by "a million homeless ghosts . . . who were listening to my cry as a radio" (50). The ostensible anomalousness of the radio and telephone in these contexts brings these objects to the fore of our attention, as if they were lit- eral prostheses or props integral to the way these creatures communi- cate and listen. They become constitutive components of the creature's sense of space and world. These commodities come to life by way of the simile, inscribing the creature into capital's global circuits of exchange. Another notable instance is the "flash-eyed mother" in *Bush of Ghosts,* whose fireball-eyes are used "at night as a flood light in lighting the whole town as electricity lights" (99). Here, the literalized simile con- veys an actual infrastructural network, gesturing toward the illumina- tion of the modern African city.

However incongruous these electric lights, radios, and telephones may seem in Tutuola's work, they are, I want to suggest, intrinsic to African modernity. The Africanness of these modern technologies re- calls Anthony Appiah's well-known discussion of a particular Yoruba wooden sculpture depicting a man riding a bicycle. Noting the signifi- cance of the bicycle, Appiah suggests, "It is not there to be the Other to the Yoruba self . . . it is there because it will take us further than our feet will take us; it is there because machines are now as African as novelists" (157). Though many technologies and commodities found in Africa have been invented or produced abroad, in other words, what actually matters is how an object is reconfigured in each cultural context as it moves through capital's global circuits. A radio in Lagos or Dakar—and certainly the radio of the "homeless ghosts" in Tutuola's surreal novel—assumes different layers of cultural significance from a radio in London or New York. In Tutuola's creatures, technologies that have traveled the global pathways of empire, mutating across cultural geographies, blur into West African cultural forms. A modern African object is formed. And, as Tutuola's fantastical fiction reveals, so too is the modern African creature.

TOWARD A GLOBAL AFRICAN MODERN

Amos Tutuola's modernist sensibility shatters the overwrought binary of tradition and modernity that persists in much Africanist discourse. These constructs fuse in his fiction, creating a new form of interstitial cultural space. An exemplary instance of this space is the "10th Town" in *My Life in the Bush of Ghosts*, which is inhabited entirely by "deads," yet has schools and hospitals built in "modern styles." A dead person can be healthy and educated in his surreal world. The afterlife is a modern life. Throughout Tutuola's oeuvre, we find a new form of life, an alter-life, emerging from the gaps and syntheses of histories and geographies. Contradiction, freakishness, and mutation are what manifest when Tutuola ruptures the dichotomies of tradition and modernity, local and global, center and periphery. His modernism collapses these figures to create a new sort of enchantment, embracing the tainted, messy, transfigured forms that tradition has become in modern Africa. And in the end, this enchanted peculiarity of Tutuola's world—his photographing trees, his folkloric biopolitical landscape—is brought to life through the enchanted peculiarity of his literary style, his blurring of literal and figurative, his stilted syntax, his meandering sentences.

This modernist aesthetic allows us to see the phenomena of the world, the relations that flow below superficial appearances. Through Tutuola's work, we see what would otherwise remain invisible to us.

His creaturely bodies comprised of disparate circulating cultural forms together constitute quite literally a sprawling sense of being-in-the-world. In them, we see the flows and contortions of a world system in perpetual motion. Understanding his nonhuman monsters as worldly multitudes effectively reinscribes Tutuola into African modernist discourse, a body of thought from which he had effectively been expelled. But Tutuola does not simply enter the fray of African modernism, conforming to its tropes of anticolonialism or the emergent nation. In his midcentury moment, he ushered in a new formation of the African modern—one that did not enclose itself in its call for liberation, but instead opened itself to the traces, contaminations, and undulations of global capital. His creatures bear the marks of these contaminations. They are freaks in their worldly excess and multitude. To be a figure of modernity, Tutuola tells us, is to be a mutant in and of the world.

Matthew Omelsky received his PhD in English from Duke University and is currently the Mellon Sawyer Seminar postdoctoral fellow in the Department of African American Studies at Pennsylvania State University. His articles on African literature and film can be found in *Research in African Literatures, Nka: Journal of Contemporary African Art,* and *The Cambridge Journal of Postcolonial Literary Inquiry.*

Notes

1. From the outset, I want to clarify some of the terms I use throughout this essay. By "modern" and "modernity" I refer most fundamentally to the historical period beginning in the mid-seventeenth century that Reinhardt Koselleck identifies as a critical turning point in the way European societies conceived of science, metaphysics, and temporality itself (Koselleck, 9–25). This period of more than a century, of course, coincides with the Enlightenment, the transition from feudalism to (merchant and industrial) capitalism, as well as the imperial expansion of European power, culture, and capital throughout the world. I therefore conceive of "modernity" as a diverse global phenomenon based on the ways in which European culture and capitalism merged with non-European cultures and economic structures since this mid-seventeenth-century moment. While capitalism is certainly not synonymous with modernity, the former is an absolutely central component of the global structure of the latter. As Fredric Jameson suggests, modernity is, above all, about the ways people conceive of themselves as modern: "If modernization is something that happens to the base, and modernism the form the superstructure

takes in reaction to that ambivalent development, then perhaps modernity characterizes the attempt to make something coherent out of their relationship. Modernity
would then in that case describe the way 'modern' people feel about themselves"
(310). If modernity is a kind of intellectual processing of base and superstructure,
Jameson usefully locates "modernism" in the superstructure—the cultural and ideological forms that correspond to infrastructural modernization. More specifically,
in terms of literary production, I use the term "modernism" to refer to the diverse
array of aesthetic practices from the late nineteenth century to the mid-twentieth
century marked by a certain break from "realist" representation and a certain degree
of formal experimentation. But modernism, indeed like modernity itself, as I argue
in this essay, took on its own shape in African cultural production, with writers
like Amos Tutuola presenting their own kind of experimentations with nonrealist
form and representation.

2. I want to be clear about the language I use to characterize Tutuola's writing.
There seems to be some consensus among Africanists that the works of Tutuola and
Daniel Fagunwa (the Yoruba-language novelist whose work arguably most influ-
enced Tutuola) are precursors to magical realism—the latter term, in the anglophone
African context, being most closely associated with Ben Okri's work. Tutuola's and
Fagunwa's writing, according to Brenda Cooper, do not qualify as magical realism
because they lack the sense of ironic distance from indigenous culture characteristic of magical realism: "These devotees and storytellers have not been torn from
their societies in the manner of those modern writers whose village is now global.
They have not distanced themselves from their belief in the supernatural, and therefore do not need to quality their depictions with the irony of the magical realist.
Their fiction is mythical, supernatural, allegorical and epic" (44). While my central
claim in this essay has to do with the sense of the global in Tutuola's fiction, Cooper
is right that the global is not conspicuous in Tutuola's novels in the way that it is
in Ben Okri's *The Famished Road*. The global in Tutuola's writing is subtler, found
primarily in his manipulations of figures of speech. Instead of magical realism, I
use the terms "fantastic" and "surreal" to refer to the interstitial generic space
Tutuola occupies between folklore and magical realism. "Surrealism," of course,
is not meant to align Tutuola with the twentieth-century European avant-garde.
I use "fantastic" and "surreal" synonymously to characterize the singular nonreal-
ism of Tutuola's writing, to have language to identify his world of shape-shifting,
fire-emitting, tapster-chasing beings. For more on Tutuola as a precursor to magical realism, see Quayson, "Magical Realism and the African Novel" (2009) and
Wenzel, "Petro-Magic-Realism: Toward a Political Ecology of Nigerian Literature"
(2006).

3. This brief overview is intended to be a sampling of the dominant currents
in African modernist writing and criticism, and is by no means comprehensive. In
addition to the scholars and texts discussed here, see also Anthony Appiah's *In My
Father's House* (1992), Simon Gikandi's *Maps of Englishness* (1996), Nicholas Brown's
Utopian Generations (2005), Michael Janis's *Africa After Modernism* (2008), and Neil
Lazarus's "Modernism and African Literature" (2012).

4. There have of course been numerous examinations of Tutuola's works over the years. One of the most influential, in addition to Lindfors's studies, is Chinua Achebe's essay "Work and Play in *The Palm Wine Drinkard*," in which he claims that the novel's protagonist at times breaks the normative distinction between work and play and "raises pleasure to the status of work and occupation" (110–12). In contrast, Achille Mbembe's essay "Life, Sovereignty, and Terror in the Fiction of Amos Tutuola," which I discuss later in this essay, unpacks notions of ghostly violence, disrupted temporality, and suspended sovereignty. More recently, in *Metaphor and the Slave Trade in West African Literature* (2012), Laura Murphy takes up related notions of terror in her examination of the historical residue of the Atlantic slave trade in Tutuola's fiction. The focus of recent Tutuolan criticism, though, has been the renewed consideration of the production and reception of Tutuola's early work. In *Commonwealth of Letters* (2013), Peter Kalliney argues that although the views of European and African critics at midcentury differed greatly, both groups paradoxically read Tutuola's novels through a similar discourse of international development. And Gail Low in *Publishing the Postcolonial* (2011) builds an intriguing case for the ways in which Faber and Faber molded the text of *Palm Wine* and its international promotion so as to establish a culturally translatable "value" for British audiences.

5. My notion of biopolitics and its emergence in the late eighteenth century comes from Foucault's observation of the development of a "new technology of power" at that time, which had less to do with the discipline of the individual than the control of the biological field, of "man-as-species" (242). That Santner and Mbembe both ground their work in largely the same body of continental thought further indicates the commonality between the biopolitical structures in the Tutuolan and German-Jewish literary traditions.

Both theorists, for instance, begin their examinations with the same theoretical model of sovereignty. "The tradition of thought I am calling 'German-Jewish,'" Santner advances, "is one that takes as its point of departure some form of the 'decisionist' logic of sovereignty articulated by Carl Schmitt" (13). And, as if in dialogue with Santner, Mbembe begins his essay on Tutuola's fiction claiming, "The ultimate expression of sovereignty resides, to a large degree, in the power and the capacity to dictate who may live and who must die" (1). With these clear common influences of Schmitt, Foucault, and others, Mbembe and Santner together demonstrate that the theoretical apparatus of biopower is not exclusively applicable to Europe, and that the instances of violence and terror in Tutuola's work in particular demand a theoretical approach related, but of course not identical, to the one Santner brings to bear on German-Jewish thought.

6. Related to Rilke's notion of the Open, taking a very different methodological approach, is Jakob von Uexküll's groundbreaking work in the field of biosemiotics. In *A Foray into the Worlds of Animals and Humans* (1934), published just over a decade after the publication of Rilke's *Duino Elegies*, the Estonian biophilosopher presents a scientific though speculative account of the ways in which insects and animals perceive the world around them. The concepts of "effect space,"

"dwelling-tone," and "self-tone" that Uexküll constructs from his speculations on animal subject positions indeed complement Rilke's observational metaphysics on the creaturely Open. When, for instance, the latter suggests in "The Eighth Elegy" that "We know what's out there only from the animal's / face," Rilke seems almost to prefigure Uexküll's systematic analyses on how ticks and hermit crabs perceive depth of visual field, time, and movement in their capacity to read the different perceptual signs in their *Umwelt* (Rilke 55).

7. This notion of hyperstrangeness bears a broad resemblance to Timothy Morton's notion of "hyperobjects," in the sense of the hyperobject's vast distribution across time and space in relation to humans. An in-depth engagement with Morton's framework would take this discussion well beyond the scope of West African modernist forms, into the realm of ecological crisis and geological time, but the "hyper" embodied by the TV-handed Ghostess—a "hyper" indeed central to the phenomenological understanding of the Tutuolan creature—does entail a related sense of geographical, historical, and ontological expansiveness. The creature is *hyper* in the sense of being exponentially "beyond itself" or "in excess of itself" on these different registers.

8. I should note that Bernth Lindfors has argued against a literal reading of the ghostess's TV hands as actual televisions. In his short essay, "Amos Tutuola's Television-handed Ghostess," Lindfors suggests that these "televisions" likely refer to nonelectronic Yoruba divination practices. He cites an anecdotal account in which a man recalls peering into a diviner's liquid-filled earthenware pot to "see the nether-world." Lindfors additionally cites Tutuola's own relationship to the technology as further support for this divination thesis: "And since we have reliable evidence that he created the television-handed ghostess without ever having seen a television set in operation, it is no doubt safe to assume that his fabrication of the ghostess's transcendental hand was inspired more by the Yoruba folk belief in the ability of professional diviners to magically tune in on a distant spirit world than it was by Western electronic technology" (76–77). Certainly it is entirely possible that Tutuola never saw an operating television prior to writing the novel, but unfortunately, Lindfors's "reliable evidence" is an insubstantial aside in the foreword to *Bush of Ghosts* in which Geoffrey Parrinder simply declares Tutuola to be "a man who has never seen a television" (Parrinder 12). Beyond this issue of evidence, however, I am still not convinced that we ought not entertain the idea of literal televisions in the ghostess's hands. Indeed, I think it would be a disservice not to take Tutuola's deliberate choice of language seriously. Surely he must have been aware of the global, technological, and communicative connotations the term invoked in the mid-1950s. What is more, the ambivalent simile that introduces the TV in the novel—"it was exactly as a television"—decidedly collapses the distinction between literal and figurative. The precision of "exactly" erodes the metaphorical register of the comparative "as," necessitating, in my view, that we at least consider the television's literalness. But perhaps the most convincing indication to take the television hands literally is demonstrated in a fleeting moment

in Nnedi Okorafor's recent *The Book of Phoenix* (2015), a cyberpunk novel replete with Tutuolaesque "juju" and freakish beings. Characteristic of the range of her literary influences, Okorafor presents a cyborgian ontology that seems to belong just as much to the matrix-world of William Gibson as to the folkloric ghostly forest of Amos Tutuola: "I see three people in the same room with skin that glows a soft green. . . . [W]hen I look more closely, I see that their skin is embedded with millions of miniscule screens" (101).

Works Cited

Achebe, Chinua. 1989. "Work and Play in Amos Tutuola's *The Palm-Wine Drinkard*." In *Hopes and Impediments* 100–112. New York: Doubleday.

Akinjogbin, I Adeagbo. 1975. "Letter from I. Adeagbo Akinjogbin." In *Critical Perspectives on Amos Tutuola*. Ed. Bernth Lindfors, 41–42. Washington, D.C.: Three Continents Press.

Appiah, Anthony. 1992. *In My Father's House: Africa in the Philosophy of Culture*. New York: Oxford University Press.

Brown, Nicholas. 2005. *Utopian Generations: The Political Horizon of Twentieth-Century Literature*. Princeton: Princeton University Press.

Bunyan, John. 1987. *The Pilgrim's Progress*. New York: Penguin.

Coetzee, J. M. 2003. *Elizabeth Costello*. New York: Penguin.

Cooper, Brenda. 1998. *Magical Realism in West African Fiction: Seeing with a Third Eye*. New York: Routledge.

Derrida, Jacques. 1994. *Specters of Marx*. New York: Routledge.

Ekwensi, Cyprian. 1968. *Burning Grass*. London: Heinemann.

Enwezor, Okwui. 2010. "Modernity and Postcolonial Ambivalence." *South Atlantic Quarterly* 109, no. 3:595–620.

Foucault, Michel. 2003. *"Society Must Be Defended": Lectures at the Collège de France 1975–1976*. Trans. David Macey. New York: Picador.

Gikandi, Simon. 1996. *Maps of Englishness: Writing Identity in the Culture of Colonialism*. New York: Columbia University Press.

Gikandi, Simon. 2007. "African Literature and Modernity." In *Texts, Tasks, and Theories: Versions and Subversions in African Literatures, Volume 3*. Ed. T. R. Klein et al., 3–20. New York: Editions Rodopi.

Hall, Stuart. 2001. "Museums of Modern Art and the End of History." *Modernity and Difference*. Ed. Stuart Hall et al., 8–23. London: Institute of International Visual Arts.

Harney, Elizabeth. 2004. *In Senghor's Shadow: Art, Politics, and the Avant-Garde in Senegal, 1960–1995*. Durham: Duke University Press.

Hassan, Salah M. 2010. "African Modernism: Beyond Alternative Modernities Discourse." *South Atlantic Quarterly* 109, no. 3:451–73.

Jaji, Tsitsi. 2014. *Africa in Stereo: Modernism, Music, and Pan-African Solidarity*. Oxford: Oxford University Press.

Jameson, Fredric. 1991. *Postmodernism, or, The Cultural Logic of Late Capitalism*. Durham: Duke University Press.

Janis, Michael. 2008. *Africa After Modernism: Transitions in Literature, Media, and Philosophy*. New York: Routledge.

Kalliney, Peter. 2013. *Commonwealth of Letters: British Literary Culture and the Emergence of Postcolonial Aesthetics*. Oxford: Oxford University Press.

Karouma, Ahmadou. 1970. *Les Soleils des indépendances*. Paris: Éditions du Seuil.

Koselleck, Reinhart. 2004. *Futures Past: On the Semantics of Historical Time*. Trans. Keith Tribe. New York: Columbia University Press.

Lazarus, Neil. 2012. "Modernism and African Literature." In *The Oxford Handbook of Global Modernisms*. 228–48. Oxford: Oxford University Press.

Lincoln, Sarah. 2012. "'Petro-Magic Realism': Ben Okri's Inflationary Modernism." In *The Oxford Handbook of Global Modernisms*, 249–66. Oxford: Oxford University Press.

Lindfors, Bernth. 1970. "Amos Tutuola: Debts and Assets." *Cahiers d'Études Africaines* 10, no. 38:306–34.

Lindfors, Bernth. 1971. "Amos Tutuola's Television-handed Ghostess." *Ariel: A Review of International English Literature* 2, no. 1:68–77.

Low, Gail. 2011. *Publishing the Postcolonial: Anglophone West African and Caribbean Writing in the UK, 1948–1968*. New York: Routledge.

Marx, Karl. 1978. "Capital Volume One." In *The Marx-Engels Reader*. Ed. Robert Tucker. New York: W. W. Norton.

Mbembe, Achille. 2003. "Life, Sovereignty, and Terror in the Fiction of Amos Tutuola." *Research in African Literatures* 34, no. 4:1–26.

Morton, Timothy. 2013. *Hyperobjects: Philosophy and Ecology After the End of the World*. Minneapolis: University of Minnesota Press.

Murphy, Laura. 2012. *Metaphor and the Slave Trade in West African Literature*. Athens: Ohio University Press.

Ngugi wa Thiong'o. 1967. *A Grain of Wheat*. Oxford: Heinemann.

Olaniyan, Tejumola. 2001. "The Cosmopolitan Nativist: Fela Anikulapo-Kuti and the Antinomies of Postcolonial Modernity." *Research in African Literatures* 32, no. 2:76–89.

Parrinder, Geoffrey. 1994. "Foreword." *The Palm-Wine Drinkard* and *My Life in the Bush of Ghosts*. New York: Grove Press.

Pritchett, V. S. 1975. "V. S. Pritchett in *New Statesman and Nation*." In *Critical Perspectives on Amos Tutuola*. Ed. Bernth Lindfors, 21–24. Washington, D.C.: Three Continents Press.

Quayson, Ato. 1997. *Strategic Transformations in Nigerian Writing: Orality and History in the Work of Rev. Samuel Johnson, Amos Tutuola, Wole Soyinka, and Ben Okri*. Bloomington: Indiana University Press.

Quayson, Ato. 2004. "Modernism and Postmodernism in African Literature." *The Cambridge History of African and Caribbean Literature*. Ed. Abiola Irele and Simon Gikandi, 824–52. New York: Cambridge University Press.

Quayson, Ato. 2009. "Magical Realism and the African Novel." *The Cambridge Companion to the African Novel*. Ed. Abiola Irele, 159–76. New York: Cambridge University Press.

Rilke, Rainer Maria. 2005. *Duino Elegies and the Sonnets to Orpheus*. Trans. A. Poulin Jr. New York: Mariner Books.

Santner, Eric. 2006. *On Creaturely Life: Rilke, Benjamin, Sebald*. Chicago: University of Chicago Press.

Tansi, Sony Labou. 1979. *La Vie et demie*. Paris: Éditions du Seuil.

Tutuola, Amos. 1994. *The Palm-Wine Drinkard* and *My Life in the Bush of Ghosts*. New York: Grove Press.

von Uexküll, Jakob. 2010. *A Foray into the Worlds of Animals and Humans with a Theory of Meaning*. Trans. Joseph D. O'Neil. Minneapolis: University of Minnesota Press.

Wenzel, Jennifer. 2006. "Petro-Magic-Realism: Toward a Political Ecology of Nigerian Literature." *Postcolonial Studies* 9, no. 4:449–64.

Williams, Raymond. 1983. "Drama in a Dramatized Society." In *Writing in Society*, 11–21. New York: Verso.

HEIDEGGER'S METAPOLITICS

Jeff Love and Michael Meng

N ational Socialism is a *barbaric principle*. That is its essence and its potential greatness. The danger is not National Socialism itself, but that it becomes disarmed in a preaching of the true, the good, and the beautiful (just as at a training seminar). And that those who want to form its philosophy do nothing more than repeat the accepted "logic" of commonplace thinking and exact science instead of realizing that precisely now "logic" comes anew into distress and needs and must arise anew.[1]

HEIDEGGER

Martin Heidegger is a philosopher of the city. He is not devoted to an otherworldly city. He creates no city in speech, no city of God. Heidegger devotes his thought to the city as the site (*Stätte*) of a history that forecloses and grants certain fundamental creative possibilities. One of those possibilities came to the fore in 1933, and Heidegger chose to seize the moment, to pursue with the utmost energy a thorough and radical program of renewal. Heidegger's choice was not an aberration, not the blundering of a naive scholar into the rough-and-tumble precincts of political life. To the contrary, this choice made good on a promise that he had not kept hitherto, the revolutionary promise of his own thought as it had developed in the 1920s. For what can one say of a thinking that claims to pose a question—indeed, *the* question—having lain dormant for more than two millennia while making no corresponding intervention in the life of the city? What kind of attitude to thought might this be, if not one of sardonic derision and dismissal? As we know from his own insistent pronouncements, Heidegger did not see philosophy as so trivial, but rather as sovereign, ruling (*Basic Questions of Philosophy*). To be sure, he did reject the direct connection of philosophy with action, but he never tired of proclaiming a far more important indirect connection, a grounding one, whereby philosophy opens up the very horizon that proscribes at any given time the possibilities for action or any series of actions: in short, a history or metapolitics in Heidegger's own words (*Überlegungen II–IV*, GA 94, 115).

We might then ask why it was that Heidegger chose to intervene in the life of the city under the banner of National Socialism. If Heidegger was not naive nor a mere opportunist, it follows that he must have found some kinship to his own thought in National Socialism. This seemingly simple conclusion has created exceptional controversy for eighty years now. Why, after all, would a thinker of Heidegger's stature side with National Socialism? The question is a cloying one because it implies that no thinker of stature could have endorsed a movement so fixated on the primitive assertion of inequality, violence, and nationalism. To think against the consensus, stemming from the Enlightenment, about equality, peace, and universality, might seem to be mere folly, an affront to the cherished end of history, that promised land of peace and prosperity whose achievement hangs over us as an unshakable imperative.

But it is precisely Heidegger who challenges this consensus as well as its accompanying imperative. He allies himself with the only stream in modern political thought that affirms this challenge: fascism. Heidegger does in fact much more than that. For Heidegger not only allies himself with fascism, he creates his own brand of fascist political thought. We are not speaking here of the ever exculpatory claims of Heidegger's "private" National Socialism, or private this or that. We have no interest in the private Heidegger. In this respect, we follow Heidegger's famous advice to ignore the private life of a thinker. And it is easy to do so, since Heidegger's thought is and was eminently public, published in books and journals, proclaimed in speeches and in the classrooms of one of Germany's more notable universities.

To avoid unnecessary misunderstandings, we do not seek to show that Heidegger is a National Socialist or that he introduces Nazism into philosophy as Emanuel Faye and his supporters are wont to claim. We find that Faye's approach, like that of Richard Wolin, takes for granted the correctness of its own presuppositions and is thus unwilling to grapple seriously with the power of Heidegger's challenge to these presuppositions. They seem to believe that it is good enough merely to show that Heidegger may not have subscribed to the modern consensus. But we do not wish to dismiss Heidegger in this manner, to suggest that one confine his works to that *enfer* that Maurice Blanchot claims, with some delight, for the works of Sade. If we do not side with mere dismissal, however, neither do we side with the other dominant view, that Heidegger's political involvement was an aberration that he corrected after the war. This narrative, elaborated in many forms by his defenders, has the comforting fit of a redemption narrative in which Heidegger finally sees the error of his ways and the truth of the consensus. To the contrary, we remain struck by the substantial continuity of Heidegger's thought, indeed his markedly unrepentant repetition of views expressed during the Nazi period as evidenced by his endorsement of the now notorious rectoral address in the famous Spiegel interview of 1966.

The upshot is that we attempt to walk a very fine line between these dominant alternatives. We wish neither to defend nor dismiss Heidegger but to present several crucial aspects of his political thinking about and of the city in as clear a light as possible *sine ira et studio*. We begin with a reading of an astonishing passage in Heidegger's important lecture course from the summer of 1935, published in 1953 as *Introduction to Metaphysics*. The publication of the course (together with the first postwar edition of *Being and Time*) was immediately controversial because of Heidegger's praise of the "inner truth and greatness" of National Socialism, a statement whose publication in 1953 shocked the young Jürgen Habermas (Heidegger, *Introduction to Metaphysics*, 222). But more shocking still, it seems to us, is Heidegger's account of the city that preoccupies much of his interpretation of the first Stasimon of Sophocles's *Antigone*. We can think of no other work in the enormity of the *Collected Works* (*die Gesamtausgabe* or "GA") published so far that more directly, extravagantly, and crudely delights in violence, and this account of violence emerges precisely in the context of the city, its founding and evolution. While it has certainly not been ignored, not enough has been made of this violence in the critical reception, and we aim to correct that state of affairs.[2]

Our own account comprises three fundamental parts. The first involves a layered reading of the *Antigone* interpretation in *Introduction to Metaphysics* having due regard to the political aspect of that interpretation. We then proceed to draw out the basic political implications of Heidegger's discussion at length. The final intention of our discussion of Heidegger is twofold: first, to show to what extent violence was crucial to Heidegger's political thought; and second, to show how that violence as a way of interrupting or delaying finality—the realm of the complete worldview—is central to Heidegger's greater concern to prevent the hegemony of technological man over *Dasein*.

To discuss Heidegger's politics is a fraught task, not only because of the sheer complexity of his thought and the esotericism of his writing style, but also because of his view of philosophy as a restless activity that avoids doctrines and unsettles everyday conventions. Philosophy concerns the few "who transform creatively, who unsettle things" (*Introduction to Metaphysics*, 11). Philosophy, or what Heidegger in his later writings calls "thinking," destroys the clichés of the polis. This view has led a number of thinkers, including perhaps most famously Hannah Arendt, to conclude that Heidegger stayed above the political fray: unlike Socrates, he avoided the city and instead cloistered himself in his *Hütte* to contemplate Being as a solitary "seeker" (Arendt, "Philosophy and Politics"). But Heidegger's understanding of the relationship of philosophy to the city appears more complex than the image of the unworldly philosopher permits. Indeed, Heidegger sees the city as the site of history. What it means to be human unfolds in the city, and this unfolding of the human is marked by cycles of tremendous violence that cannot be overcome. The founding of the city by creative individuals enacts a primordial violence against Being that, in turn, the city attempts to contain or represent as a "civilized" refuge. But the bringing into presence of the city only discloses the primordial violence or force of the overwhelming sway that Heidegger aligns with Being.

Heidegger develops this understanding of violence in a grandiloquent interpretation of the choral ode from Sophocles's *Antigone*. This interpretation appears in the key section of the *Introduction to Metaphysics* entitled "Being and Thinking" where Heidegger seeks to attack the metaphysical reduction of human thinking to certain knowledge, the reduction, that is, of *tekhnē* since Plato to rules, logic, and calculative reason more broadly. This is a significant move that appears to set up Heidegger's emerging critique of what he will call *Machenschaft* in the 1930s and "the essence of technology" after the war.[3] By recovering the "genuine sense" of *tekhnē* prior to its decay into a calculative model of knowing that fixes beings once and for all, Heidegger seems to be creating a history of Being from which his critique of technology will emerge (*Introduction to Metaphysics*, 177). His critique of technology, in other words, is predicated on aligning *tekhnē* with the flux and openness of violence and creation: technology as *Machenschaft*, however, threatens to end the strife of unconcealment and concealment that lies at the heart of *tekhnē* in its original sense as a struggle against the overwhelming force of Being. Technology portends to eliminate this strife by placing everything in one position of fixed identity and correctness. If the genuine sense of *tekhnē* stands in the tumult of strife and embraces the fragility of human life, technology seeks refuge from human vulnerability in the comforts of certainty and perfection. Humans seek to become like god through technology. But what kind of god? A "prosthetic God" in Freud's memorable phrasing, or as Heidegger might put it, a rational, realist god: a god of repetition and bureaucratic automation, a god who does not create anything new but merely repeats and implements what already exists in a self-contained system, a god who dares to make no history (Freud, *Civilization and Its Discontents*, 44).

In short, technology threatens to end history as Heidegger understands it. Heidegger recasts the conventional understanding of history first handed down to us by the Greeks and then professionalized by the positivists in the nineteenth century. He distinguishes *Geschichte* from *Historie*. If *Historie* represents the mechanical, scientific, and normative task of putting together a chronicle about the past in a way that disconnects it from the present and Being, *Geschichte* is a dynamic process of happening entangled with the present-future.[4] *Geschichte* unfolds as one of the fundamental aspects of *Dasein*'s Being; it reveals itself not as an "object" for scientific study but rather dynamically as the unsettled horizon of *Dasein*'s future possibilities. Always thrown into an already existing world, *Dasein* either takes up authentically its own future possibilities based on a creative interpretation of the past or inauthentically follows the given conventions of that world.

This ontological dimension of Heidegger's interpretation of *Geschichte* is well known. Perhaps less known is the political aspect that attends his notion of *Geschichte* as an act of creation—as an act, more precisely, of violence—that Heidegger is obviously engaged in himself: his notion of *Geschichte* and his history of Being amount to creative rejoinders to the world's increasingly technocratic condition. It would be difficult to view Heidegger's intervention in any other way in light of his interpretation of history. History is creative and violent: it destroys the accretions of tradition only then to create new ones that will eventually be overturned by another act of creation. In this sense, violence is both a basic aspect of *Dasein's* relationship to Being and of Being as a whole: Dasein brings beings out from their concealment, while what Heidegger calls the overwhelming (*das Überwältigende Walten*) conceals them. This constant strife between *Dasein* as the being who discloses and *das Überwältigende* as the force that conceals—the conflict between humans and nature (*das waltende Aufgehen* or *aufgehendes Walten*), if we wanted to put it differently—stands at the center of Heidegger's political ontologization of violence.[5]

This strife is violent in several senses. Perhaps the most basic sense characterizes the imposition of humans on nature, the violence that accompanies human interventions and creations. Humans counter and negate nature. They violate the indeterminate hegemony of nature when they force it under the yoke of any determinate order: "The violence-doers break into this sway, year by year they break it up with plows and drive the toilless earth into the restlessness of their toiling" (*Introduction to Metaphysics*, 171–72). Here Heidegger seems merely to be reprising a fairly standard view of the daring modern enterprise as an attempt to attain human mastery over nature.

But, in fact, a far more primordial violence underlies his view of *Dasein*'s subjugation of nature. This primordial violence pertains to the coming into being that overtakes humans in their endless struggle with the overwhelming force of nature or what Heidegger calls *das Überwältigende* in the sense of the overwhelming force of beings as a whole. In other words, Heidegger wishes to avoid interpreting violence as merely a faculty humans apply to nature; rather, for him violence happens in the very act through which beings are disclosed as such or what Heidegger describes as the elemental *polemos* of an original "gathering gatherdness that constantly holds sway in itself" (*Introduction to Metaphysics*, 141). The way in which beings are disclosed involves "a disciplining and disposing of the violent forces" (175).

This dynamic of violation Heidegger captures in the word δεινόν (*deinon*), which he takes from the ode's first line and translates as *unheimlich* (homeless or uncanny).[6] *Deinon* names two interrelated and opposing aspects of Being: the violent disclosure of beings by human knowledge (τέχνη or *tekhnē*) and the overwhelming violence of Being that constantly tends toward what Heidegger calls fittingness (δίκη or *dikē*), thus recasting Greek notions of justice to describe an order that has nothing recognizably human, or "just" in this narrow sense, to it. This distinction between *tekhnē* and *dikē* is central to the primordial violence of *Dasein*'s conflict with the overwhelming sway of Being. *Tekhnē* describes *Dasein*'s "struggle to set Being, which was formerly closed off, into what appears as beings" (*Introduction to Metaphysics*, 178). This struggle involves unending violence in the sense of constantly holding at bay the tendency to concealment, to resist appropriation that is the dynamic force of *dikē*. To put this in terms that violate Heidegger's elusive vocabulary, we might say that *Dasein*'s disclosure of beings is a resistance to or taming of nature that involves a violation of nature, insofar as every act of disclosure is by definition a bringing of beings into a human, not natural economy that fences them off, or defines them. Every act of disclosure places beings under the yoke of the human and thereby expresses, in violation, the pure force (*Walten*) from which they originate.[7] *Dasein* is a site of conflict, where Being as nature expresses itself in turning away from itself: *Dasein* is the site of the inherently contradictory self-restriction of Being, of genesis.

Human beings are thus not merely homeless, but the most homeless, τὸ δεινότατον: they disclose beings in regimes of truth only to rebel against those conventions of representation. Every coming into form and founding is (homeless) displacement—it is a fundamental *defamiliarization*, to recall the famous phrase of the Russian formalist Victor Shklovsky (Shklovsky, "Art as Device," 6). History represents an endless unfolding of creation and destruction, of affirmation and alienation, of being in and outside one's home: "the homeless (man) is what it is because from the ground up it controls and protects the homely (*das Einheimische*) only in order to break out of it and to let what overwhelms it break in" (Heidegger, *Introduction to Metaphysics*, 181–82). Being human involves a tragic interplay of openness and closure, of creating order and breaking out of it. Human beings are nomadic, creating for a while, and moving on once again simply so as not to stop.

This unsettledness is tragic because every inception will betray itself (*Anfang*).[8] An insistence on beginnings courses through Heidegger's work. Heidegger consistently glorifies inception as what is always greatest. This "beginning" represents a moment of pure innocence in its sheer newness, a moment when creators have violated or negated what has hitherto existed and created the openness necessary for the emergence of something wholly new (*Introduction to Metaphysics*, 17). As such, the inception is a pretemporal "moment," better, a site of fecund violence that, inevitably and tragically, collapses into a temporal configuration, a narrative, that becomes routine, doctrine, cliché. The inception never lasts in two senses: first, what has been created coalesces into a dominant and dominating mode of interpreting Being; and two, it flattens out into the conventions and dogmas of the "they" (*Being and Time*, 163–68 and 211–14). This second sense may be the most striking one: the "tragedy" of inception lies in the fact that it will always be disarmed or betrayed by those who follow in the wake of the creator. Banality will always overtake the novelty of the original act of creation as it degenerates into repetition (*Introduction to Metaphysics*, 68). What has been created will always be freed of its original danger and violence—its indeterminacy—as it spreads among the masses becoming political in a different sense from what accrues to the founding of the city—creation becomes management:

> The inception is what is most uncanny and violent (*Gewaltigste*). What follows is not development but rather flattening out as mere widening out; what follows is the inability to hold on to the inception, is the disarming (*Verharmlosung*) and exaggeration of the inception into a perversion of what is great, into greatness and extension purely in the sense of number and mass. (173)

Heidegger's claim that the *Verharmlosung* of the beginning will always happen seems to rest on an interpretation of the human being as a creature who finds it terribly difficult to deal with its fragility as a mortal being, as an uncanny being who can ask—why are there beings rather than nothing?—but would rather not ask that question. To ask that question is to ask about nothingness, to ask about one's fragile existence, to ask about the possibility of one's death (*Being and Time*, 310). To ask about death is terrible. Not only does it involve facing the possible negation of the self, but it also means confronting a most uncanny possibility: How precisely does one even describe the possibility of one's impossibility?[9] This is a dilemma that only the human appears to face. Death hovers over us as a possibility about which we are aware but about which we cannot know as we know any other things in life. This uncanny and unsettling possibility tends to go unexplored by most humans according to Heidegger. For the greatest, most primordial violence is unending indeterminacy or dissolution itself.

From this common evasion of death Heidegger advances the broader view that humans tend to prefer the banality of the familiar over the terrifying tumult of the unknown; that is to say, very few humans seem able to apprehend the tragedy and insecurity of human existence or would wish to do so. Many instead cling to truths that deny vulnerability, evade mortality, deaden creativity, and close off thought. Humans tend to settle on a dogma and hold to it for the rest of their lives. Or at least modern humans have become habituated to promises of security and permanence; indeed, the essential premise of the Enlightenment is precisely the containment, if not the elimination of contingency and imperfection. Heidegger counters this inauthentic mode of human striving for perfection with a different vision of emancipation: a freedom from attempts to overcome the uncanny being of the human. It is a freedom that embraces the essence of the human as uncanny, as a fragile and contingent being assailed by forces it cannot fully fathom. Yet, by its very nature, this kind of freedom seems limited to the "few" and the "rare," whom Heidegger calls "creators" (*Contributions to Philosophy*, 11).

The creators embrace the tumult of insecurity and enact violence in the *polis* (πόλις) by affirming rather than turning away from the fundamental violence of indeterminacy. The *polis* functions as the site where the struggle with indeterminacy unfolds as the origin of history and where creation breaks through the conventions of the everyday. The polis is the site of inception where poets, thinkers, priests, and rulers "use violence as violence-doers and become those who rise high in historical Being as creators, as doers" (*Introduction to Metaphysics*, 170). In rising as creators, the founders of the *polis* do not appear subject to the laws, traditions, and myths that they themselves establish. Rather, the creators enjoy a position transcending all positions. The creators assert themselves and are defined in their struggle with indeterminacy:

> Rising high in the site of history, they become απόλις (*apolis*), without city and site, lone-some, un-homely, with no way out amidst beings as a whole, and at the same time without ordinance and limit, without structure and fittingness (*Fug*), because they *as* creators must first ground all this in each case. (170)

Does this self-assertion ultimately involve establishing some kind of order because the creator still must act—in order to create in the first place—in the *polis*? Or does Heidegger envision an entirely new kind of politics in which the constant overturning of the conventional never allows for any one position to ground itself fully and finally? Heidegger privileges spontaneity over regulation. He seems to be after creating a new kind of thinking beyond metaphysics and preparing the way for a new kind of politics that staves off the finality of technological modernity, or finality of any kind, for that matter. Still, it would appear that the creators act both beyond and in the *polis*, suggesting once again that any engagement in the *polis* will betray itself. Creation is always ambiguous, and tragically so: the spontaneity of every historical creation is bound to coalesce into tradition and legislation.

The creators, however, seem to recognize this ambiguity, especially the thinker. The thinker apprehends the tragic strife between the disclosure of *tekhnē* and the concealment of *dikē* (Heidegger, *Introduction to Metaphysics*, 184). The thinker, who questions everything, attempts to avoid the *polis*'s need for final positions, arguments, and truths. The thinker sees the arbitrariness of any grounding and preserves a place of virtually divine freedom to create. The thinker is a gadfly in the venerable, conventional sense given that term in defense of Socrates's anodyne role in the polis; the thinker is also akin to Goethe's Mephistopheles, a seemingly clownish figure who saves human being from its tendency to fall asleep; but the thinker is also something more than these relatively benign figures—at the most extreme the thinker is the proponent of *total* revolution who seeks not merely to correct the order of his day for the apparent benefit of the city but to dispose of that order entirely, to leave it in ruins. In this latter sense, the thinker is always an apocalyptic figure declaring the most fearsome violence of all, the destruction of the current order (and, perhaps, any order). For the thinker is not merely content to express his sovereign identity with the "overwhelming sway" of Being by restricting his freedom in an act of singular creation, as if the thinker were the beneficent deity of the nominalist[10]—to the contrary, the thinker at his most radical is the purest expression of the violence of wholesale unsettlement, of wholesale displacement—the thinker is not only never at home, the thinker does not seek to be at home, the thinker is the pure and savage fury of creation unlimited by the need for norms, doctrines, or rules to live by, all of which he leaves to his disciples, those by definition unable to create as he does. Heidegger clarifies this point in another lecture where he refers to an unconventional Socrates, not a gadfly but the purest thinker of the West because he showed no need whatsoever to write, that is, to let his thinking solidify, to identify disciples, to close off definitively the possibilities of thinking by imposing his thought on the future—to create a discipline called philosophy to which even Heidegger belongs as philosopher no matter how hard he seeks to overcome the boundaries of that discipline (*What Is Called Thinking?* 17).

Heidegger may use terms such as thinker, creator, or founder, but, in each case, he seems to refer to those who by the very radicality of their violence never can become anything else than a founder whose disciples mitigate the specter of originary violence disclosed by the founder through transforming his action into a foundation that, as we have noted, always betrays the founding in its essentially dynamic aspect. For the founding is ever imperfect, incomplete, whereas the foundation points to the perfection or completion of the founding act in a structure that is no longer vibrant or in a process of transformation but finished so that it may only be repeated mechanically.

For Heidegger violence seems to be tied to possibility, to the possibility of transformation that remains in a given founding or, in its most extreme form, a formless form, pure possibility itself. Pure possibility is of course an impossible possibility since it is strictly speaking impossible to contemplate a possibility that is fully indeterminate or pure or absolute. To think this sort of possibility—which is of course not a sort—is to think what is equivalent in all salient respects to the *nihil absolutum* or absolute nothingness or, indeed, as we have already noted, the most pressing impossible possibility: death. Here we are repeating the essentially Hegelian identity between being and nothingness. But, for Heidegger, there is no one form of genesis out of this purely indeterminate origin. The "monstrous power" of the negative, of the negation of this original indeterminacy, does not proceed in the manner of the *Phenomenology of Spirit* providing what some may claim to be a full and final account of the possibilities of genesis—a meta-narrative of forms of genesis, a history of genesis or Genesis itself.

To the contrary, Heidegger's most radical gesture is to suggest that genesis may take any number of forms, that genesis indeed has no single definable course to follow. The specter of combat that Hegel brings to an end in the *Phenomenology* as a catalogue of all possibilities of genesis cannot be brought to an end according to Heidegger—indeed, it seems that Heidegger views the impetus toward finality as a perversion or destruction of the origin, his logic being precisely at odds with that of Hegel in the sense that for Heidegger the origin is properly fulfilled by not being fulfilled, whereas in Hegel an origin that does not cover itself over or cancel itself in fulfillment makes no sense at all. The key difference is this: for Heidegger the origin appears continuously as the violence of the *Riss* or the failure of completion, of harmony, of final equilibrium ("The Origin of the Work of Art," 38). For Hegel the origin appears only in its final fulfillment—the origin sacrifices itself to finality in Hegel. If we return to terms we have applied already, we might say that Heidegger asserts something like the pure unrestricted power of the nominalist deity, while Hegel hews to the realist notion of a deity that restricts itself and eliminates itself in history, the deity of kenosis, the beneficent deity who becomes flesh in the incarnation.

Thus, in the end, Heidegger retains a notion of the whole whose potential for radical transformation—i.e., violence—never restricts itself to purely human standards. There is no theodicy in Heidegger that approaches Hegel's or indeed those versions of Christian thought that see God's love for humanity in His appearing in human form, in His making Himself human. If we put the matter in these terms, we may come to a more comprehensive understanding of Heidegger's notion of violence and why he places that notion within the context of the Greeks. That is, Heidegger returns us to the awe and terror that must dawn upon us in a world that can never conclusively establish itself as secure from change, from immanent destruction, the overwhelming sway that is the current of nature in motion as it waxes and wanes indifferent to us, our fragile hopes and fears. If the overwhelming sway is ultimately inscrutable or irreducible, we can never be content with our attempts to reduce it to a truly human product—the city. The elemental violence of transformation or destruction remains always as a reminder of our frail hold on life, our own fragility amid beings.

Heidegger returns us to a primordial insecurity, or as he put it in another reading of Sophocles's *Antigone* in 1942, to our primordial condition of "not 'at home,' not homely within what is homely" (*Hölderlin's Hymn "The Ister,"* 71).[11] He seeks thereby to undermine the anaesthetized life of the modern man who wants only security, the bourgeois ideal of perfection as wealth and comfort best exemplified by the notion that, once one has made one's fortune, one may then turn to art and self-expression, a sort of capitalist twin to the ostensive dream of Marx where the workers will be freed to hunt or read Plato or paint. No surprise then that in the same lectures that contain his earlier reading of *Antigone*, Heidegger identifies Russia and the United States as "metaphysically the same," as the twin exemplars of the essentially modern impulse to fall asleep in comfort, to avoid death, to make art that is no longer tragic or comic but merely kitsch, something one might hang on one's walls so as to show that one is "with it" or "hip" or simply to avoid the barrenness or desert that seems to well up within the modern "ape of civilization" as Heidegger writes in another lecture course from the very beginning of the 1930s (*Fundamental Concepts of Metaphysics*, 5).

How can one argue that this Heidegger is not political? We are all aware of the exculpatory myth generated largely by Heidegger himself after the war. His brief and notorious tenure as rector of the University of Freiburg seems to have been an "aberration," a failed and naive venture into the dangerous political landscape of the initial year of the National Socialist revolution in Germany. After resigning from his position as rector of the university in April 1934, Heidegger kept a steadfast distance from political life. One would not confuse him with the public intellectual modeled on the engaged intellectual of postwar France: one would not imagine him at the head of a demonstration marching in solidarity with everyday people. To the contrary, Heidegger did not invite this kind of publicity. He preferred his celebrated hut at Todtnauberg, where he could retire from the strains of university life and the sort of publicity he attracted after he became famous with the publication of *Being and Time* in 1927.

Does this picture of the unworldly philosopher match the picture of the thinker Heidegger himself creates in the *Introduction to Metaphysics*?

If not, are we to assume that the distance between the philosopher and the political actor is so great that the one is in effect a parody of the other, as we have already suggested? While we may want to make this assumption, we should ask ourselves why we wish to do so. What is it in us that demands that we reject the political Heidegger as a parody of the philosopher whose works have penetrated into so many aspects of contemporary thought around the world that it is impossible to engage in the sort of intellectual cleansing that Faye would have us perform?

Let us examine once again the image of the thinker provided by Heidegger in the interpretation of *Antigone*. For Heidegger, the thinker is a founder who, as such, is not restricted by what he founds. The thinker is not only beyond any specific creation of his; he is in this sense more importantly "beyond good and evil." He takes no moral stance to the extent he takes no final stance; nothing is more repugnant to him than "the didactic praise of philosophy one finds in Seneca or Cicero" (*Nietzsche*, 1/3). Now, of course, one can argue that by taking no final stance the thinker in effect takes a final stance; the thinker merely says that no morality is possible in the sense that there is no morality that can be said to be final, determinative, applicable to all. To the contrary, Heidegger banishes all particular moral positions to the realm of ideology, as that term is usually understood: to the expression of the interests of a particular group vying for power, vying to assert itself as against other groups. To be sure, the thinker is above the fray in this respect, walled off from politics or at least derisive of them. But this position above all positions is itself negative—it offers no other consolation to authority than to put all measures of authority in question.

Yet, this too *is* a political position, one that cannot comfort those who look to the philosopher as a sage or a beneficent wisdom figure who bestows upon the polis his sagacious guidance. We may thus affirm the political nature of Heidegger's thought as forever untimely, forever "indigestible" in the polis because it stands as an affront to whatever shape the polis takes. The shadow of the thinker is a negative or violent one: the thinker is the highest criminal because the thinker refuses to accept any norms whatsoever and defines himself in this cloying negative way as one who explores or seeks so as to find only in constant seeking, this being characteristic Heideggerian indirection. Moreover, the thinker resists a clear connection to any of the positions he may take at any given time. The thinker leaves this task of clarification to those who are not thinkers in the same sense, those who are disciples or advocates. The thinker himself is a figure of ambiguity, the very ambiguity Heidegger describes as an essential aspect of philosophy in the first chapter of the *Introduction to Metaphysics* (8–14).

If this is so, then, the thinker may exploit an equally ambiguous attitude in regard to interpretation of his thought or to action that results from that thought. In this respect, the "polis-apolis" expression of the thinker's relation to the city and to political action in general is telling. The crucial point to underline here is that the thinker can always retreat to the nonpolitical position, or to that of the "apolitical," in those cases where the political winds blow in the wrong way or in a way that tries to tie the thinker down to a point of view that has been defeated or rejected in the polis. The benefit of the thinker's unrestricted freedom is that the thinker has a readymade defense when necessary, a defense that does not otherwise compromise the thinker since the thinker's essential freedom precludes being compromised in that way.

So is Heidegger's thinker simply evil in the Christian sense? Is he that thief Nietzsche describes, disturbing the sleep and comfort of the good citizens of the city? (*Thus Spoke Zarathustra*, 40). Rather more than Goethe's Mephistophelean clown, whose subjection to supreme order assures that he may only shout from his prison cell to passersby, the Heideggerian thinker sets himself up like a god, an ever errant revolutionary who may not only shout at passersby, but who may so infiltrate their way of thinking that their entire way of life in the city, "that spot where all these routes cross," may be definitively transformed (*Introduction to Metaphysics*, 169). Of course the thinker may need the assistance of his disciples and, in particular, those capable of carrying out his thoughts as quickly and efficiently as possible. For the thinker is impatient. Hence, the "natural" connection we may assume between the thinker and those able and eager to do his bidding in, let us say, efficient ways.[12] The attraction of the tyrant or those who do not shy away from radical action must be irresistible for the thinker. And not only for the thinker of Heidegger's notoriety. One wonders if Heidegger's attraction to tyranny would have been judged the same way if he had supported a radical regime prepared to do "what is necessary" to install a democracy or a more universalist, or at least politically palatable, regime.

If we put this vital question aside for the moment, we come to another, more interesting difficulty: What does Heidegger's political program enact? What political program emerges from the histrionic interpretation of *Antigone*, if any?

Surely, most sober spirits—not the founders, we may assume—will scoff at any attempt to found a political program on the kind of fanciful mytheme of the founder Heidegger creates in his interpretation of that powerful myth of transgression, *Antigone*. Of course, Heidegger does not speak to this constituency of bureaucrats, of those who write "strategic plans," not in the *Introduction to Metaphysics*, nor, for that matter, in any of his other overtly political utterances. The rectoral address is as fanciful and imaginative as the interpretation of *Antigone*, and the wits had as easy a time mocking its apparent obscurity. To these wits, we may add figures of admirable sobriety or skepticism. Karl Löwith, who very much admired the rectoral address, was, however, dismissive of the political potential in Heidegger's thought, remarking that one could not know whether to read the Greeks or march in the streets in brown uniforms with, we might add, nowhere to go (*Martin Heidegger and European Nihilism*, 217).

Heidegger is not after this kind of disciple, however. Heidegger's political program is altogether different: it is a *metapolitics*, as Heidegger himself said, not a politics, not an action plan, not the sketch of a regime, the best regime—or the worst (*Überlegungen II–IV*, GA 94, 115). It is an invitation to revolution, to violence, to strife as salvific in and of themselves. It is, in short, the devil's invitation to politics that encourages those who are willing to listen, and who are not yet paralyzed by the numbing weight of convention, to struggle against that convention, to test, challenge, and unsettle the political calm of the city. But not only that: Heidegger provides an exhortation not just to critique or to opposition, but to violent revolution, to a new founding that will in turn be toppled or modified by another founding. Heidegger provides a model of the polis that threatens to fall apart at any moment.

Now, there are those who might see a democratic aspect to this kind of thinking. Certainly, it seems to be the case that some of Heidegger's students were able to disarm his model of struggle for suitable application to democracy, by identifying Heidegger with the gadfly or critic who helps to militate the tyrannical demands of any one group in a diverse, democratic polity (Arendt, *Life of the Mind*). In an analogous move, there has been an equally intriguing attempt to disarm Carl Schmitt's advocacy of violence (which of course has many affinities with Heidegger's). The radical or "agonistic" democracy advocated by Chantal Mouffe is a case in point (Mouffe, *The Democratic Paradox*). But these attempts seem to some degree misguided, even if they may be, above all, strategic attempts to adapt a dangerous kind of thought to a milieu whose proper functioning is based on the eradication of that danger.

Heidegger's radicality cannot be so easily disarmed or, in his own term, *verharmlost*. His emphasis on violence and creation, not just critique, is too clear. The city is a site of primordial violence, a conduit of unrest, both in its creation and in its continued growth and change. This violence cannot have limits, nor be prescribed certain "proper" channels in advance—to do so would completely undermine the intimate connection of the violence enacted in the city, in a concrete context, with the seemingly unlimited violence, *das Überwältigende*, which that violence both expresses and resists. Heidegger's emphasis on the pervasiveness of violence understood this way is ubiquitous in his works where rest is everywhere referred to as a kind of motion or as derived from motion (*Basic Questions of Philosophy*, 7). Heidegger's own works are, as he famously said, "ways, not works"; they are explorations that do not conclude.

This apparently liberating or emancipating notion of inconclusiveness has its correlate in action as violence. The violent interpretive approach Heidegger takes to the many texts he reads is intended to bring them alive in strife or, to use the term he later adopts, *Auseinandersetzung* or "confrontation" (*Nietzsche*, 1/4–5). Thought is active combat, struggle, refusal to rest; "philosophy disorients," as Heidegger laconically puts it in the mid-1930s (*Überlegungen II–VI*, GA 94, 252). All we need do is eliminate the metaphoric relation in the preceding equation to come to recognize that the proper correlate to Heidegger's thinking is action that by its very nature must be violent since it seeks fundamental change and can truly seek change only at the cost of liberating primordial violence. Thus, the notion that this kind of action can tame or adjust itself to comply with the canons of proper democratic discourse merely perpetuates the brilliant ruse created by Hitler himself, whose famous legality strategy, instituted after the failed putsch of 1923, lulled many into believing that the National Socialists would honor the basic constitution of the democracy they eventually destroyed.

If violence is at the essence of Heidegger's politics as expressed in the 1930s and, perhaps, the early 1940s—in other words, the period of Nazi rule—one may well question at this point whether or not such an argument remains valid for the postwar Heidegger, the Heidegger of *Gelassenheit* (releasement or letting-be). A skeptic might claim that Heidegger retreated after the war, if not already in the late 1930s, into a position of solitude (or even resistance) from which he took up a critique of technology that insisted on passiveness, hardly the stirring violent strife celebrated in the *Introduction to Metaphysics*. He turned away from his earlier views of *Dasein*'s violent creation of a world and insisted on an almost Buddhist-like stance of emptying the self of the illusions of creation. Heidegger extracted himself from the subjectivism of will and power tentatively beginning with his critique of Nietzsche in the late 1930s and continuing with his postwar critique of the dominant and dominating technological interpretation of Being. He turned away ever more explicitly from the alleged anthropologism of *Being and Time* and developed a thinking in which Being becomes almost like the hidden God that calls and invites; that is, *Being* becomes a supreme authority to which *Dasein* hearkens. In making this anti-anthropological "turn," Heidegger insists on our limits and vulnerabilities as mortals who are called by Being to "let beings be" rather than dominate them. He thus resists the modern striving to turn us into gods who master nature by fixing all entities, including themselves, and their multidimensional relationships in the world into one regime of truth or representation. Put simply, Heidegger resisted precisely the capacity of free will granted to humans in Saint Augustine's famous and immensely influential *On Free Choice of the Will* (*de libero arbitrio voluntatis*) that would enable them eventually to imagine themselves as completely free beings who can know and dominate their world through logic, mathematics, and science.[13] We might say that he understood the inner contradiction inherent in the attempt to obtain freedom through a self-determining rationality that would have the effect of determining not only the objects of the world but also the being who sought to determine those objects in its ostensive bid for freedom.[14] The pursuit of freedom thus understood would lead to the most complete and inflexible domination yet seen on earth—the planetary reign of technology.

Certainly, Heidegger's critique of technology can and has been pushed by others in a direction that encourages us to embrace a more reflective stance toward technology in order for a greater plurality of human meanings and modes of existence to thrive.[15] As with any thinker as complex and elastic as Heidegger, his thought can be shaped to fit other political molds. But it is difficult to argue that after the war Heidegger himself became a pacifist seeking to let things be in quiet meditation, the "zen" or "hippy" Heidegger. It is equally difficult to suggest, as Hannah Arendt herself did in *The Life of the Mind*, that Heidegger embraced such a stance after realizing that he had made a terrible mistake in supporting Nazism. If it is evident that Heidegger focuses more on Being than *Dasein* by the 1930s in reaction to misunderstandings of *Being and Time* as anthropological, and if releasing oneself to Being may seem to be more passive after the war than the more overtly violent releasing of oneself to the overwhelming sway, such a turn does not correspond to a concomitant shift away from the centrality of violence to his politics—indeed a great deal hinges on what we mean by violence.

The obvious exculpatory aspect of this interpretation of Heidegger focuses largely on his supposed postwar renunciation of will as a sign of repentance for his political error and, thus, on the suitability of his thought for consumption by a generation of philosophers, writers, sociologists, and thinkers of all stripes hailing mainly from countries that suffered horribly at the hands of the National Socialists. As tempting as it may be, this exculpatory aspect should not blind us to the general thinness and ambiguity of the textual evidence. The writing most commonly mentioned in support of this interpretation is *Gelassenheit*, a short speech Heidegger gave in 1955 in his hometown of Meßkirch, later included in a volume of the same name with an added dialogue about the term *Gelassenheit*.[16] The title makes the case: releasement, letting go, calmness (as if after a storm)—terms that bespeak passivity, relinquishment, a sense that one should release oneself to the "secret" (*Geheimnis*), to "openness," to letting things be regardless of our interest in them.[17] Heidegger's own deceptive rhetoric about the status of thinking—that it has no direct effect on things—allows perhaps all too easily the redemptive view we have mentioned. But, even in this slim volume, there is strong evidence in support of a contrary interpretation. As the dialogue indicates, Heidegger may ask us to relinquish our interest in things as willing in the traditional sense, but he does so in order to free us from the notion of willing that he finds goes hand in hand with the victory of modern technology. The Heideggerian version of will—if it can be called that—is in fact the very openness to Being itself that forges the dynamic relation of shaping, of *tekhnē* that he describes in the *Introduction to Metaphysics*. In *Gelassenheit*, Heidegger merely offers another way of returning to that relation to Being without which we become the victim of technology. Releasement to Being is, in its seemingly innocuous way, no different from the releasement to the overwhelming sway that is the mark of creative Dasein. To confuse the notion of *tekhnē* Heidegger describes in the *Introduction to Metaphysics* with the closed *tekhnē* of technology is to make the mistake of assimilating the creative "sway" of the thinker or founder to subjective will.[18] Heidegger does not recant after the war. He makes his central point—that we must return to our original rootedness in a relation to Being in a variety of different ways and using a variety of different vocabularies just as he did in the 1920s and 1930s.

Perhaps the more challenging locus of the narrative of relinquishment is the Nietzsche lectures, which Heidegger published in 1961. Yet, even in these lectures, whose enormous size and complexity preclude more than a casual glance here, we find a similar, albeit much more deftly variegated, attack on the notion of will as essentially eradicating becoming, that is, struggle, difference, creative violence in favor of a full and final picture of the world that we may claim to establish. Thus, even though Heidegger realizes an affinity to Nietzsche, who, for Heidegger, takes the full measure of the challenge presented to the human by nihilism, the attempt to achieve that final picture—an attempt whose mightiest fruit is technology—he rejects Nietzsche's various means for combatting nihilism, such as the will to power, the eternal return, or creative overturning (*Umkehrung*), claiming that they are all in thrall to the very metaphysical "logic" of completion they seek to overcome. Nietzsche, the "last metaphysician," is as such also the first to point the way beyond metaphysics.[19] Heidegger brings to the foreground a basic tension in Nietzsche's work as well as a great deal of what is violent, resistant, and outrageous in Nietzsche—one has only to recall Heidegger's famous analysis of the significance of *Rausch* or frenzy in Nietzsche's understanding of art—and this tendency is hardly the sign of a thinker ready to relinquish violence in passive resignation. Indeed, the framing of Heidegger's interpretative stance as a *confrontation* with Nietzsche bears witness to an utterly contrary intention.

Moreover, we recall that Heidegger published *Introduction to Metaphysics* in 1953, right in the midst of West Germany's postwar transformation into a peaceful liberal democracy. This move has significance, beyond its sheer audacity, because the text itself represents the early stages of Heidegger's critique of what he will call *"Machenschaft"* in the late 1930s and the essence of technology after the war. As we have already noted, Heidegger emphasizes there the violence of Being and the violence of unending creation: the "genuine" sense of *tekhnē* describes a dynamic process of "putting Being to work in beings" that never completes itself. *Tekhnē* opens up and keeps open as it restlessly holds off the end and breaks through the familiar.

If we wanted to explain Heidegger's interpretation of *tekhnē* using a different terminology, we might say that he is attempting to describe here and elsewhere a form of knowing or thinking that is katechontic. The *katechon*, from the Greek κατέχον meaning "holding," is a cryptic force described in 2 Thessalonians 2 that prevents the apocalypse from prematurely occurring against God's divine plan. The author of the verse, probably Paul, sets out to describe what will take place prior to the coming of Christ: the "lawless one" will be revealed and then be defeated by Christ. In the interregnum, the "restrainer" or *katechon* holds evil at bay until God determines when the last day will come. Following Heidegger's own confrontation with Christian concepts, we can interpret the katechon as *tekhnē* in the sense of that term found in Heidegger's work of the 1930s.[20] Genuine *tekhnē* constantly holds back finality, completion, and order; it preserves a condition of incompletion and resists the end state of stability. It precludes the end of time from ever coming by insisting on novelty and incompletion. No final dispensation or interpretation of Being can ever emerge.[21]

But such an end may be falsely asserted: Heidegger seems to fear that Western civilization has reached a point at which the metaphysical interpretation of Being in its current form of mathematical-technological reason may be able to declare itself successfully as "the sole and definitive interpretation of Being" (*Introduction to Metaphys-ics*, 203). He seems to fear that the modern striving to turn the human subject into a rational God or master of the world will usher in the apoc-alyptic end of history in which creation would end, no new thought would ever again come into existence, and the scientific disclosure of the world would reign supreme over all other possibilities of disclo-sure—indeed, that there are other possibilities of unconcealment would be utterly and finally forgotten.[22] The threat is that the essence of tech-nology will overtake us by answering once and for all the question of what it means to be human: we will become bureaucratic cogs or, in Heidegger's language, *Bestand*. In the end, we will destroy ourselves as sentient beings in our modern pursuit of self-deification: we will cease to exist in the world as creative historical individuals with mul-tiple possibilities open to us.

This possible end state seemed terrifyingly likely to Heidegger as the most profound manifestation of the forgetting of Being and of turning away from the nothingness of *Dasein* from which creation and meaning arises ("The Question Concerning Technology," 56). In 1941, he embraced the destruction of humanity over its continuation as *ani-mal rationale* in the technological-bourgeois comfort of modern life that seeks as much as possible to palliate or diminish the contingencies of finite human existence in dreams of constructing a perfect world free of suffering. For Heidegger, the elimination of suffering is the end of *Dasein* as a creative being. Thus, he claimed that the last act of the highest consummation of technology would be that "the earth blows itself up in the air and present-day humanity vanishes." This destruc-tion of humanity would not be a "calamity, but the first purging of Being of its deepest deformity through the supremacy of beings" (*Überlegungen XII–XV*, GA 96, 238).

Could this fate be averted? Heidegger always held on to the pos-sibility of a radical transformation of his time into something "com-pletely other" (*Überlegungen VII–XI*, GA 95, 48).[23] In the early 1930s, he believed that an overturning of the Western metaphysical tradition could be prepared through a transformation of *tekhnē* into a spirit of questioning and continuous change during the Nazi revolution (*Reden und andere Zeugnisse*, 111). Heidegger nurtured the possibility that a new form of thinking beyond the exhausted paradigms of the phil-osophical tradition could prepare the way for an alternative mode of human existence. Although his enthusiasm for Nazism waned in the face of bureaucratic resistance to his plans for reforming the German university, he never relinquished hopes for a new beginning and searched incessantly to find a way of thinking that might prepare for its possible occurrence, for the arrival of a new or "last" god.

"Only a God can save us," remarked Heidegger in his famous interview with *Der Spiegel* in 1966, by which he seems to have meant not the old God or gods but rather something like an apocalyptic event that would bring one era to an end and allow for an entirely new kind of human existence, a new inception, a renewed relation to Being (*Reden und andere Zeugnisse eines Lebensweges*, 652–83). Only such a revolutionary new inception could save us now from technocratic nihilism by overturning no less than 2,500 years of history since Plato. This new inception would radically affirm and keep affirming human beings as not merely displaced, but the most displaced, τὸ δεινότατον. It would embrace the primordial violence and impermanence of human existence by katechonticly resisting completion, closure, and finality, by embracing rather than avoiding being held out into the nothing (*die Hineingehaltenheit in das Nichts*). This kind of violence expresses an event of fundamental displacement and unsettledness, an opening to the ineluctable strangeness of Being—*Ereignis*, the apocalyptic event grounding a transition away from the first beginning that steps toward "a wholly other domain of history" (*Contributions to Philosophy*, 179).[24] To sustain this opening is the most difficult and violent political task of all. The meanings and beliefs cherished within a community teeter constantly at the edge of collapse as the possibility of new creations interrupts the routines of the community, transforming and renewing it.[25] The cost of such violence is freedom, the very freedom which the pursuit of perfection in technological mastery seeks to eradicate once and for all. The violence of Being is the violence of freedom, imperfection, the muddle of human delight and pain from which technological perfection seeks to insulate us permanently unless a catastrophic god should intervene to save us, a terrible god, a god of the most thorough destruction and renewal, a god of *Ereignis*.

Jeff Love is professor of German and Russian at Clemson University. He is the author of *Tolstoy: A Guide for the Perplexed* (2008) and *The Overcoming of History in War and Peace* (2004). He has also published an annotated translation of F. W. J. Schelling's *Philosophical Investigations into the Essence of Human Freedom* (2006), a coedited volume, *Nietzsche and Dostoevsky: Philosophy, Morality, Tragedy* (2016), and an edited volume, *Heidegger in Russia and Eastern Europe* (2017).

Michael Meng is associate professor of history at Clemson University. He is the author of *Shattered Spaces: Encountering Jewish Ruins in Postwar Germany and Poland* (2011). He is writing a book on death, history, and salvation in European thought.

Notes

1. Heidegger, *Überlegungen II–IV*, GA 94, 194.
2. See, for example, Geiman, "Heidegger's *Antigones*," 161–84. Geiman's approach is interesting in its own right but suggests a change in Heidegger's thought after the war, with which we disagree.
3. See Heidegger, *Mindfulness*, 12. Emad and Kalary translate *Machenschaft* as "machination," an ingenious translation that we avoid, however, because of its connection with political calculation. The other sense of the word—that one is literally turned into a machinelike being or inventory—though very apt, is perhaps also too fanciful a translation of the German.
4. See Fried, *Heidegger's* Polemos.
5. See Derrida, *The Beast and the Sovereign*, 30–44.
6. For an extensive discussion of "unheimlich" in Heidegger and its relationship to Freud's "uncanny," see Withy, *Heidegger on Being Uncanny*.
7. One need only recall Heidegger's discussion of the famous phrase from Heraclitus, "nature loves to hide" (φύσις κρύπτεσθαι φιλεῖ), both in the context of Being and appearance (*Sein* und *Schein*), in the *Introduction to Metaphysics* and *Walten* from the important lecture course Heidegger gave in the winter semester of 1929–30. See *Introduction to Metaphysics*, 126, and Heidegger, *Fundamental Concepts of Metaphysics*, 27.
8. We use the peculiar term "inception" here to translate the German *Anfang*. We note that Heidegger draws a distinction in German between "inception," as denoting a founding beginning, and "beginning," as marking the first step in a process that is analogous to the distinction between *Geschichte* and *Historie*. Fried and Polt use "inception" to capture the notion of founding and beginning to capture the notion of a first step.
9. Putting the matter more technically, the issue comes down to this question: What kind of possibility is the possibility of the impossibility of *Dasein*? Conventionally, we understand possibility as something that may be actualized, opted for, or confirmed. None of these ways of understanding possibility applies to *Dasein*'s possibility of impossibility. Death appears to be a pure possibility. A pure possibility,

as Heidegger explained in his Leibniz lecture course, means that "what is essential in beings, the ideas of things, regardless of whether or not such an idea is ever actualized. To become actual, something must be intrinsically possible, but everything intrinsically possible need not also become actual" (*Metaphysical Foundations of Logic*, 44). See also John Haugeland, *Dasein Disclosed*, 89 and 196–220.

10. By this we mean the distinction between the *potentia ordinata* and the *potentia absoluta* developed by the nominalist movement in the late Middle Ages. The nominalists focused their attention on the will of God and concluded that there can be no restrictions on that will—it is absolute power or *potentia absoluta*. God voluntarily restricts that will from his own benevolence, creating an order his subjects can rely on, and this voluntary restriction of power is called the *potentia ordinata* or orderly power. See the supremely lucid discussion in Funkenstein, *Theology and the Scientific Imagination*, 117–52.

11. Although it is certainly true that the strife of *tekhnē, dikē,* and *Walten* does not appear in Heidegger's second interpretation of Antigone in 1942, this absence does not amount to a downplaying of violence in his understanding of the human as τὸ δεινότατον. In this second reading, Heidegger affirms displacement as fundamental to the essence of the human being and views the polis as the site in which history unfolds. If there is a shift in his thinking from *Introduction to Metaphysics*, it is largely in terms of the manner in which he describes the primordial strife that characterizes the human relationship to Being: he sees man as an "unhomely" (*Unheimische*) creature that strives to become "homely" (*Heimschwerden*). This seeking out of the homely "balks at no danger and no venture" (*Hölderlin's Hymn "The Ister,"* 74).

12. See Kojève, "Tyranny and Wisdom," 164–65.

13. See Arendt, *Life of the Mind*, 84–110; Dihle, *The Theory of Will in Classical Antiquity*, 123–44.

14. This notion of reason is described well by Alexandre Kojève: "Man is only man to the extent he *thinks; his* thought is only *thought* to the extent that it does not depend on the fact that it is *he* who thinks it." In other words, reason must transcend the concrete individual; it is not *we* who have reason, but reason who has *us*. See Kojève, *Identité et Réalité dans le "Dictionnaire" de Pierre Bayle*, 15.

15. Arendt, *The Human Condition*; Marcuse, *One-Dimensional Man*; Feenberg, *Questioning Technology*.

16. The dialogue included in the published volume was written in 1945; the full version appears in Heidegger, *Country Path Conversations*.

17. Heidegger uses the terms, "*das Geheimnis*" and "*die Offenheit*" that tie *Gelassenheit* to his crucial talk, "On the Essence of Truth," first given in 1930. There too the emphasis is on openness and "letting beings be" (*das Seinlassen von Seiendem or des Seienden im Ganzen*). While violence is not stressed, the orientation to "openness" must be of extraordinary violence since it places an entire world in suspension, in a moment of almost apocalyptic realization, timeless and terrifying in its putting into question all one had hitherto believed—this is a primordial experience of homelessness. See "On the Essence of Truth," 124–32.

18. We should recall that Heidegger explicitly refers to this interpretation of *tekhnē* as a poetic form of thinking that disrupts and questions at the ostensive height of his official involvement with Nazism. The key text in this regard—which Heidegger continued to cite long after 1933–34, including in the *Der Spiegel* interview of 1966—is "Die Selbstbehauptung der deutschen Universität," in Heidegger, *Reden und andere Zeugnisse eines Lebensweges*, 107–17.

19. This attitude is captured nicely in a passage from the *Black Notebooks* from 1939: "*Nietzsche*—in what sense alone is Nietzsche a transition (*Übergang*), to wit: the preparation for another beginning of the history (*Geschichte*) of beyng . . . Nietzsche is *only* a transition because he anticipates metaphysically the completion of the modern age and thereby sets out the end in a beyng-historical way and *with* this end, which he himself is *not* able to recognize or know as such because he still— and as the final, conclusive one—thinks metaphysically, readies the possibility of preparation for the decision in favor of the other inception" (*Überlegungen XII–XV*, GA 96, 11).

20. See Geiman, "Heidegger's *Antigones*," 161–82.

21. Our invocation of the *katechon* may immediately invite a comparison to Carl Schmitt, who insisted on the importance of the *katechon* as the delaying force that precludes the end of history from happening now. In the end, Schmitt turns to the *katechon* to advance his dogmatic assertion of a political order defined by political conflict. Heidegger wishes to transition to a new dispensation of human existence that overcomes precisely the attachment to finality and stability that Schmitt evinces. See Hell, "*Katechon*: Carl Schmitt's Imperial Theology and the Ruins of the Future."

22. Perhaps Heidegger's frankest expressions of concern about modernity's ability to assert itself as the end of history appear in the *Black Notebooks* (see *Überlegungen XII–XV*, 110).

23. For a different reading that stresses Heidegger's fatalistic resignation in the face of technology, see Dreyfus, "Heidegger on Gaining a Free Relation to Technology."

24. See also the discussion of the "eschatology of Beyng" in *Anmerkungen I–V (Schwarze Hefte 1942–48)*, GA 97, 302, 335, 343, 392.

25. As Heidegger says in another context in *Being and Time*: "The level which a science has reached is determined by how far it is *capable* of a crisis in its basic concepts." One might expect the same to apply to the city. See *Being and Time*, 29.

Review Essays

A PASSION FOR SAMENESS: LEO BERSANI'S ONTOLOGY OF NARCISSISM

THOUGHTS AND THINGS
BY LEO BERSANI
(Chicago: University of Chicago Press, 2015)

Mikko Tuhkanen

> . . . *we are already out there.*
>
> —Leo Bersani and Ulysse Dutoit, *Caravaggio*

In his most recent texts, Leo Bersani frequently refers to Michel Foucault's argument, in his 1981–82 Collège de France seminar, concerning the importance of Cartesian philosophy in articulating the mode in which the moderns conceptualize their relation to the world. Foucault sees "the Cartesian moment" as a pivot where the ancient forms of "the care of the self" (*souci de soi*; *epimeleia heautou*) were overtaken by modernity's emphasis on epistemology as philosophical practice *par excellence.*[1] If modernity begins with Descartes, it is driven by epistemophilia. But, according to Bersani, what Foucault misses in dividing, like Pierre Hadot, ancient philosophical discipline from modern regimes of thought is the way in which neither ancient practices nor modern epistemophilics "puts into question a more general assumption common to both: that of a difference of being between the subject and the world" (2015, 62).[2] Both the care of the self and modern science depend on an understanding of the subject as distinct from the object-world; both rely on confluent conceptualizations of otherness.

One of the twentieth century's articulations of the Cartesian subject is what has come to be known in contemporary critical theory as "the divided subject." The divided subject, whose history in Western thought is frequently traced to the Freudian version of the unconscious, has functioned in the field as an antithesis to, an escape from, the alleged certainties of the imperial, essentialist subject, often, since Aristotle, articulated in terms of grammatical logic. It is, in turn, the "antiessentialist" notion of the divided subject that critical theory has keenly appropriated for the ethical work of destabilizing philosophical assumptions about subjecthood and otherness. Yet in his latest book, *Thoughts and Things* (2015), Bersani suggests that the divided subject may not be as radical or novel a notion as we have assumed. Freud, he argues, rearticulated in psychoanalytic terms the split subject of the Cartesian weltanschauung (61–63, 67–68). There is a false dialectic at work in celebrations of the divided subject: we have understood it as an attack on the autonomous self, the grammatical subject, of Western essentialism; Bersani suggests, by contrast, that, as much as "essence" can be thought in terms unrelated to those describing the target of antiessentialist critiques,[3] there is *an undivided subject* that cannot be identified with the self-possessed essence of *ousía*, the subject whose fraudulence, according to Jean Laplanche, Freudian theory revealed.

One way to describe the Bersanian oeuvre—if we can call it such[4]—is to say that, throughout his work, Bersani seeks alternatives to the divided subject. His original example of the antagonistic relation between the subject and the other is the Proustian world, which he begins to map in his first book, *Marcel Proust: The Fictions of Life and of Art* (1965). In the early 1970s, psychoanalytic theory, particularly Freud's and Laplanche's, comes to supplement *À la Recherche du temps perdu* as texts to which Bersani will most frequently, and with a productive ambivalence, return in his subsequent work. Over the years, a number of (literary, painterly, cinematic) texts emerge as counterpoints to psychoanalysis and Proust—as "ontological laboratories" (Bersani and Dutoit 1998, 59, 63) in which alternative hypotheses are tested. In the opening pages of *Thoughts and Things*, Bersani gestures toward his collaborative work with Ulysse Dutoit, where they locate "models for an aesthetic ethic of correspondences between the self and the world, a community of being in which the recognition of various degrees and modes of similitude is itself a sensually appealing deconstruction of the prestige of knowledge" (5). Examples can be found in *The Forms of Violence: Narrative in Assyrian Art and Modern Culture* (1985), where Bersani and Dutoit trace aesthetic repetitions in Assyrian art that seduce the spectatorial gaze away from the reliefs' imperial war narratives and their sadistic pleasures; in *Caravaggio's Secrets* (1998), where they find the painter's later work increasingly de-emphasizing the human figures' "sexual" appeal in favor of a "sensual" communication between human and nonhuman forms; and in *Forms of Being: Cinema, Aesthetics, Subjectivity* (2004), which illustrates such ontological crossings in Jean-Luc Godard, Pedro Almodóvar, and Terrence Malick.

The title of Bersani's new book immediately announces his focus on divided subjecthood: it refers to what one scholar has called "the striking Cartesian independence of thoughts from things" (Hundert, 48). The chapters of *Thoughts and Things* offer varied alternatives to "the ontological premise of a subject-object dualism" (Bersani 2015, 4–5). The first chapter, for example, centers around Claire Denis's film *Beau Travail* (1999), in which Bersani locates something of an answer to the question he and Dutoit ask in *Arts of Impoverishment* (1993): Is it possible to conceptualize "a nonsadistic type of movement" (Bersani and Dutoit 1993, 147; Bersani 2015, 1)? If the libidinal object in Proust and Freud is figured in terms of an enigmatic otherness whose secrets the subject must excavate to complete its self, the form of relatedness expressed in the choreographed movements of the film's foreign legionnaires escapes such fascinated, sadistic possessiveness.

In its effort to think desire otherwise than as a force of the other's incorporation, the opening chapter of *Thought and Things* concludes with a characteristically Bersanian move. Bersani suggests that, rather than "subverting" or "contesting" more familiar conceptualizations of the world (such as the divided subject), artworks like *Beau Travail* remain eminently *indifferent* to extant models. If the Freudian subject's fate is tangled up with oedipal enigmas, Denis's film demonstrates that such traps may be neutralized by "stand[ing] up and simply leav[ing] the family tragedy by which Western culture has been oppressed at least since Oedipus's parricide" (13). Similarly, the second chapter, in which Bersani continues his engagement with Jean Genet, includes a brief critique of the politics of same-sex marriage, about whose limits Bersani writes: "It is not, for example, that gay marriage is an inadequate transgression of the social order; rather, the problem is that it is *only* a transgression" (22). Again, as with oedipalized identities, marriage for him constitutes a mode of social bonding whose "fortress" may "simply be deserted" (23). And then, in his ongoing critique of Butlerian-inflected queer theory, Bersani, reading Todd Haynes's film *Safe* (1995), proposes that, rather than "subversively parody" our identities, we may "simply disappear" from their reach (35). It is such indifference, where modes of negation are replaced by a "simple" evacuation, that frequently marks Bersani's relationship to thought whose limits he seeks to exceed.

Spent in the company of Descartes, Proust, Freud, and Godard, chapters 3 and 4 continue the articulation of an ontology that posits a "oneness of being" (xii, 64). Previously, Bersani has explored the shapes of such ontology particularly in the aesthetic experimentations of his Dutoit collaborations. These texts turn to aesthetics—mostly painting and cinema—to think modes of being whose central organizing principle is named after the Baudelairean notion of "correspondence of forms." In chapter 5, "Far Out," Bersani, with the help of Godard's cinema, rethinks such being in terms that extend the idea of "correspondence": "incongruity" or "analogy without similitude" (64, 65). Similarly, the question of *the nonhuman* has been a consistent topic in Bersani's work (again, particularly in the texts cowritten with Dutoit); "Far Out" turns to speculative astronomy to continue conceptualizing existence in a way that demotes the human from its place of centeredness and subjecthood vis-à-vis the nonhuman world. The book concludes with something of an incongruous note in "Being and Notness," the densest of its chapters. Here Bersani exercises what he calls "speculative license" (80) on *La Casse* (1994), Pierre Bergounioux's short, as-yet untranslated novel. While, as Lee Edelman notes in his blurb, *Thoughts and Things* may surprise readers who have associated Bersani's work with queer theory's unrelentingly "antisocial" ambitions, the concluding chapter strikes more familiar notes as it "qualif[ies Bersani's] utopic tendencies by giving the last word to an uncompromising negativity" (xiii).

Rather than detailing more carefully each of the chapters in this review, I propose to situate *Thoughts and Things* in Bersani's oeuvre by taking up his theory of *narcissism*, which briefly appears in the chapter "Far Out." A synthesis of various theories of narcissism yields a perspective through which Bersani approaches the question of being's "oneness." To put it simply: the undivided subject has a narcissistic ontology. In what follows, I trace the development of the Bersanian theory of narcissism from its earliest emergence in "Persons in Pieces," the final chapter of *A Future for Astyanax: Character and Desire in Literature* (1976), to the most recent work, particularly as it informs the reading of Plato in *Intimacies* (2008, coauthored with Adam Phillips), and the cosmological speculations of *Thoughts and Things*.

Bersani's returns to narcissism over the decades draw out one of his thought's "fundamental notes," as Proust would call them (see Bersani 1965, 111–21). For over half a century now, his oeuvre has been marked by such repetitive returns. In the 2013 preface to *Marcel Proust*'s second edition, Bersani speaks of "a profound continuity" in his body of work (xix). From early on, he identifies, with the help of literary and philosophical texts, a set of problematics that he pursues with a singular insistence. He anticipates his emerging thought's cohering shape when he asks in 1970: "could it not be argued that, except for Shakespeare and perhaps Picasso, a certain kind of 'variety-without-identity' in art is the sign of an imagination which has never sounded its most intense, and intensely particularizing[,] interests?" (1970, 306). From its beginning, Bersanian thought is marked by a profound suspicion of "variety" or, to use a more familiar philosophical term, "difference." "I'm not interested in variety very much," he continues in a recent interview. "People have said to me, 'You already said that twenty years ago.' Well, fine. That simply means that it was an important idea and it's remained an important idea but I've found ways to recategorize it, to play with it in a different way, adding something, changing something" (2014, 294). This movement of repetition and difference—of what Bersani most recently calls "recategorization" (2014, 294; 2013, xi–xii)—is characteristic not only of the Bersanian method but also of what we can call Bersanian ontology. It is in the theory of narcissism—which he initially draws from Freud and Laplanche but then locates also in Plato and contemporary astrophysics—that Bersani finds a way to scramble twentieth-century philosophy's prioritization of difference as the ethical category *par excellence* by intensively thinking the question of "sameness," of the undivided subject.

PRIMAL SCENE OF NARCISSISM: A FUTURE FOR ASTYANAX

Bersani equally often cites Foucault's call, in his 1981 interview "Friendship as a Way of Life," to experiment with and bring into existence "new relational modes." According to Foucault, homosexuality, as it is lived in the final quarter of the twentieth century, may have a privileged place among possible sites of such experimentation and becoming. "Homosexuality," he famously writes, "is a historical occasion to reopen affective and relational virtualities, not so much through the intrinsic qualities of the homosexual but because the 'slantwise' position of the latter, as it were, the diagonal lines he can lay out in the social fabric allow these virtualities to come to light" (1997b, 138). Nothing inherent in homosexuality—no transhistorical mode of desiring or being—explains this privilege; rather, homosexuality can be activated in the task of reinventing relationality because of its immanent position in the modern identity regimes. For reasons that Foucault leaves unspecified—for reasons he didn't have the time to explore—homosexuality may be a weak point in the armor of such historically specific constellations. He finds in friendship one of the most usable relational modes for putting pressure on modern identity arrangements.[5]

Despite fully agreeing with Foucault's admonition to rethink relationality,[6] Bersani diverges from his colleague considerably on the question of homosexuality. This divergence can to a large extent be attributed to the differing ways in which the two thinkers position themselves vis-à-vis psychoanalytic theory. Almost without fail, Foucault considers psychoanalysis comparable to the fin-de-siècle sexological discourses, part and parcel of the historical rise of biopolitics that he traces in *The History of Sexuality*'s first volume.[7] For Bersani, on the other hand, psychoanalytic theory has a specificity that renders it not so easily dismissed. Its influence has been such that in its formulations we can observe our extant ways of desiring, being, and relating; the efficiently disseminated lessons of psychoanalysis constitute some of our culture's most important training manuals on *how to be*. Yet the muddled formulations of psychoanalytic theory may also contain unexplored potential that, like the virtualities Foucault speaks of, can help us imagine other modes of relatedness, whether to one's self or to others.

For Bersani, such psychoanalytic virtualities largely concern homosexuality and narcissism, or homosexual narcissism. They are *virtualities* insofar as they point to sites of thought and practice where an unactualized potential can be activated through what Bersani often calls "speculative" work. The earliest of such speculations takes place in the final chapter of *A Future for Astyanax*. In "Persons in Pieces," Bersani seeks to outline modes of desiring by turning, on the one hand, to Jean Laplanche's reading of Freud—this is the first substantial appearance of both in his work—and, on the other, two mid-1950s French erotic novels: Pauline Réage's (i.e., Anne Desclos) *Story of O* (1954) and Jean de Berg's (Catherine Robbe-Grillet) *The Image* (1956). Initially, Réage's and Berg's novels exemplify the two ways in which, according to Laplanche, and Bersani after him, Freud understands the child's relation to the otherness of the outside world: nonsexual mastery (found in *Story of O*) and erotic sadism, derived from the pleasures of masochism (illustrated in Berg's text). The argument about erotic sadism in the final chapter marks the first appearance of the theory of *ébranlement* in Bersani's work. Yet, having contrasted the approaches to otherness illustrated by the two novels, Bersani further complicates the argument by identifying two discrete modes within the violent but detached desire represented by Réage; this distinction returns in a more explicit and elaborated form in his later work in the difference between self-shattering, whose inspiration we find in Laplanche's reading of Freud, and the dynamic Bersani comes to call "inaccurate replications" or, after Charles Baudelaire, "correspondence of forms."

Réage's novel tells the story of a woman who receives "training" in becoming a sexual slave by the secret society to which her lover, René, introduces her. He stipulates that she submit particularly to his stepbrother Sir Stephen, an older man, before she is sent to join a society of women to get further instruction in masochistic compliance. While the novel's depiction of sadomasochistic sex precipitated something of a literary scandal in 1954, with calls for censorship and legal action, Bersani notes the oddly "asexual" atmosphere of its tableaux of torture: the scenes of sadism appear to be informed by "a nonerotic imagination" (1976, 300). The emotional distance of the executors of punishment from the suffering indicates their failure to be at all perturbed by the excitements of sadistic violence: the men approach the erotic scenes, as Réage writes, with "a certain attitude of detachment" (80). Turning to Freud's explanatory schema in "Instincts and Their Vicissitudes" (1915), "'A Child Is Being Beaten'" (1919), and "The Economic Problem of Masochism" (1924), Bersani suggests that the detached masters of *Story of O* exemplify what "Instincts and Their Vicissitudes" argues is the child's initial, nonsexual relation to the world, one of attempted mastery. But as Laplanche observes in *Life and Death in Psychoanalysis* (1970), Freud vacillates about the primacy of (nonsexual) sadism in the subject's constitution. He originally postulates that one's initial orientation to others is that of control, and that sadistic impulses become eroticized only in the drive's subsequent vicissitudes: "A primary masochism, not derived from sadism," he writes, ". . . seems not to be met with" (1915, 125). Yet, in a moment of hesitation that Laplanche highlights, a footnote added in 1924 to "Instincts and Their Vicissitudes" (125 n.3) directs us to a later text, "The Economic Problem of Masochism," where we find Freud speculating about the existence of a masochism prior to the stage of nonsexual sadism (1924, 418–19). We seem to have two forms of sadism in Freud. There exists, as Bersani writes in his subsequent book *Baudelaire and Freud* (1977), "an 'original,' nonsexual sadism which seeks to master the world, and a derived, sexual sadism which is actually a pleasurable fantasy-identification with the intense (sexualized) pain of the victim" (79). As Bersani's quotation marks around the term "original" indicate, for Laplanche the sadistic pleasures of the psychoanalytic subject rest on a prior, masochistic jouissance: "the masochistic moment is first," Laplanche writes. "The masochistic fantasy is fundamental, whereas the sadistic fantasy implies an identification with the suffering object; it is within the suffering position that the enjoyment lies" (1985, 91). Bersani echoes in *A Future for Astyanax*: "We are erotically stimulated by someone else's pain because we identify with it, having already experienced pain as pleasure: that is, sadism is projected masochism" (301). This form of *projected masochism* or *derived sadism* doesn't perturb *O*'s men; they are not moved by the remembered excitements of masochistic—shattering—intensities that produce sadistic pleasures.

If *Story of O* demonstrates the nonsexual detachment of the observer from the scene of suffering, *The Image* describes the sadist's visceral identification with masochistic jouissance, an identification that, according to Bersani, reenacts the shattering mobilization of primary masochism. Berg's novel illustrates Freud's understanding of derived sadism in that in its scenes of punishment we find "both the sadist and the masochist experiencing excitement as a direct result of physical pain": "the sadist responds as if his body were being stimulated erotically, but what stimulates him (or her) are someone else's sensations" (Bersani 1976, 303). Like *The Image*'s male narrator, the sadist is drawn into the spectacle of punishment by the scene's infectious jouissance; the novel's sadists thus exemplify "the Freudian suggestion that sadism is projected masochism. We can be excited by the pain of others because we have ourselves already experienced pain as sexually exciting" (303). In Berg, Bersani locates an illustration of Laplanche's argument according to which "the sadist himself finds masochistic enjoyment in the pain he provokes in others through an identification with the suffering object" (Laplanche 1999, 204). The absence of the sexual, defined in these terms, from Réage's text suggests to Bersani that its violent scenes constitute a narrative whose choreography is interrupted neither by sexuality's absorptive intrusions nor by inassimilable otherness; in *The Image*, by contrast, sexuality becomes a force of otherness in its destabilization of the enjoying subject. What we find in Bersani's depiction of *The Image* are early examples of *ébranlement*. Already in *A Future for Astyanax*, Bersani seeks, as he puts it in a 1997 interview, "to move to a different relation to otherness, not one based in paranoid fascination but one that might use the masochistic element in the confrontation productively" (2010, 177).

Yet having illustrated the distinction between nonsexual and derived sadism with *Story of O* and *The Image*, respectively, Bersani complicates the comparison: he proposes that *O*'s nonsexual sadism bears within it *two forms* of disengagement. There are, first, *O*'s heterosexual men, captured by her irresolvable difference, the dark continent of femininity. The enigma of otherness propels the subject onto a process of violent investigation: in a crucial passage, Réage's narrator describes René's persistent attempts "to understand the *raison d'être*, the truth which must have been lurking somewhere inside Jacqueline, under that golden skin, like the mechanism inside a crying doll" (182). Similar scenes abound in the Proustian world, Bersani's privileged example of a literary imagination enthralled by enigmatic otherness. In "Contre Sainte-Beuve," Proust describes the fascinated exploration of otherness into which one is led by women's beauty: "Beauty multiplies the possibilities of happiness by its particularity. Each being is like an unsurmised ideal that opens before us" (1958, 47). Curiosity about the other impels the subject to take apart the object of his desire as a child would dismantle a mechanized toy in an effort to understand its principle of operation; as Bersani writes in *The Culture of Redemption* (1990), Proust gives us "a desire that exuberantly dismembers its objects" (22). The lover of difference is captured by the promise of a truth hidden behind appearances, the truth whose discovery will necessitate the irreversible undoing of the object.

In "Persons in Pieces," the obvious (and obviously ethical) counterpoint to the violent responses elicited by such enigmatic difference is the shattered and shattering mobility of Berg's sadists. They are shaken by their own *ébranlement* before they can annihilate the other. Yet if this provides us an ethical model, the logic of the argument in "Persons in Piece" moves along a more involutive path, one on which Bersani is to continue in later decades: he implicitly contrasts the response of O's men to another form of immobilized· witnessing, one that emerges in scenes of (male and female) homosexuality. He identifies it in René's "nonsexual idolatry" of Sir Stephen (1976, 293), calling O's lover's "fascinated worship" of the older man "'homosexuality'"—although, importantly, rendering the diagnosis in quotation marks (295).

Bersani emphasizes the two men's absolute obedience to, and success in following, the protocols of heteronormative masculinity. Even with his "homosexuality," René perfectly fits into what Bersani identifies, in the larger structure of the novel, as "a kind of fantasy-blueprint of pure heterosexual desire, a mad dream of the 'ideal' resolution (especially by men) of Oedipal conflicts" (1976, 293). The "purity" of heterosexuality comes from its having rendered (sexual) difference absolute: the other can be desired only as a constitutive lack on this side of difference, and consequently the object to be annihilated. Yet this model entails not only the ossification of sexual difference into two incompatible realms, but also the transparency of one's "own" sex to oneself, its readiness for narcissistic recognition. As Bersani writes, "the post-Oedipal heterosexual male may no longer find any mystery of sexual identity in himself or in other men" (293). As a paradigm of difference, heterosexuality may enable a desire not driven by what it can understand as difference. Because René, O's successfully oedipalized male subject, cannot conceive of any real difference between himself and other men (nor within himself), his "worship" of Sir Stephen must, to the system of hetero-desire, register as desire for the same and, hence, not as desire at all. For Bersani, René's worship of the older man escapes the annihilative drive that marks the fascinations of difference because *it tempts the subject with nothing that he does not already, in some form, have.* The subject of what we can call homo-narcissistic desire is drawn not by the other's enigma but by the repetition, perhaps enhancement, of a familiar form. The homo-narcissist's relation to his or her object of desire is not driven by the kind of enigmatic otherness that we find in Proust. Rather, Sir Stephen is "worshiped without curiosity": "René, unlike a Proustian lover, isn't trying to penetrate the secret of someone else's mysteriously different 'formula' for sexual excitement" (294). Instead, we find in his desire a desire for nonenigmatic sameness, which remains unmotivated by the epistemophilia that Proust illustrates throughout his novel.

It is thus through Freudian and Laplanchean psychoanalysis—as well as some literary experimentation—that Bersani comes to agree with Foucault concerning homosexuality's productively "slantwise" position in the modern era's relational arrangements. Or, to be more precise, he *anticipates* Foucault's early-1980's argument about men's same-sex friendships. Already in 1976 he begins to imply what Foucault will hypothesize in 1981: that the "affective intensities" (Foucault 1997b, 137) of male same-sex attachments constitute a resource for contemporary identity regime's reorganization. Bersani's argument in "Persons in Pieces," let us also note, is contemporary with Carroll Smith-Rosenberg's groundbreaking work on nineteenth-century women's romantic friendships. The implications of what Smith-Rosenberg calls the "emotional intensity" and "richness" (59, 60) of such female companionship are further explored by subsequent scholars whose goal, like Lillian Faderman's, is to help revitalize dormant forces of becoming in the histories of our heteronormative social imaginary.[8] If Bersani formulates his argument through psychoanalysis and literary readings, Smith-Rosenberg and Faderman (writing, like Foucault, in the early 1980s) approach their topic via historical and sociological studies; but they share the ambition, which is also Foucault's, to "writ[e] the history of [our] present" (Foucault 1982, 31)—to disrupt "the now" through genealogical analysis.

In "Persons in Pieces," we find emerging two concepts that Bersani elaborates in his subsequent work: that of *shattering*—exemplified by *The Image*'s derived sadism—and that of *sameness*, in the form of O's homo-narcissism.[9] Shattering and sameness share some aspects: both enable what might be called *the self's immobile dispersal*. The shattered subject finds himself scattered in the world in a movement where the distinction of the inside and the outside is undone. Similarly, the homo-narcissist finds pieces of the self beyond his self: the self, or more precisely some of its constituent parts, is found, narcissistically recognized as, already inhabiting the outside. If the dispersal of the self amounts to a form of movement, Bersani suggests some of its characteristics when he assesses the respective appeals of hetero- and homo-desire in *Story of O*: "Women are desired because they are different," he writes, "but the stimulating lack in desire is perhaps no match for the ecstatically calm contemplation of one's own self, for a kind of self-effacement in the name of the self" (1976, 295). We find the latter form of desire not only between René and Sir Stephen, but also between women: "Homosexuality is, for O, a way of briefly leaving herself in order to observe herself" (295). Homo-narcissism, its "passion for sameness" (306), produces an "ecstatic" form of mobility; as Bersani and Dutoit write later, such ecstasy constitutes a movement in which "being is transferred without being moved" (2004, 4), an "ecstatic oneness with the world" (172).

René does not reach for Sir Stephen across the kind of ontological divide that distances Réage's and Berg's hetero-desiring subjects from their objects. Similarly, René's admiration of the older man is unmoved by the epistemophilic pressure of knowing the other, for in the system of sexual difference there is nothing to know in a subject of one's own sex. If we read Bersani's later analysis of André Gide's Michel, in *The Immoralist* (1902), as a recategorization of these early observations, we can note another collapsing duality: that between the human and the nonhuman. If "Gide imagines homosexuality as a gliding into an impersonal sameness ontologically incompatible with analyzable egos," what attracts the protagonist is not the human other in his psychological complexity but something like nonenigmatic spatiality: "homosexuality is a matter of positioning rather than intimacy" (1995, 125, 124). Homosexual sameness, theorized in narcissism, often evokes the unraveling of humanist subjectivity and the uncanniness of the nonhuman. (Some of John Rechy's narratives are exemplary here.) Bersani seeks in such dehumanizing connotations an aesthetics in which Western modernity's dualisms, including that between the human and the nonhuman, are eroded. The analysis of *The Immoralist* in *Homos* is inaccurately replicated three years later in the description of Caravaggio's later work in *Caravaggio's Secrets*, where Bersani and Dutoit observe "the possibility of spatial interests not defined or directed by the imaginary secrets of the other. Perhaps the exploration of this possibility requires a suspension of strictly human interests, a removal from those existential contexts in which paranoid fascination is the human subject's spontaneous response to the other's soliciting (or even interested) gaze" (1998, 42). The Dutoit collaborations outline, as Bersani writes in *Thoughts and Things*, "exchanges and correspondences between the subject and the world, exchanges that depend on the anti-Cartesian assumption of a commonality of being among the human subject and both the human and the nonhuman world" (62).

Bersani returns to these emphases—the work of "reinvent[ing] the relational possibilities of narcissism" (Bersani and Phillips, 76)—in his latest work. We find the minor-key argument about homo-narcissism in "Persons in Pieces" recategorized not only in the Socratic theory of love explored in *Intimacies* but, most recently, in the cosmological speculations of *Thoughts and Things*.

PLATO'S CHARIOT: *INTIMACIES*

In his collaboration with Phillips, Bersani turns to Plato's *Phaedrus*, particularly to the chariot allegory in Socrates's second speech. Contesting the notion (first articulated by Phaedrus, who recounts Lysias's speech, and then by Socrates himself) that it is better for the lover to prefer the calculative reason of a nonlover over the lover's passion, the palinode presents love as a mode of remembering the soul's preembodiment past. According to the myth, before their descent to earth, souls travel in a god's chariot in the heavens, where "abides the very being with which true knowledge is concerned; the colourless, formless, intangible essence, visible only to the mind, the pilot of the soul" (Plato 1956, 247c [288]). Once on earth, the soul obscurely recalls what it has experienced. No earthly poet will ever sing fully of the heavens to which the immortal gods ascend, yet all have varied degrees of access to "the recollection of those things our soul once saw while following God" (249c [290]). "Every human soul," as Bersani writes, "remains in touch, through memory, with the god it followed" (Bersani and Phillips, 79). What we have in the allegory is a version of the Platonic theory of Forms: all have witnessed incorporeal perfection in heaven; our earthly ambition is to recall "beauty, wisdom, goodness, and the like" (Plato 1956, 246e [287]) when prompted by various embodied objects. The experience of love is elicited by the lover's more or less obfuscated memory of beauty; the lover is a subject "who, when he sees the beauty of earth, is transported with the recollection of the true beauty" (249d [290]).

Like Caravaggio and Gide, Plato offers Bersani ways to think beyond anthropocentric models of desiring and being. Socrates indicates that we share the god's chariot with other souls. On earth, we obscurely recognize our fellow travelers. The lover, as Bersani comments, chooses an object that "already belongs to the lover's type of being" (Bersani and Phillips, 82); such an object "makes the lover remember both the heavenly Beauty and the god with whom the lover's soul had flown" (83). Because of the principle of reincarnation (παλινγενεσία, *palingenesía*) that is included in the myth, the likenesses that elicit one's recognition may include other forms than human. If the psychoanalytic subject is always the human subject, with Plato Bersani attempts to deprivilege the human by exploring "forms of being" that proceed irrespective of the divisions that initiate anthropobecoming. In *Phaedrus* and other works of art, "the subject, no longer constrained by a theory of human nature ultimately sanctioned by a Christian metaphysics, is set loose in its newly discovered finite universe and, perhaps most startlingly, discovers its possible affinities with the inanimate" (Bersani 1990, 77). Aesthetics allows us to observe "a world of ontological play . . . where the human and the nonhuman are no longer related as subject and object, but rather in the mysterious and nonnarrative 'unity' of inaccurate replications" (197).

Bersani connects Socrates's allegory to Freud's famous observation about object-love: that "the finding of an object is in fact a refinding of it" (Freud 1905, 145). "Love, which we like to think of as a discovery," he writes, "is inseparable from memory" (Bersani and Phillips, 72), for Freud the memory of the infant's satiety at the mother's breast. On the one hand, there is a "profound continuity" between the Freudian and Socratic accounts of love: in *Phaedrus*, as in Freud's *Three Essays on the Theory of Sexuality*, "love is a phenomenon of memory, and an instance of narcissistic fascination" (80). *Phaedrus* provides a myth that psychoanalysis rearticulates: love is self-love, indeed a "narcissistic extravagance" (76). On the other hand, however, Socrates's "is a form of narcissism that the psychoanalytic version of narcissism, which it appears to resemble, makes it difficult for us to understand" (80). Psychoanalytic accounts of narcissism differ from what Bersani considers its Socratic mode not only because of their inevitable pathologization of the concept but also the subject that they presume. "Despite its interest in narcissism," writes Tim Dean, "psychoanalysis has not been especially helpful in rationalizing this attraction [of sameness], primarily because it pictures de-differentiation as almost exclusively terrifying and traumatic" (38). As Dean indicates, psychoanalysis's explicit theory of narcissism relies, as do so many other psychoanalytic concepts, on the notion of *trauma*, that is, irrecuperable privation. In the context of originary trauma, a return to the same signals the approach to the zero-degree tension of death (in Freud's drive theory) or the proximity of the real (in Lacan). The pathology of Narcissus is his lethal attachment to nonbeing.

Socratic narcissism needs to be distinguished from "the specularity of a personal narcissism" (Bersani and Phillips, 82), where sameness evokes an uncanny terror. The Socratic self is not the being we find in the Lacanian mirror, the ideal ego whose appearance the disorganized being of infancy meets first with jubilation and then with aggressiveness. With Plato, Bersani recategorizes the theory of narcissism he has observed in Freud and *Story of O*: the account of (self-)love as "narcissistic fascination" Bersani locates in *Phaedrus* repeats his earlier argument, in "Persons in Pieces," about René's homo-narcissistic, "fascinated worship" of Sir Stephen. If René finds in Sir Stephen his ideal, he observes in the older man nothing he has lost but an intensification of, a correspondence with, his own form. His "fascination" with Sir Stephen is not premised on difference and privation, trauma and loss; and, consequently, it does not tempt him with promises of *redemption* from such injured being. For Bersani, redemptive models, whether in philosophy or art, imagine a world in terms of a puzzle that solicits our interpretive desire when some of its pieces have gone missing. Like the Lacanian *objet petit a*, the primordially lost pieces instigate our *wanting*: their promise is seen in objects that necessarily confuse, as Lacan would say, the object-cause of desire with objects of desire. This mode of desire characterizes psychoanalytic ontology: Bersani claims that Lacan "promot[es] . . . castration from an Oedipal fantasy to the meta-genital status of a lost plenitude of being" (2010, 54). The mode of recognition that informs homo-narcissism is premised on an economy where that which fascinates is not lacking or lost but—as Bersani increasingly frequently puts it in his later work—persists in a *virtual* form.[10] Such figurations aspire not to divinity but, through correspondences, to phenomena of "familiarity" or "solidarity"—Bersani speaks of "the particular families of forms to which we belong" (1995, 121), familiarities that express a "solidarity . . . of being" (Bersani and Dutoit 2004, 120). If homo-narcissism is a mode of correspondence of forms, its movement is—to borrow from Baudelaire—not *vertical* but *horizontal*.[11]

In this way, Bersanian ontology has a narcissistic shape; when Bersani speaks of narcissism, he is alluding to a mode that has emerged over some thirty years in his engagement with the Freudian concept. Homo-narcissistic love exhibits, as he puts it in "Persons in Pieces," "a passion for sameness" (1976, 306). Knowingly or not, Adam Phillips repeats the phrase in *Intimacies*: "Bewitched by the armor of singularity, of a picture of individual identity that has to be fought for and fought over, the question for Bersani is, how can we allow ourselves— or, how can we remind ourselves of—our passion for sameness?" (Bersani and Phillips, 108). In *Phaedrus*, Bersani finds, in Phillips's words, "the flourishing of the lover and his beloved through narcissistic mutual recognition, through the cultivation of sameness" (108). This describes René's narcissistic attraction for Sir Stephen in *Story of O*.

Yet Phillips's statement needs some modulation. If we are "bewitched" by "singularity," by the promise of "individual identity," what is the individuality at stake here, the one that claims us in fascination? Bersani frequently insists that we must distinguish between two modes of individuality, suggested by the French terms *individu* and *individuel*. Identical to what Phillips calls "individual identity," the former is synonymous with what everyday language designates as "personality"; in Western modernity, its secret core, as Foucault has suggested, consists of the truth of our sexuality. Bersani contrasts this "psychological individuality" with "metaphysical" (1990, 82) or "depersonalized individuality" (2013, xiii). This individuality—*individuel*— denotes a mode that is "distinct from subjectivity," an "individuality indifferent to the human subject" (Bersani 1990, 82). It is a singularity "individualized not in the way that personalities are, to our modern psychological understanding, individualized. Rather, it has what might be thought of as a general, universal, individuation" (Bersani and Phillips, 82). Glossing the terms again in *Thoughts and Things*, Bersani writes that *individuel* is the monadic being whose virtual potential is only partially actualized in the corporeal form of *individu*; it signals "a singular universal property distinct from the multiple particular individuals that embody it" (88; see also Bersani 2013, xiv). Art, as Bersani continues, expresses such impersonal individualities; their expression is, as in *Phaedrus*, a function of memory: "the individual in art is located at a subjective depth where, mysteriously, we 'remember' a type of being that came to us originally from elsewhere, from the artist's unknown, lost homeland, which even he has forgotten and which he remembers only in his art" (2015, 88). By contrast, the psychological individuality of *individu*, which "constitutes us as unique persons," provides us "our difference, a difference we are ready to defend ferociously, both in our individual self and in our various group selves (ethnic, racial, national, sexual)" (83). Pairing *individu* and *individuel*, Bersani articulates the competing ethics of otherness that has occupied him throughout his career: while *individu* names a being relating to its others in terms of difference, the concept of *individuel* assumes an ontology of sameness, correspondences, and homoness—of "impersonal" narcissism.

OUT THERE: *THOUGHTS AND THINGS*

In *Thoughts and Things*, Bersani implicitly elaborates his account of narcissism, one with which he hopes to escape not only the epistemophilics that he observes organizing Western thought, but also the ontological divide posited between the subject and the world. He recategorizes his theory of narcissism by engaging contemporary cosmological theory. He begins the chapter "Far Out" by referring to the cosmologist Lawrence Krauss's suggestion that our bodies contain atoms of far-off heavenly bodies, long ago extinguished: bearing the residue of exploded stars, we are, as Krauss puts it, "star children" (quoted in Bersani 2015, 77). Without naming Henri Bergson, Bersani proposes we think of this celestial residue as evidence of something like "ontological memory": "we can obscurely remember," he writes, "our origins almost 14 billion years ago" (2015, 77).[12] Krauss's argument about our bodies' recall of their remote celestial ancestry—"neural memories of our beginnings" (80)—constitutes a scientific recategorization of the texts we have seen Bersani read, all of which recast the question of narcissism. While outlining his cosmology in *Thoughts and Things*, he, for example, returns to *Phaedrus*. Referring to his discussion, in the Phillips collaboration, of the "kind of self-love," "a love for a different sameness" that he had observed in Socrates's story, he suggests that we regard the Platonic myth, itself something of a variation of what psychoanalysis will theorize as narcissism, as a version of Krauss's cosmological observations: as much as the Socratic lover remembers the species to which he belonged in the heavens, "Krauss gives us a cosmic version of this identity of being," of "primal correspondence" (2015, 84).

Despite his ongoing critique of Proustian onto-ethics / aesthetics, Bersani finds further resonances of such cosmological propositions in the theory of art prompted by the fictional composer Vinteuil's music. Listening to a sonata and a septet, Marcel observes "resemblances, concealed, involuntary, [breaking] out in different colours" in the divergent compositions; such correspondences and analogies in separate pieces point to "profound similarities" expressed in art (Proust 2006, 2.655). Art is a mode of re-calling a forgotten "homeland" (Bersani 2015, 88) where the artist—perhaps, a charioteer—once dwelled. "Each artist," Marcel observes, "seems . . . to be the native of an unknown country, which he himself has forgotten, different from that from which will emerge, making for the earth, another great artist"; even when artists can't remember "the country of [their] heart[s]," "each of them remains all his life somehow attuned to it; he is wild with joy when he is singing the airs of his native land" (Proust 2006, 2.656). The memory inscribed in art constitutes a "call" or "summons" (Bersani 2015, 87, 92). Already in *Homos*, Bersani speaks of our being summoned by "formal affinities that diagram our extensions, the particular families of forms to which we belong" (121). This solicitation by sameness, whose early example in Bersani is the appeal of Sir Stephen's familiar form to René, constitutes a mode of narcissistic relatedness. Yet, as Bersani and Dutoit write elsewhere, "what might have been seen as a specular narcissism should rather be read as the subject's recognition that in approaching otherness, he is also moving toward himself. A nonantagonistic relation to difference depends on this inaccurate replication of the self *in* difference, on our recognizing that *we are already out there*" (1999, 72). Rather than fortifying the ego, impersonal narcissism

demands that our selves be deliriously unbound so that we can actual-
ize "our *extensive identity* in the world, an identity forgotten or repressed
by the authoritative self intent on reinforcing its boundaries in order
to know better what lies beyond them. Self-absorption . . . is an activity
that replaces us in the world" (Bersani and Dutoit 1993, 207). Rather
than moved, like the Cartesian subject, by the love of knowledge, the
narcissistic being of Bersanian ontology responds to the call of the world
aesthetically. This narcissistic aesthetics is indicated by a fleeting shot
in Alain Resnais's film *Providence* (1977) where the protagonist's failing body is momentarily overlaid, as if in an x-ray image, by the reflection of tree branches in a car window. For Bersani and Dutoit, writing
in *Arts of Impoverishment*, this impression suggests a world getting ready
to welcome the dying human entity into its "families of forms": "At
any moment that reflection in the car window may reappear, and the
veins so carefully protected by our skin are once again, as they always
were, out there, circulating" (Bersani and Dutoit 1993, 208).

The chapters in *Thoughts and Things* render inescapable what should
have been evident about Bersani's work for a while now: that it is speculative and—to cite an assessment concerning Walter Benjamin's—
"unapologetically ontological" (Cowan, 59); it proceeds heedless of the
commonplaces of contemporary continental philosophy, where "the
terms 'speculation' and 'metaphysics' [have] been reduced to insults
for attacking mere guesses and weird supernatural ideas" (Schweppenhäuser, 55). It is, some might say, out there. The most important
of contemporary commentator in dressing down ontology has been
Jacques Derrida, who, extending the Heideggerian critique of Western ontotheology, has analyzed philosophy's assertions about "being"
in terms of "supplementarity," "*Nachträglichkeit*," and "*différance*." I
have suggested elsewhere that Bersani's early encounter with Gilles
Deleuze's work (in *Balzac to Beckett: Center and Circumference in French
Fiction* [1970]) enables his untimely engagement with being (Tuhkanen
2018, esp. chap. 1). That Bersani reads Deleuze before the Derridean-
ization of ontological thinking has crucial ramifications: with Deleuze,
he takes on the question of ontology in a way that would become difficult if not impossible after deconstruction's impact was felt in the
Anglo-American academia later in the 1970s and subsequent decades.
He comes to share Deleuze's indifference to "the anti-ontological trend
of much of twentieth-century philosophy" (May, 16).[13]

Bersani's language in *Thoughts and Things* indicates his indifference to decrees that, perhaps reductively, have been identified with Derrida's philosophy. Bersani frequently makes metaphysical statements about "the oneness of all being" (83; see also 64, 69 n.13), echoing what he has earlier called "the total relationality of being" (Bersani and Dutoit 1993, 140) or the "essentially mysterious connectedness in the universe" (Bersani and Dutoit 1985, 46). Such statements point us toward some allies to the Bersanian project. Most notably perhaps, in Baruch Spinoza's monist metaphysics we find ontology conceptualized in ways that agree with Bersani's effort to think being. Like Bersani, Spinoza undoes the Cartesian prioritization of cogito as the ground from which the object becomes conceivable. For him, as a recent commentator writes, "there is no subject/object gulf between me and the objects that I cognize"; rather, Spinozian metaphysics offers us "a state of being that is at home in the universe" (Almog, 94, 95). It is through its Deleuzean resonances that Bersani's thought can be rearticulated in Spinozist terms.

While Bersani, echoing Deleuze, suggests that we haven't quite finished with the question of ontology, he also, as would be his wont, betrays his own nondeconstructionist bent. In *Homos*, speaking of the reorganization of the relational field through the concept of "homoness," he writes that we need to think difference as "the nonthreatening supplement to sameness" (7). Repeating the phrase several times (see Bersani and Dutoit 1999, 72; Bersani 2010, 33, 100),[14] he indicates his agreement with the Derridean rendering of being's self-sameness as a ghostly presence conjured into existence, *après-coup*, by supplemental difference.

When Bainard Cowan writes of Benjaminian philosophy that it is "unapologetically ontological," he is referring to the influences of Judaic messianism on Benjamin's thought. His choice of words indicates that in a critical field defined by the "linguistic turn," the mysticism that Benjamin's friend Gershom Scholem studied constitutes something of an embarrassing anomaly. Bearing in mind Bersani's unequivocal rejection of Benjamin's work as too redemption-oriented—it amounts to a "postlapsarian dirge" (Bersani 1990, 53)—it is striking that the chapter "Far Out," in *Thoughts and Things*, culminates in a reference to the philosophy of Sufism (84–85). Does Bersani's latest work approach something like mysticism?[15] And if it does, how much of a derogative or dismissal does that term constitute in the critical field that has witnessed the recent emergence of "speculative realism" and "materialist vitalism"? How receptive might critical theory, which some are suggesting is undergoing an "ontological turn," be to the kind of speculative work that one finds in *Thoughts and Things*?

Bersani sees us living in the midst of an epistemic rupture, one whose central feature is a reorganization of the relation between the subject and the world; consequently, "connectedness," as he writes in the preface to *Thoughts and Things*, "is the subject of this book" (xv). For him, twentieth century's rethinking of the other as preceding or inhabiting or supplementing the self has but solidified familiar antagonisms. Yet as much as one can turn, for example, to Sufism for alternative ontologies, Bersani suggests that we find unprecedented experimentations with onto-ethics / aesthetics also in the texts that constitute the most prestigious articulations of our Cartesian moment: the modern canon of, for example, Freud and Proust. Approached slantwise, they point to new ways to think and live being. Newness inhabits our most familiar terrain, camouflaged like a guerrilla: Bersani indicates this by turning and returning, over the past half a century, to the villain in the mirror, the villain whose passion for sameness reduces— we have thought—the other to a mere echo.

Associate professor of English at Texas A&M University, **Mikko Tuhkanen** is the author of *The Essentialist Villain: On Leo Bersani* (2018) and *The American Optic: Psychoanalysis, Critical Race Theory, and Richard Wright* (2009). He is also the editor of *Leo Bersani: Queer Theory and Beyond* (2014), as well as the coeditor, with E. L. McCallum, of *The Cambridge History of Gay and Lesbian Literature* (2014) and *Queer Times, Queer Becomings* (2011).

Notes

1. For Foucault's use of the term, see Foucault 2005, 14; see also his description of the Descartes in Foucault 1997a, 294. For Bersani's discussion, see Bersani 2010, 62, chap. 11; and 2015, 38, 46, 62.

2. On Hadot and Foucault, see Davidson, 480–82. For Hadot's own commentary, see Hadot 1995.

3. On this, see Tuhkanen 2018.

4. See Bersani's observations of the term in 2010, 190–91.

5. On the implications of "friendship" in Foucault and after, see Roach 2012.

6. In a 1997 interview, Bersani speak of "what [he] think[s] is our most urgent project now: redefining modes of relationality and community, the very notion of sociality" (2010, 172). Writing in 2000, he goes on to attribute the same phrase—"our most urgent ethical project" (2010, 102)—to Foucault and his discussion, in "Friendship as a Way of Life," of relationality's new possibilities.

7. As Didier Eribon writes, describing Foucault's attitude, "Psychoanalysis is intrinsically linked to this apparatus [of sexuality], and indeed makes up a large part of its machinery, and so the attack against the apparatus is necessarily an attack against psychoanalysis itself" (79). Eribon also assesses the differences between Foucault's and Bersani's readings of psychoanalysis (84–85). For a recent reconsideration of queer theory that insists on Foucault's dismissal of psychoanalysis, see Huffer.

8. For some of this work, see Rothblum and Brehony.

9. In order to highlight this shift, my above reading—let me now admit—inverts the chronology of the theoretical narrative in "Persons in Pieces." In the chapter, Bersani moves from noting René's attraction to Sir Stephen in *Story of O* to a consideration of Réage's male subjects' torturing of their female victims to accentuating the "shattering" involved in the derived sadism of *The Image*. The story's narrative ordering—where we shift, paradigmatically, from lesser details to the climactic dénouement—suggests Bersani's prioritization of what he finds in *The Image* as the solution to the ethical dilemma of otherness's annihilation in desire. Whereas Bersani ends his theoretical narrative with the ethical importance of *ébranlement*, I have scrambled this line of argumentation, moving from shattering (or derived sadism) to the kind of worship of sameness that we find in René's "homosexuality," that is, his "nonsexual adoration" of Sir Stephen. I do this to anticipate the shift that Bersani undertakes in his subsequent work, one by which *ébranlement* is deprioritized in order to investigate the ramifications of the sameness—the homo-attraction—an example of which we find between René and the older man.

10. For some commentary on this term, see Bersani 2014, 281.

11. Baudelaire remains one of Bersani's most important sources: see esp. Bersani 1977; and 1990, 63–86.

12. In *Creative Evolution*, Bergson insists on the metaphysical connectedness of all beings in a way that Bersani might approvingly quote: "we shall find [the individual] solidary with each of [his remotest ancestors], solidary with that little mass of protoplasmic jelly which is probably at the root of the genealogical tree of life. Being, to a certain extent, one with this primitive ancestor, he is also solidary with all that descends from the ancestor in divergent directions. In this sense each individual may be said to remain united with the totality of living beings by invisible bonds" (43). In *Thoughts and Things*, Bersani quotes passages from Deleuze's *Bergsonism* (56, 77) that are paraphrases of Bergson's statements such as the above (2015, 88n.).

13. On the divergence of Deleuzean and Derridean thinking, see Smith, chap. 16.

14. There is also a near-repetition of the phrase in Bersani and Dutoit 2004, 63.

15. See Bersani's brief reaction to the term in 2014, 293. Alluding to Sufism, Bersani references Joan Copjec's recent work; Copjec is in turn indebted to Henry Corbin's groundbreaking studies. For another critic writing in English who has recently engaged Corbin and Sufist philosophy for thinking ontology and politics, see Hallward, 2001, 2006.

Works Cited

Almog, Joseph. 2014. *Everything in Its Right Place: Spinoza and Life by the Light of Nature*. Oxford: Oxford University Press.

Berg, Jean de. 2006. *The Image*. n.p.: Wet Angel.

Bergson, Henri. 1911. *Creative Evolution*. Trans. Arthur Mitchell. Mineola: Dover.

Bersani, Leo. 1965. *Marcel Proust: The Fictions of Life and of Art*. New York: Oxford University Press.

Bersani, Leo. 1970. *Balzac to Beckett: Center and Circumference in French Fiction*. New York: Oxford University Press.

Bersani, Leo. 1976. *A Future for Astyanax: Character and Desire in Literature*. New York: Columbia University Press.

Bersani, Leo. 1977. *Baudelaire and Freud*. Berkeley: University of California Press.

Bersani, Leo. 1990. *The Culture of Redemption*. Cambridge, Mass.: Harvard University Press.

Bersani, Leo. 1995. *Homos*. Cambridge, Mass.: Harvard University Press.

Bersani, Leo. 2010. *Is the Rectum a Grave? and Other Essays*. Chicago: University of Chicago Press.

Bersani, Leo. 2013. Preface to the Second Edition. In *Marcel Proust: The Fictions of Life and of Art*, ix–xix. 2nd ed. Oxford: Oxford University Press.

Bersani, Leo. 2014. "Rigorously Speculating: An Interview with Leo Bersani." In *Leo Bersani: Queer Theory and Beyond*. Ed. Mikko Tuhkanen, 279–96. Albany: State University of New York Press.

Bersani, Leo. 2015. *Thoughts and Things*. Chicago: University of Chicago Press.

Bersani, Leo, and Ulysse Dutoit. 1985. *The Forms of Violence: Narrative in Assyrian Art and Modern Culture*. New York: Schocken.

Bersani, Leo. 1993. *Arts of Impoverishment: Beckett, Rothko, Resnais*. Cambridge, Mass.: Harvard University Press.

Bersani, Leo. 1998. *Caravaggio's Secrets*. Cambridge, Mass.: MIT Press.

Bersani, Leo. 1999. *Caravaggio*. London: BFI.

Bersani, Leo. 2004. *Forms of Being: Cinema, Aesthetics, Subjectivity*. London: BFI.

Bersani, Leo, and Adam Phillips. 2008. *Intimacies*. Chicago: University of Chicago Press.

Copjec, Joan. 2012. "The Fate of the Image in Church History and the Modern State." *Política Común* 2: n.p. Web. 28 February 2016. http://dx.doi.org/10.3998/pc.12322227.0002.003

Corbin, Henry. 1998. *Alone with the Alone: Creative Imagination in the Sufism of Ibn 'Arabī*. Trans. Ralph Manheim. Princeton: Princeton University Press.

Cowan, Bainard. 2005. "Walter Benjamin's Theory of Allegory." In *Walter Benjamin: Critical Evaluations in Cultural Theory*. Ed. Peter Osborne, 2.56–69. 3 vols. London: Routledge.

Davidson, Arnold I. 1990. "Spiritual Exercises and Ancient Philosophy: An Introduction to Pierre Hadot." *Critical Inquiry* 16, no. 3 (Spring): 475–82.

Dean, Tim. 2002. "Sameness without Identity." *Umbr(a): A Journal of the Unconscious*, 25–41.

Deleuze, Gilles. 1997. *Bergsonism*. Trans. Hugh Tomlinson and Barbara Habberjam. New York: Zone.

Eribon, Didier. 2014. "Toward an Ethics of Subjectivation: French Resistance to Psychoanalysis in the 1970s." In *Foucault Now: Current Perspectives in Foucault Studies*. Ed. James D. Faubion, 71–87. Cambridge: Polity.

Faderman, Lillian. 1981. *Surpassing the Love of Men: Romantic Friendship and Love Between Women from the Renaissance to the Present*. New York: William Morrow.

Foucault, Michel. 1982. *Discipline and Punish: The Birth of the Prison*. Trans. Alan Sheridan. Harmondsworth: Penguin.

Foucault, Michel. 1990. *The History of Sexuality, Volume 1: An Introduction*. Trans. Robert Hurley. New York: Vintage, 1990.

Foucault, Michel. 1997a. "The Ethics of the Concern of the Self as a Practice of Freedom." Trans. P. Aranov and D. McGrawth. In *Essential Works, Vol. 1: Ethics: Subjectivity and Truth*. Ed. Paul Rabinow, 280–301. New York: New Press.

Foucault, Michel. 1997b. "Friendship as a Way of Life." Trans. John Johnston. In *Essential Works, Vol. 1: Ethics: Subjectivity and Truth*. Ed. Paul Rabinow, 136–40. New York: New Press.

Foucault, Michel. 2005. *The Hermeneutics of the Subject: Lectures at the Collège de France, 1981–1982*. Ed. Frédéric Gros. Trans. Graham Burchell. New York: Palgrave Macmillan.

Freud, Sigmund. 1905. *Three Essays on the Theory of Sexuality*. In *Pelican Freud Library*, 7.31–169.

Freud, Sigmund. 1915. "Instincts and Their Vicissitudes." In *Pelican Freud Library*, 11.105–38.

Freud, Sigmund. 1919. "'A Child Is Being Beaten (A Contribution to the Study of the Origin of Sexual Perversions).'" In *Pelican Freud Library*, 10.159–93.

Freud, Sigmund. 1924. "The Economic Problem of Masochism." In *Pelican Freud Library*, 11.409–26.

Freud, Sigmund. 1974–86. *The Pelican Freud Library*. Ed. and trans. James Strachey and Angela Richards et al. 15 vols. Harmondsworth: Penguin.

Hadot, Pierre. 1995. "Reflections on the Idea of the 'Cultivation of the Self.'" In *Philosophy as a Way of Life: Spiritual Exercises from Socrates to Foucault*. Ed. Arnold I. Davidson. Trans. Michael Chase, 206–13. Malden: Blackwell.

Hallward, Peter. 2001. *Absolutely Postcolonial: Writing between the Singular and the Specific*. Manchester: Manchester University Press.

Hallward, Peter. 2006. *Out of This World: Deleuze and the Philosophy of Creation*. London: Verso.

Huffer, Lynne. 2010. *Mad for Foucault: Rethinking the Foundations of Queer Theory*. New York: Columbia University Press.

Hundert, Edward M. 1995. *Lessons from an Optical Illusion: On Nature and Nurture, Knowledge and Values*. Cambridge, Mass.: Harvard University Press.

Laplanche, Jean. 1985. *Life and Death in Psychoanalysis*. Trans. Jeffrey Mehlman. Baltimore: Johns Hopkins University Press.

Laplanche, Jean. 1999. "Masochism and the General Theory of Seduction." Trans. Luke Thurston. In *Essays on Otherness*. Ed. John Fletcher, 197–213. London: Routledge.

May, Todd. 2005. *Gilles Deleuze: An Introduction*. Cambridge: Cambridge University Press.

Plato. 1956. *Phaedrus*. In *The Works of Plato*. Ed. Irwin Edman. Trans. Benjamin Jowett, 263–329. New York: Modern Library.

Proust, Marcel. 1958. "Contre Sainte-Beuve." In *On Art and Literature, 1896–1919*. Trans. Sylvia Townsend Warner, 17–76. New York: Meridian.

Proust, Marcel. 2006. *Remembrance of Things Past*. Trans. C. K. Scott Moncrieff and Stephen Hudson. 2 vols. London: Wordsworth.

Réage, Pauline. 1973. *Story of O*. Trans. Sabine d'Estrée. New York: Ballantine.

Roach, Tom. 2012. *Friendship as a Way of Life: Foucault, AIDS, and the Politics of Shared Estrangement*. Albany: State University of New York Press.

Rothblum, Esther D., and Kathleen A. Brehony, eds. 1993. *Boston Marriages: Romantic but Asexual Relationships among Contemporary Lesbians*. Amherst: University of Massachusetts Press.

Schweppenhäuser, Gerhard. 2009. *Theodor W. Adorno: An Introduction*. Trans. James Rolleston. Durham: Duke University Press.

Smith, Daniel W. 2012. *Essays on Deleuze*. Edinburgh: Edinburgh University Press.

Smith-Rosenberg, Carroll. 1985. "The Female World of Love and Ritual: Relations Between Women in Nineteenth-Century America." In *Disorderly Conduct: Visions of Gender in Victorian America*, 53–76. New York: Oxford University Press.

Tuhkanen, Mikko. 2018. *The Essentialist Villain: On Leo Bersani*. Albany: State University of New York Press.

BOOK REVIEWS

Cultural Critique's commitment to cultural and intellectual debate and discussion is bolstered by the regular inclusion of reviews of both new and not-so-new books. Generally, books reviewed will have appeared within the past three years, although reviews of older books that are emerging or reemerging in intellectual debates are also welcome. As an academic publication, *Cultural Critique* sees itself as having a responsibility to devote space to authors whose work may not be otherwise reviewed. For *Cultural Critique*'s special issues, book reviews should share the issue's thematic focus. *Cultural Critique*'s book review editors solicit writers, books, and ideas for future contributions to this section of the journal. Please contact the book review editors at cultcrit@umn.edu or *Cultural Critique,* Department of Cultural Studies and Comparative Literature, 216 Pillsbury Drive S.E., 235 Nicholson Hall, University of Minnesota, Minneapolis, MN 55455–0229.

PRISING OPEN THE
CONTRADICTIONS OF EMPIRE

THE LIFE OF CAPTAIN CIPRIANI:
AN ACCOUNT OF BRITISH GOVERNMENT
IN THE WEST INDIES
WITH THE PAMPHLET THE CASE FOR
WEST INDIAN SELF GOVERNMENT
BY C. L. R. JAMES (Introduction: Bridget Brereton)
Duke University Press, 2014

Andrew Smith

The Life of Captain Cipriani: An Account of British Government in the West Indies was the first full-length work of nonfiction by the West Indian Marxist and pioneering historian of black resistance to oppression, C. L. R. James. Drafted sometime between 1929 and 1931, while James was living in Trinidad, the study was originally published by a small local printer in the northern English town of Nelson in 1932. James had moved to the UK that year with the encouragement and support of the cricketer Learie Constantine, whose ghost-written biography he also brought with him, and to whom he dedicated this study. Before he settled in Lancashire, James had opted to spend time in the intellectual circles of Bloomsbury—an experience on which he reported for the *Port of Spain Gazette* (see James 2003)—and it was at the suggestion of Leonard Woolf that he produced, in 1933, a radically abbreviated version of the original text for the Hogarth Press, which drew out his underlying critique of Crown Colony government in the West Indies (as the revised title makes clear: *The Case for West-Indian Self Government*). These two early works are brought together and republished here for the first time as part of the excellent Duke University Press series on James, edited by Robert A. Hill. The historian Bridget Brereton provides an insightful introduction that offers valuable context, including a detailed account of the original reception of James's study in the Caribbean.

At the outset James insists that his text is to be understood not as a conventional biography, but as "a political biography" (39). In this respect, as Brereton points out, it can be thought of as lying at the beginning of a long line of efforts on James's part to think through the relationship between leaders and the social movements of which they are part. He would return repeatedly to this relationship with regard to a series of (always male) political figures including, inter alia, Toussaint Louverture, Leon Trotsky, Kwame Nkrumah, Frederick Douglass and, in a slightly different sense, Frank Worrell. Cipriani, from a family of Corsican descent, had been a captain in the British West Indies Regiment during World War I and became, on his return, president of the Trinidad Workingmen's Association, a campaigner for social and political reform in the colony, and an advocate of self-government. James takes Cipriani as his focus, then, not so much for his own sake, but because he was one of the "leaders of the democratic movement in the West Indies" (165). Indeed it seems clear that what James has in mind when he describes the book as "political biography" is not so much the biography of someone who happens to be a political figure but rather biography that has, itself, a political purpose, biography as a means of doing politics. This is made evident at the end of chapter 1, for example. Here James provides a sociological synopsis of the relationships of colonial society in Trinidad from which Cipriani is more or less absent. It is only at the end of the chapter that James segues into the start of his account of Cipriani's life with a kind of "crane shot" overview of rising popular discontent across the region, which ends up by panning back even further, and positioning that discontent as part of a wider shift in the relations of empire as a whole: "It is strange that the British official, with his long experience of having to pack his traps and go from Canada, Australia, New Zealand, South Africa, Egypt and Ireland, while yet the people of India speed the parting guest, despite all this has not yet learnt to recognize when he is outstaying his welcome" (60). In this way, James has Cipriani ushered onto the stage of his own biography, as it were, by the movement of history: "That is why it [his life-story] is presented here. . . . That is why it is presented now" (60).

James's later work, especially the political writings he produced with Grace Lee Boggs and Raya Dunayevskaya during his time in America, provide a significant attempt to define and describe a critical, humanist Marxism. Still somewhat undervalued, and not yet systemically collected, it is body of work that deserves to be read alongside that of, for example, Henri Lefebvre, Erich Fromm, E. P. Thompson, Frantz Fanon, and Agnes Heller. In that context James came to defend a version of historical materialism that recognized and was interested in the characterful specificity of individuals, and which emphasized the capacity of human beings to make history as well as the extent to which they are made by it. He became especially concerned with the ways in which popular struggles to realize the creative and expressive potential of human beings could open out into wider struggles against capitalism's circumscription of such potential. James would write, in this respect, about the need to be attentive to the "volcano that is clamped down in every human being" (1996, 326). That interest in the individual and his or her political agency might be taken to be implicit here in James's early decision to write a biography rather than a straightforward historical or political study. It would also of course be an interest entirely befitting the aspiring novelist that he was at this point. More than once in the course of his account one feels that James is trying out literary styles and turns of phrase, especially in those passages that deal with Cipriani's own life, where he frequently slips into the voice of an omniscient narrator: "Old Dr. de Boissiere passed through the rooms and examined them" (61). Yet, for the most part, and despite these novelistic flourishes, Cipriani remains a rather absent figure in his own *Life* as James tells it; we get no really vivid sense of him as a person the way that we do, for example, in some of the wonderful sketches that James provided of the great West Indian cricketers in later years. The contemporary reviewers that Brereton cites, who criticized the book's failings as a biographical study, did so with some justification. Even in the short chapter at the end of the book in which James tries to provide a summarizing portrait of his subject as an individual—"to complete the picture" (155)—he comes across as an agglomeration of principles rather than as a recognizably human being.

But then, this may also be the point. It is possible that James is being rather more knowing here than his detractors at the time gave him credit for. The Cipriani that he presents us with—an opponent of racism, a man who holds British officers to their own rules in defense of black soldiers, and who acts according to the principles that the British proclaimed as being at the core of their empire, but that they continually violated—is perhaps the figure that James needed as a means of giving voice to his own political perspectives. James may, in a sense, have created the Cipriani that he wanted to see, or to use, as the agent of critique against British rule. Indeed, James comes close to saying as much at the outset of the book, when he describes the biography as "the best means of bringing before all who may be interested the political situation in the West Indies to-day" (39). Half a century later, in *Beyond a Boundary*, his famous study of cricket in the Caribbean, he would talk of significant political and cultural figures "filling a need," insofar as they serve to articulate social and political demands that have no other immediate means of articulation. His biography presents the reader with a Cipriani whose life becomes an articulation in just that sense, and which therefore serves as the context for James's own attack on the racism and political inequality that characterized colonial society. Although, ostensibly, each chapter (apart from the first) is focused on a significant episode from Cipriani's life, James repeatedly ends those chapters by mining the events for a political lesson about the treatment of colonized peoples in the Caribbean and about the absence of popular political representation: "We need not go an inch out of Captain Cipriani's life to see it [Crown Colony Government] on every conceivable occasion doing its damnedest" (120), he concludes, at the end of a section that deals with Cipriani's struggles for reform within and against the island's Legislative Council. The same pattern is evident in the chapter that deals with the formation of the British West Indies Regiment, and that describes the racism encountered by black troops in that context and the refusal of the local colonial government to challenge that racism. Here again, James ends by reiterating that these events make clear the "smug complacency" (83) that typifies imperial rule: "So it has been, so it is, and so it always will be until the day that these colonies govern themselves" (83).

That smug complacency has already been emphasized in James's opening to the same chapter. Here he begins, clearing space for himself, by saying: "A detailed history of the B.W.I. Regiment in the War will be told some day. Crown Colony Governments will not interest themselves in any such thing. But it will be one of the early though minor duties of a Federated West Indies Legislature to ask for and support the production of this necessary piece of West Indies history" (69). There is an absolutely characteristically Jamesian confidence in that assertive "it will be." By and large, one feels, his interest in Cipriani here lies not so much in what he was in himself, nor just in what he said or did, but in the fact that his *Life* provides the occasion for moments such as these, moments of critique that are also moments of invocation; what a later James, speaking in more Hegelian terms, would call the struggle to summon up the future in the present.

One danger of such an approach, of course, is that in making Cipriani a means of articulating a critique of colonial rule, James risks losing his critical grip on his supposed subject. Brereton's introduction shows in detail the limitations of his account of Cipriani's responses to various contemporary political decisions. This includes the latter's volte-face on the question of reform to divorce legislation in the colony, something that James tries to finagle his way around in the penultimate chapter, but which marked the start of an increasingly conservative trajectory in Cipriani's politics. In general terms, it seems clear, James overstated the depth of Cipriani's relationship to emerging forms of popular discontent. "He represents the people so well," he writes near the end of the study, "chiefly because he is so much one of them" (155). A concern with figures of whom this could be said remained at the heart of his work for the next half a century. But whether it was an appropriate characterization of Cipriani, even at the point at which James was writing, is a very different question. His willingness to ditch the autobiographical aspects of the study in the subsequent Hogarth Press pamphlet suggests that James may, himself, have harbored some doubts. It is notable that in Ralph de Boissière's novel *Crown Jewel*, which was published in 1952, but that looked back to militancy in the Trinidadian oil industry in the late 1930s, a thinly disguised version of Cipriani appears as a figure of intransigence and reaction.

For many readers, in any case, the interest in this text is likely to lie less with what James's study tells us about Cipriani as a historical figure, and more with what it tells us about James and his early political perspectives: James's subtitle, we might say, has probably come to matter more than his title, an inversion that *The Case for West-Indian Self Government* had already enacted. By James's own later account, his political worldview changed radically during the period following his arrival in Britain. This was the case, not least, because of his encounter with popular traditions of trade unionism and Marxism in the north of England, and because of his growing involvement in the networks of diasporic anticolonial struggle in London, an involvement catalyzed by protests against the Italian invasion of Abyssinia in 1935 (for James's time in Britain, see Hill 1981; Høgsbjerg 2014; Howe 2003). Nevertheless, it is worth recalling that, unlike many of his contemporaries, James did not leave Trinidad as a young man in order to pursue an academic or professional career. By contrast, he left in his thirties, and as someone with well-established political interests and writerly ambitions. As Selwyn Cudjoe (1992, 1997) and others have emphasized, James was shaped in significant and enduring ways by the intellectual traditions of the Caribbean, including a long local history of contestation against colonial racism. *Life* is an intriguing text in that respect because it straddles, as it were, James's formative experiences in Trinidad and his remarkably sudden emergence as a prominent political theorist and organizer of the non-Communist left during the six or so years that he was in Europe.

There are certainly plenty of moments here that make clear that James in the early 1930s was no Marxist, and that suggest that in many ways his outlook was—as he himself recalled later—that of an "English intellectual." The "case" that the text makes, after all, was not the case for decolonization but for "self government" along the lines granted to the other dominion territories in whose company James imagined a future, federated West Indies belonging: Canada, Australia, New Zealand, South Africa. In some places, such as his reporting of the experiences of black troops in World War I, for example, James's tone is perhaps best described as Edwardian: "Recognition [of the B.W.I.R.] by a personal visit from the great solider [General Allenby] was a very great compliment, and one which will always be remembered by officers and men" (75). Politically (and tonally) there is an astonishing distance between statements of this kind and, for example, the pamphlet that James authored for the Workers Party in America a mere decade later. In the latter case, the voice he adopts is demotic rather than patrician, and the message is an unequivocal one of popular resistance to the war: "I went to the last war. I was treated like a dog before I went. I was treated like a dog while I was there. I was treated like a dog when I returned. I have been played for a sucker before, and I am not going to be played again" (1996a, 22).

Yet even those moments that, at first reading, appear to reveal an as-yet-unchallenged deference on James's part are not without a certain ambivalence. So when, for example, he seeks to contest racist stereotypes about the black population of the islands, he does so by calling on the testimony of a series of former colonial governors (50–53), in a way that appears to unduly privilege English intellectual authority. But James is also careful to insist, having cited these voices: "I could have said all these things myself. I preferred to let Englishmen, and Englishmen of the official class, say them" (53). He had indeed already said many of these things himself, having publically rebutted, in 1931, a racist attack on black intelligence from another relatively privileged Englishman who taught at the Imperial College of Tropical Agriculture (discrimination at the college is raised in *Life* as well [111–15]). Here, as in other instances, one feels that James's willingness to let "Englishmen of the official class" make his points for him is at least as much a matter of cool strategic choice as it is a matter of a colonial mind-set.

In the same way, James's knowledge of European political and cultural history is evident throughout the text, and he clearly enjoys making it so. Thus his critique of the workings of the Legislative Council cites Burke and Voltaire and refers to the details of British constitutional history, but it does so, again, to a point: this is unquestionably an act of "writing back" on James's part, allowing him to impugn the practice of colonial government by comparing it to the ideological self-image by which it justified itself. In a famous passage, he makes this tactic rhetorically explicit (I cite here the version as it appears in *The Case for West-Indian Self Government*:

> At home he [the Englishman] was distinguished for the liberality and freedom of his views. Hampden, Chatham, Dunning and Fox, Magna Carta and Bill of Rights, these are the persons and things (however misconceived) which Englishmen, undemonstrative as they are, write and speak of with a subdued but conscious pride. . . . But in the colonies any man who speaks for his country, any man who dares to question the authority of those who rule over him, any man who tries to do for his own people what Englishmen are so proud that other Englishmen have done for theirs, immediately becomes in the eyes of the colonial Englishman, a dangerous person, a wild revolutionary . . . a reptile to be crushed

at the first opportunity. What at home is the greatest virtue becomes in the colonies the greatest crime (175).

That interjection—"however misconceived"—is especially telling. As with James's insistence that he could have "said all these things" himself, could have dismantled the stereotypes of colonial racism in his own terms, it keeps open an important critical space with regard to the justificatory ideologies of imperial rule, and makes clear that James reserves the right to judge the English and their own self-presentation. Here as elsewhere James is clearly involved in a deliberate and knowing act of immanent critique, turning the claims of British—and indeed European—political and cultural traditions against themselves.

Yet this strategy is not without a dangerous double edge. James's demand for self-government rests in a crucial respect on his insistence that West Indians deserve political representation because they are the products of "Western culture." "These people are not savages," he insists, at the start of *Life*, referring to the islands' "coloured" population: "they speak no other language except English, they have no other religion expect Christianity, in fact, their whole outlook is that of Western civilization modified and adapted to their particular circumstances" (49). A few years later, in his masterpiece, *The Black Jacobins*, James emphasized the pivotal location of the plantation economies of the Caribbean within the emerging capitalist world-system. His reading of the Haitian revolution rests on his recognition, as Christian Høgsbjerg has emphasized, of "the modernity of Atlantic slavery and so also of slave experience and slave resistance" (2014, 178). In one respect perhaps, we can see in *The Life of Captain Cipriani*, and in James's insistence here on reading West Indian history as a part of the history of "the West," a distant precursor to that later argument. Yet a thoroughgoing encounter with Marxism, and with an analysis focused on class rather than cultural tradition, lay some years in the future. In *Life*, James's tendency is to represent the peoples of the region, not as part of the making, shaping, and contestation of capitalist modernity, but rather more as the successful adepts of a Western civilization inherited from elsewhere. In that respect, his concern to contest colonial racism as it applied to the Caribbean—his desire to dispel the stereotypes of readers who imagined "savage people, speaking primitive languages, worshipping heathen gods, walking about in the sunshine . . . in fig leaves and feathers" (44)—sometimes operates, as it does implicitly in this quote, by juxtaposing the successfully "Westernized" West Indian with other colonized peoples, who, it is presumed, remain "savage." At various points in the study he cites figures who make comparative judgments of this sort: the Major, for example, who contests the handling of the British West Indies Regiment troops on the grounds that they should not have been treated "as if they were of the same status as the native labourer from the Fijian Islands" (77), or Cipriani's own claim that "Crown Colony rule may still be ideal for the primitive races . . . for the jungle and the wilds of Africa, but it has outlived its usefulness in these Colonies" (135). These are not James's own words, but he reports them without comment or contradiction and, on one occasion at least, says much the same for himself: "Bad as this [political arrangement] is in a colony where the population is divided into whites and native tribes, it is intolerable in a West Indian community, where in language, education, religion and outlook, the population is essentially Western" (99). So while repeatedly in this text James claims the right to critique colonial rule in and through an appropriation of the terms in which it justified itself, that critique is also shaped in troubling ways by empire's characteristic process of racist divide-and-rule.

Having said all of this, and while it is the case that in places James's account unquestionably bears the marks of someone who was the product of one of Trinidad's elite colonial schools, it is worth reiterating that, in general, what one is struck by is the self-confidence with which he goes about unpacking and critiquing the relationships of empire. He may have considered himself an English intellectual at the time that he left the Caribbean, yet there are numerous passages here where it is clear that James had not internalized that identity in any straightforward sense. He opens the first chapter, indeed, by constructing "the English" and later the "Colonial Englishmen" quite explicitly as objects of skeptical study rather than of emulation. His rhetoric in this section is drawn directly from the canons of imperial ethnography with its tendency to make sweeping, essentialist judgments about the characters and capacities of colonized peoples. In this case, though, such judgments rebound back onto the colonizer, whose "good nerves" and "good temper" James praises, but who is also described as being "uninterested in things of the mind and concerned with culture only as a means of personal advancement" (42). More tellingly still, James says of the English that they are "despite their long experience of Empire, the most prejudiced people upon the face of the earth" (43). The portrait thus provided, James says, is not a complete one, but is enough to do "justice to the sitter from the angles which concern us most" (43). One feels that his intention, in opening his essay in this way, is as much performative as it is substantive; it is about providing a demonstration of the ability of the colonized to subject the colonizer to their own critical gaze.

There is more to James's account, though, than discursive contestation. There are passages here—although only passages, rather than a developed argument—that suggest a potentially interesting, structurally inclined interpretation of the nature of imperial relationships and of the racism that organized those relationships. More than once, for example, James talks fascinatingly about the "unreality" that besets (elite) colonial society. He seems to have in mind here two related facets of that society. First, the fact that colonial officials lived lives segregated from the people over whom they ruled: "These heads of department mix almost entirely in clubs and social gatherings with the more wealthy element of the white creoles, whose interests lie with the maintenance of all the authority and privileges of the officials against the political advancement of the coloured people" (99). There is a straightforward sociological argument here about the effects of this estrangement on the cultural and intellectual life of colonial rulers and their comprador allies: he talks of their "shallowness . . . self-sufficiency and . . . provincialism" (101). But, at the same time, James notes that this elite social world comes to constitute a distorting "magic centre" (102) within the colony, access to which is the overriding ambition of any local person with the requisite talent, wealth, opportunity, or skin color. James has plenty of satirical fun pointing out the sycophancy of those local "coloured" men who try to inveigle themselves into this charmed circle of white colonial society, and his long-standing love of Thackeray is nowhere clearer than in his descriptions of those local politicians whose ambitions are limited to whether the Colonial Secretary sees fit to distribute to them the "nod distant, the bow cordial, the shake-hand friendly, or the cut direct" (104). Yet he is also at pains to emphasize that this behavior is the product of a particularly structured set of relationships. White commentators and officials, he notes, treated this obsequiousness as evidence of the inherent servility of colonized peoples, and therefore as proof of the continued necessity of white rule (103). James's careful sociological interpretation of colonial society is specifically aimed at contesting such a view, emphasizing instead that "these men are not so much inherently weak as products of the social system in which they live" (ibid.). His point, in this respect, is that the identities and relationships of colonial society have to be read as expressions of the system that makes them as they are; that structural reading of those relationships emerges here as a means of contesting the way in which colonial authorities sought to naturalize the inequalities on which their positions depended. It is clear, in this regard, that Cipriani is significant for James, at least in part because he heralded the possible emergence of a local political class willing to turn its back on the "magic centre" and willing to speak from, and for, the real lives of ordinary men and women in the colony.

I have already referred to the second, related point, and this is the gap between what we might call the form and content of empire; between its ideological justification (through the rhetoric of the civilizing mission, of trusteeship, the white man's burden, for example) and its utterly self-interested political and economic practice. James traces this contradiction closely through the workings and arrangements of the colonial government in Trinidad, noting: "There is a further unreality," which besets those arrangements, which is that "the Government can always win when it wants to" (98), not least because the governor acted simultaneously as the representative of the Crown, the equivalent of the prime minister and the chair of the Legislative Council ("an incomprehensible personage," James adds drily, "three in one and one in three" [106]). For all the talk of democracy, then, the colony was run as a form of oligarchy such that the formal procedures of government served an essentially decorative function: James describes them as "the ancient covering for what in reality amounts to this. We have the power in our hands and we shall hold onto it as long as we can" (117). It is these "unrealities" that James prizes opens here in order to make space for his demand for self-government.

That demand in itself is somewhat underwhelming, but much more potentially explosive is his argument that this lacuna between imperial ideology and imperial practice is already well recognized in

popular understanding: "All of this is and has been common knowledge in Trinidad for many years" (104). Thus James insists that it is
those who have to struggle with and against the injustices of empire
who are best placed to recognize its contradictions; it is the colonized
who understand most penetratingly the nature of colonial relations.
This is, it might be noted, a more consistent theme of his later work than
has been sometimes recognized. On a number of subsequent occasions,
he would describe it, half-jokingly perhaps, as the "law of historical
compensation." In *The Black Jacobins*, of course, he was to take this point
further, insisting that it was the rebellious slaves of San Domingo who
understood most urgently and who defended most unambiguously
what was at stake in the French Revolution's declarations of liberty.
Contrastingly, of course, as James notes, the beneficiaries of the racist
structures that underpinned colonial society and its modes of production had every reason to overlook these lacunae: "Englishmen or white
men do not wish any discussion of matters of race. They go where
they like, do what they like, travel in any part of a ship, are eligible for
any position. They stand to gain nothing by talk about racial discrimination, and they stand to lose a great deal" (114).

So even in this very early study we can see evidence of what would
become a characteristically Jamesian insistence on the ability of the
oppressed to make critical sense of the social and political arrangements that organize their oppression, and *Life* makes clear how far this
insistence was informed, specifically, by his reflections on the nature
of colonial society. He shares this point of emphasis, of course, with
a number of other writers who have reflected on the experiences of
racialization and colonization. One thinks classically, for example, of
the way in which W. E. B. Du Bois's (much misinterpreted) metaphor
of the veil drew attention to the willful blindness of white communities to the practices and effects of racism in the segregated southern
states of America, and of his corresponding recognition of the skeptical "second sight" that the daily encounter with racism made possible for black communities, with regard to the dominant ideologies of
American political life.

In James's case this leads, among other things, to a nuanced account
of the politics of popular culture. *American Civilization* provides the
incomplete theorization of his position in this respect, while *Beyond a*

Boundary provides a compelling exemplification of his approach (see Smith 2010 for a more detailed discussion). Thus James would insist that even commodified "mass" cultural practices and forms needed to be approached as spaces of unresolved political struggle, shaped by the ideological demands of their producers but simultaneously appropriated to the insurgent angers and longings of their audiences. In the face of readings of popular culture which tend to emphasize its role in the reproduction of hegemony and of acquiescence with the world-as-it-is—one thinks classically of Theodor Adorno, or more recently of some aspects of Pierre Bourdieu's work (although see Fowler 2006 for a careful defense of Bourdieu in this regard)—James's two-sided reading of its political potential is an important resource, not least because it never slips over into a naive celebration of the popular.

Finally, we might note that all of this also leads James, in *Life*, to some striking comments about the nature of colonial racism more generally. The white official who arrives in the colonial context, he notes, finds himself occupying a dramatically elevated class position: "Bourgeois at home, he finds himself after a few weeks at sea suddenly exalted into the position of being a member of a ruling class" (43) and a ruling class whose position is defined and justified not by virtue of its achievements, but by virtue of its very being. The colonial Englishman finds himself, James says, in a world no longer defined by the categories of European bourgeois society, but rather in the position of being "an aristocrat without having been trained as one" (45). Hannah Arendt, in a provocative but largely unelaborated comment, noted that modern "race-thinking" drew in important ways upon the premodern conception of personhood as an attribute of birth: "modern race ideologies . . . helped anybody feel himself an aristocrat who had been selected by birth" (1973, 73). James, intriguingly, recognizes something similar here. His comments are also unelaborated, but they point to a potential reading of colonial racism as a particular product and expression of capitalism's uneven development, rearticulating a feudal understanding of innate inequality as a means of quashing the contradiction that existed between the liberal ideologies of representative government and individual freedom that Europeans proclaimed domestically and the absolute denial of those freedoms in colonial societies. And in those latter contexts, such as Trinidad, James notes, one of the further and pernicious sociological effects of this understanding was that it created conditions in which perceptions of relative racial difference became deeply invidious, leading the white creole population of the island, for example, to distance themselves symbolically and politically from the majority: "the mere fact of his being white, or at least of skin fair enough to pass as white, makes him a person of importance" (49). Again, one recognizes that Cipriani may have mattered to James because he (appeared to) reject the aristocracy of whiteness, endorsing instead the alternative possibility of class solidarity. Whether he really did signify this possibility is a different question, as I have noted already, and Brereton also points out that James was overoptimistic about the prospects of intercommunal solidarity in the Caribbean, and especially between populations of African and Asian descent: "There is no communal problem in the West Indies" (57) was his untroubled judgment on the issue.

In general, *The Life of Captain Cipriani* is an uneven piece of writing. Brereton describes it, nicely, as an "apprentice" text. There are plenty of provocative passages, and some telling aperçus and insights, but it lacks the wonderful intellectual control of James's greatest work, and the theoretical organization and clarity that emerged from his commitment to Marxism. There are relatively long passages that consist of little more than quotations drawn from the records of the colonial government in Trinidad, although James—as did Marx with the "Blue Books" before him—often uses these official reports to damning effect, nowhere more so than where he records the investigation into the conditions of children working in gangs on the plantations. (Here, as elsewhere, James is at pains to point out that these working conditions have "long been common knowledge among the people" [88].) Having these previously difficult-to-obtain texts available in this form, and with Brereton's valuable introduction, is nevertheless something to be warmly welcomed. There is much that is likely to be valuable here for historians of the region and of the wider currents of Atlantic radicalism (including an important account of the revolt of black troops against the racism of their South African commander at Taranto in 1919) and much to be learned also by those interested in James and his intellectual career. In many ways the brilliance of the best of James's later work rests precisely in his ability to successfully bring together many of the currents and concerns that are already to be found swirling together here: the politics of antiracism and anticolonialism with the politics of organized labor; the novelist's turn of phrase with the historian's concern for context; a respectful engagement with popular culture with a mastery of European intellectualism. These things are not yet brought into a compelling synthesis in this text, but James's ambition is already evident, as is his confidence in his own ability and his enduring faith in the future. These might not have been surprising attributes for the relatively young man he was at this point, but neither the self-confidence nor the optimism ever left him.

Dr. Andrew Smith is reader in sociology and head of the sociology subject area at the University of Glasgow. He is author of *C. L. R. James and the Study of Culture* (2010) and *Racism and Everyday Life: Social Theory, History, and "Race"* (2016) and coeditor of the forthcoming Duke University Press volume *Marxism, Colonialism, and Cricket*, a collection of new critical essays focused on C. L. R. James's pioneering text *Beyond a Boundary*. He is a co-investigator in the ESRC Research Centre on the Dynamics of Ethnicity (www.ethnicity.ac.uk).

Works Cited

Arendt, Hannah. 1973. *The Origins of Totalitarianism*. New York: Harcourt Brace and Company.

Cudjoe, Selwyn. 1992. "The Audacity of It All: C. L. R. James's Trinidadian Background." In *C. L. R. James's Caribbean*. Ed. P. Henry and P. Buhle, 39–55. Durham: Duke University Press.

Cudjoe, Selwyn. 1997. "C. L. R. James and the Trinidad and Tobago Intellectual Tradition, Or, Not Learning Shakespeare Under a Mango Tree." *New Left Review* 1, no. 223: 114–25.

De Boissière, Ralph. 2006 [1952]. *Crown Jewel*. Enfield, UK: Lux Verbi Books.

Fowler, Bridget. 2006. "Autonomy, Reciprocity, and Science in the Thought of Pierre Bourdieu." *Theory, Culture and Society* 23, no. 6:99–117.

Hill, Robert A. 1981. "In England, 1932–1938." *Urgent Tasks*, no. 12:19–27.

Høgsbjerg, Christian. 2014. *C. L. R. James in Imperial Britain*. Durham: Duke University Press.

Howe, Stephen. 2003. "C. L. R. James: Visions of History, Visions of Britain." In *West Indian Intellectuals in Britain*. Ed. Bill Schwarz, 153–74. Manchester: Manchester University Press.

James, C. L. R. 1980 [1938]. *The Black Jacobins: Toussaint L'Ouverture and the San Domingo Revolution*. London: Allison and Busby.

James, C. L. R. 1983 [1963]. *Beyond a Boundary*. New York: Pantheon Books.

James, C. L. R. 1996. *Special Delivery: The Letters of C. L. R. James to Constance Webb, 1938–1948*. Ed. Anna Grimshaw. Oxford: Blackwell.

James, C. L. R. 1996a. *C. L. R. James on the "Negro Question."* Ed. Scott McLemee. Jackson: University of Mississippi Press.

James, C. L. R. 2003. *Letters from London*. Ed. Nicholas Laughlin. Port of Spain: Prospect Press.

Smith, Andrew. 2010. *C. L. R. James and the Study of Culture*. London: Palgrave.

"IN ORDER TO LIVE, THE OTHER MUST DIE": THE LOGIC OF BIOPOLITICS

EARTH POLITICS: RELIGION, DECOLONIZATION, AND BOLIVIA'S INDIGENOUS INTELLECTUALS
BY WASKAR ARI
Duke University Press, 2014

Grant Farred

A single movement, Alcaldes Mayores Particulares (AMP). Within it the short history of twentieth-century indigenous political aspiration in Bolivia. But such brevity of description is deceptive because the history of the AMP encompasses so much. There is, to begin with, colonialism, racism, segregation, religion, revolution ("Movimiento Nacionalista Revolucionario"—the Bolivian National Revolution, 1951–71), assimilation, language (whether or not to speak Spanish, as the mestizos did and as the cholos later would; or, to speak Aymara, as the AMP activists insisted, as a matter of national self-determination), Indian law (which is, in turn, mobilized, publicized, rejected) and the irrepressible question of sovereignty. That is to say nothing of equally pressing issues such as the act of inhabiting indigeneity (what clothes the Aymara, the Quechua, and Urus wore was an implacably political decision, a marker of modernity or "backwardness"), the role of women in the struggle against colonization, the distinct approaches favored by different generations of AMP intellectuals, the tensions between the indigenous and the cholos, naming (were the indigenous "Indians," as they saw themselves, or "campesinos"—peasants?, as the revolution of 1951 tried to make them, in order to "dissolve" the revolutionary nation into universal verisimilitude), the racially inflected conflict between modernity (as envisaged and desired by the Bolivian state in which the Spanish, the mestizos incarnated modernity—a status to which the cholos could aspire and, eventually, achieve) and indigeneity (the Indians were not civilized, they were anachronistically bound to "old times"), and the struggle between ethnicity (Indianness) and class (the indigenous were not Indians but "campesinos"). All this can be acknowledged and still the list of questions taken up by Waskar Ari in *Earth Politics: Religion, Decolonization, and Bolivia's Indigenous Intellectuals* (Duke University Press, 2014) remains incomplete.

Earth Politics is focused on the long half-century of indigenous struggle against the mestizo Bolivian state, from the 1920s through the 1970s, and contains within it all the key events in twentieth-century Bolivian history: the founding of the AMP, the Chaco War (between Bolivia and Paraguay, 1932–35), the BNR (1951), of course, which led to the "long cycle of revolution (1951–71)" during and because of which the AMP "reinvented their movement to address new forms of coloniality"; these two decades included military dictatorships and "administrations," land reform, industrialization (mining), the formation of pro-state unions (at once a Keynesian articulation of labor-state relations and a symbiosis antithetical to radical politics) largely antagonistic to the AMP cause, and, regrettably, the decline of the AMP itself. But not, as Ari points out, the end of the movement's influence. *Earth Politics* begins and ends, gesturally, with a nod to the election of the current Bolivian president, Evo Morales, "an Aymara from Oruro," who for Ari "represents the legacy of the AMP." For Ari Morales's election marks the revitalization of a "legacy," the fulfillment of indigenous political promise, after decades of fallowness, during which the AMP's mantle of determined opposition to the ruling mestizo class was assumed by other movements—most notably the "Indianista and Katarista civil rights movements." Morales may trace, as Ari asserts, his political lineage to the AMP, but the later "civil rights movements" (Indianista, "an Aymara or *originario* who seeks an Indian revolution"; Katarismo, those activists who "argue in favor of indigenous rights") are unquestionably the (more) direct source of the presidents' politics and his 2006 electoral victory. After all, Morales effected "an Indian revolution," the likes of which the Bolivian elite had never previously encountered and, in truth, which the AMP could never have hoped for or envisaged. (It seems, to Ari, that such an imagining, an indigenous person as president of Bolivia, as a modern state, was not deemed possible. Perhaps it was not even, given the movement's ethnic particularity, desirable.)

In salient ways, Morales's remove—through chronology, history, ideology, political instinct—from the AMP is symptomatic of a larger strain of argument in *Earth Politics*. Morales's symptomaticity derives from the ways in which everything in Ari's work turns on difference, division, and a Marxist sense of moment; if, that is, we take Marx's notion of contingency as articulated in the "Eighteenth Brumaire of Louis Bonaparte" as our point of departure—we do not make history under conditions of our own choosing. Ari documents the movement's rise and decline ("fall" is too precipitous and categorical a term) by charting the AMP's history through its four dominant figures: Gregorio Titiriku, Toribio Miranda, Melitón Gallardo, and Andrés Jach'aqullu. Broadly speaking, the first three belong to the founding generation. Their vision for the AMP is entirely a response to the racism, discrimination, and exclusion of Indians from Bolivian public life—political disenfranchisement (which can be said to have begun with the 1874 "agrarian reform," which "officially eliminated allyus, dissolved Indian representation, and openly appropriating Indian land in the name of civilization and modernity"), deracination (the "hacienda expansion that began in Bolivia in the late nineteenth-century had pushed community leaders and activists to search for ways to prevent appropriation of indigenous lands"), disparagement of Indian modes of dress (indigenous men were forbidden from wearing ponchos and had to don Western suits; Indian women's ethnic dress was tolerated, but they had to use nonindigenous fabrics in making their garments; for Jach'aqullu, "cholo or Western dress was evidence of coloniality"), a lack of access to education, which later turned out to be an issue "ethnicized"—*particular*-ized—by the AMP leadership.

The AMP's suspicions about "universal" education that the Bolivian state insisted on turns out to have been well founded because this educational model undermined the AMP's desire for autonomy over the syllabi in which their children would be instructed. AMP's dreams of *particular* curricula designed for Indian children, especially in relation to language, had its moment, but it never achieved the ideological heights or the numerical scale that the organization needed to insulate indigenous children from the reach of the Bolivian state. As a result, "education ensured that more of the younger generation would speak Spanish and assimilate to the new version of the nation-state."

Assimilation trumped, in the classroom and beyond, particularity; from the moment of the revolution, the AMP—especially for Jach'aqullu's generation, the last in the AMP's history ("In contrast to Miranda and Titiriku, who mostly confronted segregationist policies, Jach'aqullu had to confront the assimilationist or integrationist context that followed the national revolution")—found itself struggling against the Bolivian state's drive toward incorporating the indigenous peoples as individual subjects (the project of modernity writ large: founding the subject in history) denuded of their ethnic particularity an ethnic identity that placed them, historically, at odds with the Bolivian state. In order to protect the indigenous from the effects of the MNR, the "second generation of the AMP shaped their discourse more in terms of rights, reelaborating the Indian law to oppose forced participation in peasant unions and other MNR policies enacted after agrarian reform in 1953." Jach'aqullu's AMP had to use every resource at its disposal to withstand the attack that the MNR had unleashed in the name of "revolution."

The obstinate truth of the MNR is that it reveals a discomfiting reality: the revolution is (very) bad for the indigenous peoples. This is a strange prospect (the revolution as damaging, devastating, even, for the subaltern) and yet not, given what history has taught us about the event of the revolution—from the Soviet Union to China, from the United States to Cuba, the revolution is, it would seem, unfailingly hostile to minorities or those whose difference (otherness) represents an implicit challenge to the grounds and the logic of the revolution. For the MNR, the message to the indigenous peoples was clear: the revolution will not be ethnicized.

The revolution, as we well know, is as retrograde in its imposition of conformity ("assimilation," "integration" as "official state policy"; the myth of equality—all "comrades" enjoy the same standing), as über-nationalism. In the Bolivian case, the revolution proved life-threatening to the being and the cosmology of the indigenous. "Crucial to de-Indianization," Ari writes, "integration started to affect ethnic and racial identities." In the face of the Bolivian state's determination to integrate the indigenous, Jach'aqullu's AMP mobilized the only—the most, certainly—effective defense against integration: the intensification of fidelity to Indianness itself. Jach'aqullu vivified ethnic identity, from the promotion of indigenous religion to the assertion of native modes of dress to the insistence on speaking the indigenous language(s).

CLASH OF CIVILIZATIONS

In order to resist expropriation of their lands, the indigenous population was faced with a choice. They could, as some did (Marka T'ula most prominently), follow the logic of the "Leyes de Indias" (Law of the Indies and search for "colonial titles to back their claims"— that is, use colonial history and its legal decrees to protect their property in order to produce a "reinterpretation and re-elaboration of the seventeenth-century colonial Law of the Indies"); or, and here Titiriku's intervention is crucial, they could declare that "written records such as property titles were irrelvevant to indigenous people and their beliefs. Titiriku argued that continuing to pay rent to the *hacendados* and levies to the state harmed the foundations of the indigenous religion that the Quechuas, Urus, and Aymaras shared." The indigenous either worked within the regime of colonialism or not only rejected it entirely but pronounced it inapplicable to the worldview—the cosmography— of the "Quechuas, Urus, and Aymaras." In so doing, Titiriku not only "brought the Aymara gods, such as Pachamama and Achchilas, back into discussion" (foregrounding, mobilizing, indigenous religion), but he announced a clash of civilizations. Any indigenous compromise with the mestizo state was tantamount to apostasy—one could serve only one god (or, gods, as the case might be). The indigenous could serve only their gods; Mammon represented an intolerable incursion into the life of the indigenous and as such had to be disobeyed and resisted; in the process of which, of course, Titiriku was engaging, speaking to, and confronting the very colonial law that was the source of the colonized's subjugation. An astute political organizer, it was this "invocation of the Aymara gods to delegitimize the tactic of searching for colonial land titles that set Titiriku and his network apart from their contemporaries." Not resistance, as such, but a higher order of political action: the refusal to engage at the level of colonialism or the Bolivian state. Titiriku reinscribed the very core of indigeneity itself through his insistence that the Indian was not subject to the law because that law itself was alien to the place (Bolivia) of the indigenous.

What Titiriku was advocating was, for want of a better term, a certain autochthonous relationship between the indigenous and the "soil" of Bolivia ("blut und grund," to cast the matter in a very different historical register). Autochthony is inscribed in the ways that "Melitón

Gallardo referred to indigenous peoples as *jall'p sangres* (the 'blood of the earth')," and Titiriku proclaimed "we are the blood of the Qullasuyu" ("Aymara territory in pre-Inka times"). Whenever "blood" is invoked, as we well know, we are face to face with nationalism and nationalist (or "Qullasuyu") language of the most intense variety. "Blood" and soil denotes nothing less than blood and sacrifice, as Gallardo so vividly reminds us—an evocation of violence (taken here as the consequence of colonial violence against the Aymaras, Urus, and Quechuas) that comingles with a fierce determination to retrieve the blood-soaked land (such sacrifice adds meaning to the land, of course) so as to give biopolitical meaning to those lives sacrificed in defense of the "jall'p." In the face of such a call, how does one gainsay the affective lure of the "blood soaked" land as a rallying cry? No wonder then that Foucault issues such a stern warning against biopolitics in the closing section of "*Society Must Be Defended*." Foucault is especially wary of what he understands as the "suicidal" impulse at the heart of the biopolitical project because he recognizes the perversity of the biopolitical logic that venerates "exposure to death."[1]

THE NATIONALIST CORE OF ARI'S EARTH POLITICS

Ari's work is an explicit attempt to define the nationalist politics of the Bolivian indigenous peoples. Ari's definition of nationalism is offered both at the start and at the end of *Earth Politics*. In both instances he privileges, in the spirit of Titiriku and his colleagues, the role of indigenous religions, the first of which leads to the most important conceptual shortcoming of *Earth Politics*, the second of which intensifies this critique—in no small part because it elaborates what it is Ari fails to do theoretically. To begin with, "A major ideological component of this decolonization project . . . advocated for two separate republics: one Indian and the other white (or Spanish). Titiriku legitimized the Indian republic through an Aymara religious and cultural worldview that reflected the beliefs of a new ethnic movement I am calling earth politics." Ari concludes, "Earth politics encompassed ideas about land, territory, nation, faith, religion, rights and Indianness—all issues that resonate in contemporary Bolivia." Again, the inescapable figure is Morales, the trajectory that haunts is the one that leads—even, or, because it peters out in the 1970s, leaving the "civil rights movements" to, as it were, connect the historical and ethnic dots—from the AMP to Morales.

Resisting first segregation (Titiriku, Miranda, and Gallardo), until circa 1951, and then assimilation and integration, it would be fair to say that the AMP's struggle—from Titiriku through Jach'aqullu, all "alcades majors" (high level leaders), they are united in this—is for indigenous sovereignty: "two separate republics," the Aymaras, Urus, and the Quechuas constituting out of their many and varied "ayllus" (large economic and political communities), a sovereign people divided from the Spanish, the mestizos, the "*indigenistas*," the whites, the cholos—those Indians who had thrown off their ethnic identity but have been only nominally assimilated into mainstream Bolivian society. Very few of them were accepted into the middle class, and the chutas—those indigenous peoples whose rural origins marked them as distinct, even from their cholo cousins, in urban Bolivia. Titiriku was utterly contemptuous of the cholos and the chutas, condemning them as "'whitened Indians' (*vueltos en blancos*)." Titiriku's pejorative is rooted in nothing other than Indian purity. Any compromise, in any form, by the indigenous with the political realities of colonialism or to evince any interest in modernity is to act criminally against the Indian community; such criminality must be met with, and, as such, implicitly discouraged, the force of exclusion. The other must be named other by its own (*vueltos en blancos*) in such a language as to distinguish clearly between the pure and the impure. This is the force of Titiriku's Indian nationalism at work: he is the political activist convinced of the cultural purity and racial particularity of the indigenous; he is intolerant of any concession to modernity, whether that be a Western suit or a national educational system that sought to incorporate, for whatever political purposes, indigenous children.

It is not, however, as an Indian nationalist that Ari fails in his critique of Titiriku. It is, rather in his inability to hold Titiriku the "indigenous intellectual" accountable as a thinker—as a thinker who advocates nationalism. In order to critique nationalism, in whatever guise it presents itself, it is necessary to identify, from both within political organizations and outside of nationalist movements, how these structures circumscribe the world and what the effects of their mandates (behavior, language, dress, and so on) are for individuals within their communities. Moreover, if the work of the intellectual is, before all else, to think, how is it possible to delimit thought? How is it possible to maintain an absolute division (purity) between the "two republics" when the revivification of one (the indigenous republic) turns, with the full weight of the colonial encounter and all the violence entailed in that historical exchange, on thinking its relation to the other (the mestizo state)? In fact, is it not possible to argue that the first fidelity to the nationalist project is to think its being as the emergence out of violence, which means that it cannot be conceived as a settled, predetermined polity?

The nation not as historic but as historicized, which invariably demands an accounting outside of any prohibitive strictures. If the nation already is, then there would be no—at least no immediate—urgency or need to struggle for it. (As such, the nation is always to come.) It is, then, not nationalism, for all the critiques that can be leveled against it, that is inherently against thinking. It is, rather, the proponents of nationalism who make fidelity to the project contingent upon a resolved past, which makes the glorification of that past both nationalism's first articulation and its apparatus for resolution. But in *Earth Politics* that is the less egregious offense. Much more troubling is Ari's refusal to hold Titiriku accountable for the limits of his thinking.

Engaging Titiriku as a thinker means, at the very least, to move beyond the description of his politics of exclusion (and to contemplate its effects) and then to name that nationalist limit as the failure of thought. What kind of intellectual delimits? Is such a figure, political activist and indigenous proponent though he be, an intellectual? Titiriku might have strategic reasons for treating the past as a settled matter, but this is where it is imperative for Ari to insert himself as the critic of Titiriku's shortcomings. The work of the thinker is to apprehend the project, not to implicitly—through either omission or commission—underwrite it as Ari does. A rupture, violent though it may be, is required; a break, between critic and subject, intellectual and project, must be enacted.

It is precisely this break that the state as such, Giorgio Agamben argues, militates against. Thus Agamben in his rumination on the event of Tianamen: "The State, as Alain Badiou has shown, is not founded on a social bond, of which it would be the expression, but rather on the dissolution, the unbinding it prohibits." The "unbinding" Titiriku will not tolerate, making of the "social bond" an entirely repressive mechanism; an "unbinding," one suspects, Ari will not permit him-self, latter-day activist in Titiriku's cause that he is; inheritor of the proscription in the moment after, the Titiriku moment that lingers, as all nationalist causes tend to do. The only figure in this morbid mise-en-scene, so overwrought with the fear of "whatever," who is "with-out an identity," is the intellectual. The intellectual is the only figure who can achieve "dissolution."

THE QUESTION OF SOVEREIGNTY

It is for this defining issue, sovereignty, that Ari will not reserve a moment in which he might reflect upon it. Sovereignty is a concept invoked (as the very political utopia, at least the dream, of the AMP and the "alcades majors") by *Earth Politics* but never theorized. Or, at the very least, questioned—subjected to a thinking. After all, as we have known since Carl Schmitt's work, sovereignty is—in addition to being so famously determined by the "exception"—indivisible. There cannot be two sovereignties in a single nation—the very notion is polit-ically unsustainable. The Qullasuyu cannot coexist with (or within) the Bolivian state, in whatever formation—pre- or postrevolutionary; only one can hold sway; in order to achieve sovereignty for the indig-enous peoples the mestizo nation would have to have been overcome; that is, one mode of politics, indigeneity or coloniality (or neocolonial-ity), will have to have triumphed. If the Aymaras, the Urus, and the Quechuas were to become sovereign, it would first have been neces-sary to oust the mestizos and their ilk. As Foucault phrases it in *Soci-ety Must Be Defended*, the logic of biopower is emphatic: "In order to live, the other must die" (Foucault, 255).

The biopolitical logic that Foucault delineates in *Society Must Be Defended* echoes Schmitt's founding division, friend/enemy, in that Foucault's biopower works insistently toward the elimination of the biological threat to the self. The biopolitical imperative is to ensure the safety (*securitas*) for the self, an end which can only be achieved at the expense of the other—"In order to live . . ." It is in regard to the problematic of sovereignty that *Earth Politics* fails itself concep-tually. How did Titiriku or Jach'aqullu imagine an "independent" (if sovereignty and independence might be thought coterminously, even interchangeably) Qullasuyu? Who would have constituted this sovereign nation? Would all the indigenous peoples have been equal, especially if the logic of self is coterminous only with itself? Would those from the "Aymara-speaking highlands" and those from the "Quechua-speaking southern Andes" have equal status? What of those in the cities? Do the political ambitions of these two constituencies coincide exactly? Were there no intra-Quechua or Aymara tensions? What of the *vueltos en blancos*? Where would the cholos and the chutas find their place? Would all the deities have had the same standing? Would Qullasuyu sovereignty have coincided with the borders of the Bolivian state? And could—or would—all the indigenous groups have wanted to coexist in the same space—and cosmography—with one another?[2]

Under this kind of philosophical pressure it is easy to imagine a moment of radical fracturing, that moment when, say, the Aymara and the Quechua sought to achieve a sovereign nation in, respectively, the highlands or the southern Andes; that is, a singularly Aymara nation, with its own boundaries, in which only its customs and culture obtains. Under these conditions, the Aymara could thrive and, as Foucault says, "proliferate" in a space that is "pure" Aymara; within any other political configuration, the Aymara render themselves precarious to the other. The struggle for sovereignty is nothing other than a war for the self in which the self is, by turns, in turn, first one and then the other, risked and hypostasized.

The thrust of identity politics, of which ethnicity is, at base (albeit a complicated and expanded one), an articulation, particularity (signaled in *Earth Politics* via modes of dress, self-representation, forms of religious worship, ancestry); or, as it is also conceived, difference. These are both terms and political modalities that resonate within the context of the AMP's project, most obviously with the *escuelas particulares*, the AMP's call for a cultural and political education for Indian children tailored to their particular history and experience—indigenous children had to be apprehended and instructed differently from their nonindigenous Bolivian peers. This divide, again, returns us—again—to difference and ethnicity because, if the national curriculum is designed for mestizos and whites, what would constitute a suitable or proper curriculum for indigenous children? And who would instruct them? Following what pedagogical model? How does one instruct the nation? Or, more precisely, how does one teach the nation to itself? The specter that haunts all of these inquiries is the matter of how sustainable such a model of sovereignty would be.

In this way the shadow of Morales's 2006 victory, at once anticipated and anachronistic, hangs over *Earth Politics*. That shadow is inescapable because it manifests itself in equal measures as the haunting and salient question of whether Morales's election means the final death knell for a vision such as the AMP's; a death knell inaudible in, say, 1971 (when the prospect of an indigenous Bolivian president who dressed as such, who claimed his past and his ethnic identity proudly, seemed a pipe dream), and yet, strangely, always present at the core of—constitutive of, as a ghostly conjuration, the political translation to come ("Katarista")—the AMP's political project. The ghost, however, always presents itself in the form of a question, so one must ask whether Morales's electoral victory resolves, once and for all, the question of an indivisible sovereignty. Resolve it "negatively," that is, because it signals at once and by turns the impossibility of the Qullasuyu and—or, is that through?—the usurpation of the mestizo elite, the indigenistas, the cholos, the chutas into, to phrase this as a matter of historical irony, the "vuelta en blanco" AMP project. Modernity, in the guise of the sovereign (indivisible) nation-state, "ethnicized," made indigenous, and yet only nominally so; the modern sovereign state incorporating into itself indigenous peoples, mestizos, whites, cholos, chutas; the modern sovereign state absorbing into itself Quechuas and Aymaras, with equal ease (or, unease), distinguishing between them and yet not; indigenous people taken up by the state as, one is compelled to inquire, as Indians or as "campesinos" ("peasants")?; or both?; all of the divisions articulated and mobilized by both the Bolivian state and the AMP folded into itself, conjoined by the Liebnizian fold. These divisions, if history is our teacher, that one expects to reemerge again at the most unpropitious of times. The untimely irrepressibility of difference. Is this, to argue in a fashion entirely contrary to Ari, the final legacy of the AMP? The legacy to come that is already, incipiently, here?

ENVIRONMENTALITY

Morales's victory, the AMP dream realized only insofar as it has had to adapt itself to the logic of the contemporary modern state, which is adept at recognizing, mobilizing, absorbing and, yes, neutralizing the difference of difference; subtending the 2006 victory is the ordering of difference, allotting a place to indigeneity that is very much in keeping with the ideological tenor of the times. There is, then, something biopolitically apt about Ari's title "Earth Politics" because it is limned with environmentality. Not only autochthony, the rootedness of the indigenous in the Bolivian earth, but also a Romantic relationship to the land—venerating a past in which the Indian is the (only) native of the land, the Indian is the land made native to itself; the singularity of the Indian as a historical figure who is simultaneously historic (an "ancient" belonging, devoid of, say, Heine's critique of unifying the past) and contemporary (the political actor issued up by the land). That is, in our era of environmental politics (where the struggle to preserve the earth's resources against degradation is an ever more vital battle internationally), *Earth Politics* resonates with the call to native stewardship (where "native" functions as both the signifier of the indigenous and the entire Bolivian nation, since all are, technically, if not spiritually and ideologically, native), a responsibility that Morales's Bolivian government publicly embraced with its "Law of the Rights of Mother Earth" (Ley de Derechos de la Madre Tierra), known as Law 071, which gives nature the same rights as humans and defines the earth as a collective subject of public interest." Ari, again, produces only an adumbrated rendering of environmentality. It is present only as the faintest articulation when elaboration and theorization are called for to properly address the (obvious) link between the history of his project and the ways in which it speaks to the political tenor of our moment. Ari's title demands it.

Earth Politics, then, is most effective in sketching the political biographies of its principal figures (Ari gives them all equal attention and he has a keen eye for the particularities of their eras) and translating that as the biography of a Bolivian nation that is, there is no escaping this, at war with itself; and of course at war with something else. That is, the war within, Quechua, Aymara, mestizo, cholo, and so on, in struggle with one another and themselves, that can ever only be temporarily resolved. At the very least, a struggle now conducted against the backdrop of a nation in which the mestizo elite and their allies have few qualms about doing violence to the indigenous populations— racism, land appropriation, unbridled discrimination on the grounds of language, dress, appearance, to state only the most egregious offenses. What Ari is less skilled at executing is transcribing the extant conditions into a higher-level critique. This is a critique, we might name it abstraction or theorization, that would have imbued the project with the kind of political language—the geopolitical vocabulary of sovereignty, to begin with—that would have revealed the stakes of the AMP's ambitions with greater clarity. Such an abstraction would have given the theoretical claims of *Earth Politics* the opacity it requires. What Gallardo and Miranda might have wanted, for all the contradictions and the conceptual insufficiencies as well as the remarkably ingenious political drive and vision that sustained their project, and deserved, was a more ruthless interrogation of their undertaking. For all its strengths, and they are not inconsiderable, *Earth Politics* is most disappointing when it does not pursue the theoretical questions that Ari has worked so scrupulously to raise.

Grant Farred teaches at Cornell University. His most recent publication is *Martin Heidegger Saved My Life* (2015). His forthcoming publications include *The Burden of Over-Representation: Race, Sport, and Philosophy* (2018) and *Entre Nous: Between the World Cup and Me* (2019). He is also the editor of the series *Untimely Interventions*.

Notes

1. Michel Foucault, *"Society Must Be Defended:" Lectures at the Collège de France, 1975–1976*, trans. David Macey (New York: Picador, 2003), 260. Foucault's conception of what we might name the thanatos instinct at the core of the biopolitical project derives, of course, from his critique of Nazism, which was for him the most brutal exemplification of a modernized, refitted biopolitics that emerged in the wake of nineteenth-century colonialism. Foucault offers this in his memorable formulation: "A racist State, a murderous State, a suicidal State" (260). There is, naturally, no correlation between the AMP's politics and those Foucault is attacking, but the recognition of death as constitutive of its politics does lend credence to Foucault's notion that the tendency toward—as well as the interplay between—violence (the "absolutely murderous State") and self-destruction (the "absolutely suicidal State") "is in fact inscribed in the workings of all States" (Foucault, 260). At what point—which is the question lodged in Foucault's analysis of sovereignty—does the willingness to die for a political objective such as the state become suicidal? Or, rather, how is it possible to prevent the inclination toward such an outcome?

2. In *The Coming Community*, Giorgio Agamben argues, based on the Talmu-dic notion that "two places are reserved for each person," for an "unconditioned substitutability . . . an absolutely unrepresentable community" (*The Coming Community*, trans. Michael Hardt [Minneapolis: University of Minnesota Press, 1993], 24.5). In this way, Agamben raises the prospect that every individual can be sub-stituted for, establishing an unbreakable relation between self and Other, forging new links between self and neighbor. In *Earth Politics* this would mean that, say, the Aymara and Quechua can "share" or inhabit the space that is Bolivia in such a way as to render each of them nonthreatening to and almost coextensive if not interchangeable with each other. However, it is precisely the specificity of the "rep-resentable community," of each "representable community," that Ari's indigenous intellectuals seek. Always lurking, sometimes more ominously than others, is the precarity of the bonds that connect these struggles to each other.

UNRAVELING THE BEING OF MATERIALITY

INSISTENCE OF THE MATERIAL: LITERATURE IN THE AGE OF BIOPOLITICS
BY CHRISTOPHER BREU
University of Minnesota Press, 2014

Antoine Traisnel

Christopher Breu's *Insistence of the Material* opens with the disarming image of the author's own body summoned yet again to the operating table. Diagnosed as a child with a benign condition known as hypospadias—a form of intersex—Breu underwent a surgery that aimed to return him to an imagined state of normalcy. This first unnecessary operation was followed by fourteen surgeries over more than three decades, all caused by unforeseen medical "complications." Thus Breu's body acts both as a testament to the overmedicalization characteristic of the second half of the twentieth century and to the flesh's unobliging tendency to challenge the medical corps' binaristic conceptions of sex and gender. Failing to conform to dominant cultural and medical scripts, the body is the traumatic site from which arises the titular demand to recognize and theorize what Breu calls the "insistence of the material," that is, materiality's obstinate "resistance to and divergence from the dominance of biopolitical forms of governance" (x). Yet from the outset also looms the specter of the body's complete obliteration, not just under the invasive scrutiny and practices of the medical establishment, but also under the biosubject's own introspective eye, as the image on the cover of the book suggests. This image, a haunting embroidered photograph by Peruvian artist Ana Teresa Barboza, shows a female chest torn apart by the subject's own hands and literally unraveling under its own gaze. Allegorized by threads of yarn, the body's materiality simultaneously appears and disappears in its figuration. It is precisely the matter of figuration in the age of biopolitics—and, more specifically, the potentials and limitations of lit-erary figuration—that Breu's book proposes to examine.

From ailing and laboring bodies to the material elements that make up our late-capitalist ecosystems, "the material" for Breu names that which appears eminently vulnerable yet ultimately resistant to the uni-versal solvent of biocapitalism. Probing literature's capacities to attend to the "way in which material life is shaped in ever more intimate ways by biopolitics, thanatopolitics, and biopolitical production" (2), the book's main contention is, paradoxically, that language is *essentially inadequate* when it comes to heeding "the various forms of materiality in contemporary social existence." By dint of this very inadequacy, and even while he recognizes on occasion the linguistic as a specific "reg-ister" or "form of materiality" (38), Breu surreptitiously aligns language with the dematerializing forces of biocapitalism. Indeed, by positing an axiomatic allergy of the material to the forces that shape it—an abso-lute impermeability of substance to form—he claims that the "cultural and linguistic turns" have been historically complicit with the virtu-alizing tendencies of the post-Fordist era (4–7).[1] Pushed to its logical (though not fully acknowledged) conclusion, Breu's thesis is that neo-liberal reason is at bottom *linguistically structured*. Given this deep-seated suspicion toward language and "the linguistic," it is surprising that he would look to literature—and postmodernist fiction to boot, often caricatured as "pure metafictional play, as the irresponsible aes-thetic of a dominant class of cultural producers" (25)—as a site for theorizing the intrinsic resilience of the material. In this paradox lies the book's compelling if contentious ambition to identify within "the reviled object that is postmodern literature" a countertradition "en-gaged with tarrying with the material unconscious of late-capitalist existence" (25–27). I say contentious because the vein of experimen-tal fiction that Breu names "late-capitalist literature of materiality" is not valorized because it circumvents the self-reflexiveness and hyper-referentiality often celebrated by postmodernism, nor even because it figures itself as a materialist practice,[2] but because of its uniquely *negative* capacity to "recognize" and "attend to" traces of a materiality that eludes linguistic logic. In other words, Breu is not arguing that lan-guage takes on its own materiality but that it traces in shadow the prob-lem of biopolitics as language, positing thereby a clear-cut fracture between language and matter. Before examining in greater detail Breu's treatment of language and its purported "necessary contradiction" with materiality (198), I will briefly retrace some of his book's most notable theoretical gestures.

Wrestling with the recent "material turn" in Western critical theory, *Insistence of the Material* weaves together an eclectic array of theoretical approaches—from new to old materialisms, from biopolitics to queer theory, from Lacanian psychoanalysis to Object-Oriented Ontology—in hopes of doing justice to the material in an era marked by the simultaneous development of biopolitical governance (wherein material bodies are subjected to ever more invasive economic and political calculations) and a growing fascination with the virtual (which Breu equates with the immaterial and the textual). Instead of seeing these two tendencies as mutually exclusive, Breu proposes that the "transcendence" promised by the dematerializing logic of post-Fordist America is in fact the vanishing point of a biopolitics that dreams of infinitely docile and malleable bodies. In this, he follows Hardt and Negri's claim that "biopolitical production" has a propensity to present itself as "immaterial" when it is, in fact, anything but.[3] Breu, however, quickly distances himself from the two philosophers, whom he accuses—despite their insistence that immaterial production is always predicated on (the disavowal of) material production—of falling prey to the fascination of the virtual. "For all their value," Breu concludes, "theories such as Hardt and Negri's run the danger of becoming junk-fueled fantasies of transcendence" (51).[4] This disagreement is key to understanding Breu's concept of the material: whereas Hardt and Negri try to think the dematerializing effects of the globalized neoliberal machine *as material processes*, Breu wishes to redeem the material as the pure "other" eroded by virtualizing linguistic-economic-biopolitical apparatuses.

Seeking to present a materialist counterpart to the notion that there is no (place for theorizing) death in biopolitics, Breu understands the material as the blind spot and breaking point of biopolitical governance: "Materiality . . . can be likened to biopolitics and virtuality's unconscious flip side—one that resists integration with the world of biopolitical control" (2). Only once it is able to account for the material's irreducible residuality, Breu predicts, will biopolitical critique realize its full critical and political potential. "This is not to situate the body or materiality as fully outside the sphere of culture," he insists:

Indeed, as much biopolitical thought has demonstrated, the history of the last half century can be productively thought of in terms of the increasing ability of culture to shape and discipline the body and for it to socialize and commodify ever more fully different aspects of everyday life. Yet this is also [sic] to refuse to make the material and the cultural coincident, for even as the cultural and the discursive shape our bodies in ever more intimate and subtle ways, the materiality of our bodies resists and interacts with such dynamics in ways neither fully controllable nor predictable. . . . In an era in which the dominant ideology of digitization is the virtual imagined as a process of dematerialization, it becomes especially important for reasons both political economic and ecological to attend to the material resources and still very material forms of production that underpin these fantasies of virtuality (18–19).

To appreciate the dematerializing urge of neoliberal biopolitics, Breu proposes to situate recent theories of globalization and late capitalism within the purview of the material turn. He accounts for the post-Fordist fantasies of immaterial production by reworking Marx's theory of commodity fetishism. According to Marx, the commodity appears imbued with a life of its own because of an active forgetting of the human labor that conditioned its existence. Thus tending to the commodity "for itself" does not mean tending to its objective features or materiality—which for Marx "have absolutely no connection with the physical nature of the commodity"[5]—but rather buying (into) the fetishism of the commodity. Whereas in industrial capitalism it is social relations that are mistaken for material relations, in the virtualized economies of late capitalism, it is the material itself—our own bodies, material dimensions of economic production, the raw material of which our commodities are made, and so forth—that appears abjected, if not entirely negated. There would thus be a new form of fetishism specific to late capitalism, which Breu calls "avatar fetishism." With this second-degree fetishism, Breu calls the bluff on the ostensible immateriality of immaterial labor and production for two reasons. First, the dream of a transcendable materiality is just that, a dream, since the material never fully complies to biocapitalist scripts. Second, this dream is only available to a privileged few since virtualization rests on the disavowal of a still very material production outsourced to obscure colonial elsewheres.[6] Hence avatar fetishism's paradoxical corollary, *embodiment envy*, a principle according to which "those who have the privilege of imagining that they can transcend

embodiment become envious of those who are defined as exces-
sively embodied through their lack of access to avatar fetishism and
their relationship to the more material dimensions of the production
process" (23).

Embodiment envy is presented as the racist and colonialist obverse
of avatar fetishism. In the imperialist context described in Thomas Pynchon's *V.*, for example, the colonizing subject fantasizes the colonized
other as possessing a more immediate access to materiality and a greater
enjoyment of her body. From the colonizer's structural jealousy, Breu
infers a "fetishistic logic of genocide" that simultaneously underwrites
and undermines the fantasy of biopolitical control. Thus Pynchon is
said to present "biopolitics and thanatopolitics not merely as aggres-
sive forms of power . . . but also as a defensive reaction of those in
power to the growth of the subject / object antinomy and the forms of
political-economic contingency produced by it" (87). Pynchon's biopolitics, contra Foucault, Agamben, and Esposito, is but a "rationalized
form of fetishism—a fantasy of disciplinary and political control that
is inherently elusive and structured around a disavowal" (87). Breu's
engagement with these three authors is rather elliptical, and I find it
difficult to take sides in the polemic he initiates. That said, his concepts of avatar fetishism and embodiment envy add a compelling psychological layer to the still too rare analyses of the racist and colonialist
underbelly of bio-, thanato- and necro-politics.[7] Breu's astute critique
of the fetishistic logic of globalization informs each of the five novels
studied in *Insistence of the Material*, all of which work to make manifest
the profound political, economic, and material asymmetries on which
neoliberal biopolitics is predicated.

In contrast to the metafictional and metaphyiscal proclivities of
postmodern literature, late-capitalist literature of materiality is claimed
to use "language experimentally to engage the increasingly obscured
yet ever proliferating material underpinnings of everyday life in the era
of late capitalism" (26). The counter-canon identified by Breu does not
so much belie the notion according to which experimental literature—
just like experimental theory—is *de facto* conniving with the fetishism of
immateriality but rather, rebuffing the lure of self-reflexivity, acknowledges the materiality that purportedly eludes language. Borrowing
from Enrique Dussel the rubric of "transmodernity," Breu also endows
the literature of materiality with the unique capacity to register the

profound disparities precipitated by globalization and modernization. Breu's transmodern novels therefore present us with alternative temporalities and geographies "situated simultaneously inside and outside the histories of modernity" (152). William Burrough's *Naked Lunch*, for instance, follows a double trajectory that "points backward to early twentieth-century experimentalists such as the Dadaists and surrealists and forward to our time of postmodern and 'post-postmodern' experimental fiction, globalization, neoliberal biopolitics, and so-called immaterial production" (35). Thomas Pynchon's reflections on plastic surgery and subjectivity in *V.* excavate a "prehistory of late capitalism, tracing the emergence of biopolitical forms of control in both the first-world metropole and the colonial periphery" (31). Insisting relentlessly on the hard infrastructural reality that subtends the fallacies of immaterial production, J. G. Ballard's *Crash* appears symptomatic of the repressed violence of what Breu calls "the late-modern unconscious." Dodie Bellamy's fictional memoir *The Letters of Mina Harker* "insists that a truly progressive feminist and queer politics needs to attend to the domains of the body that are constituted as abject or real but also those aspects where biology asserts its imperative separate from our cultural scripts" (32). Finally, Leslie Marmon Silko's *Almanac of the Dead* reads as an ecological allegory that "engages modernity and late capitalism yet represents Indigenous forms of subjectivity and political community that cannot be completely reduced to the space and time of modernity" (152).

Treating experimental literature as a privileged site for uncovering unexpected affinities between biopolitics, globalization, and late capitalism is doubtless an important intervention. It is not always clear, however, even for an essay whose credo is to theorize objects as "actants in their own right" (12), how the novels act *as literary objects*. How does the late-capitalist literature of materiality do politics "as literature," to borrow Rancière's locution? Can literature, one wonders, do more than passively acknowledge or register the existence of the material? More than negatively "recognize" and "attend to" matter as language's unconscious or disavowed counterpart? What, in other words, are the specifically literary techniques that enable Breu's novels to insist on the material, if language is a priori unfit to present or represent materiality? And why choose experimental texts? Does the experiment interact with, inflect, or alter a more general political-economic tendency, or is the experiment merely symptomatic of this tendency (in which case the specter of a vulnerable, impassive materiality problematically resurfaces)? One of the rhetorical strategies that, according to Breu, enables the leap from the semiotic to the somatic is the recourse to what he calls "radical parataxis," a process by which William Burroughs is said to generate a fundamental disruption in his prose in order to move "beyond representation" (41). It is no accident if one finds in radical parataxis an echo to Object-Oriented Ontology's infamous litanies, for Breu claims that parataxis' unhinged signifiers "take on a life of their own, glowing with asyntactic vitality" (42). Admittedly, parataxis indexes a "refusal of narrative"; yet it does not necessarily entail that the sentences' unsubordinated syntagms become "entities unto themselves," let alone present "the being of objects unshackled from the gaze of the human in their being-for-themselves" (Levi Bryant, quoted by Breu, 42). One could easily reverse Breu's logic to suggest that the ontological atomization into discrete units of being imagined by OOO may in fact serve the speculative reason of late capital even as it purports to escape our all-too-human epistemological and linguistic economies.[8] Besides, contrary to what Breu advances, parataxis is *not* asyntactic—it does not create "discrete *subsyntactic* units" (42, my emphasis)—but merely nonhypotactic. And not only is parataxis a highly syntactic resource, but it is also a very old trick in the modernist and postmodernist book, and it is not evident what makes Burroughs's use of parataxis so "radical" or so different from that of writers like, say, Stein, Beckett, or Ashbery.

To be fair, Breu recurrently acknowledges that language is no less material than the bodies that produce and use it. Yet it is essential for his project that language and matter remain fundamentally distinguished and distinguishable if we want "to *fully attend to* the materialities of our bodies" (9, my emphasis).[9] The implicit consequence of this requisite is that literature can only proceed *analogically* if it is to heed the material. When Breu's experimental fictions foreground the materiality of language, they can only insist by association on "other forms of abjected materiality" (41). By this logic, however, the signifier's materiality is valorized, ironically, for nothing if not its symbolic potential, that is, for its capacity to stand in for—indeed to *represent*—the nonlinguistic materialities referenced in the text. More remarkably still, in the chapter he devotes to *Naked Lunch*, Breu calls for a resymbolization of the material as a means to account for its irreducibility to the symbolic. Similarly, his otherwise incisive reading of Bellamy's *Letters* ends on a surprising plea to "symbolically accept[] our relationship to bodies and to forms of materiality that exceed and set limits on . . . our subjectivities" (148). With this remarkable return to the symbolic, we are left to wonder if and to what extent literature has effectively moved beyond the old representational paradigm that Breu decries (a task that is all the more urgent if we agree with Foucault's contention that biopolitics marks a shift from the "symbolics of blood" to the "analytics of sexuality").[10]

What becomes apparent is that Breu's insistence on the separation between text and matter stems from a tacit equation of materiality with ontology.[11] I don't dispute his analysis that our neoliberal age fetishizes the virtual and dreams of a materiality that could easily be written off. I also fully recognize the urgency to recover the traces of the racialized, gendered, wounded, and exploited bodies that biocapitalism wishes to eclipse. What I recuse is the need for the turn to the material to be predicated on *ontological difference*. For all his claims to resist any simple language/matter binarism, Breu depicts language as, at best, a technology complicit with biocapitalism's dematerializing aspirations, and, at worst, an authoritative apparatus hostile to vulnerable yet resilient bodies (which, it should be noted, are almost always human bodies). For all his protestations that we ought not to conceive the body as "a *tabula rasa* upon which biopolitics and thanatopolitics inscribe their insistent and sometimes terrifying scripts" (188), Breu dogmatically holds on to the notion of an absolutely asemiotic, uncoded "real." His overt "frustration" with the linguistic turn spurs his desire to re-dialectize theory by drawing a strict demarcation line between "language" and its supposed other (the material and all its cognates: objects, things, the body, the flesh, the real). But by being so skeptical of language's alleged "transcendence" of the material, Breu runs the risk of turning the material into a transcendent category.

Ultimately, Breu's argument revolves around the recognition of a tenacious disavowal of the material characteristic in our biopolitical, neoliberal, and postmodern moment. I am tempted to extend this diagnosis to his own relationship to language, whose alleged inadequacy to material objects—but is adequacy to the material what we expect of literary and critical language?—turns it into a dematerializing force aligned with biopolitical production and ultimately situates it, by con-tamination, on the side of the immaterial or even the transcendent. What Breu disavows is not so much the materiality of language itself, since he recognizes ways in which the signifier comes to matter in the late-capitalist literature of materiality, but rather of a number of important conceptual debates about the materiality of language. One thinks, for instance, of the theories developed by thinkers like Mau-rice Blanchot, Fredric Jameson, and especially Paul de Man, one of the key figures of the so-called linguistic turn, but also of more recent performative, affective, or biosemiotic theories of language. Instead of somewhat conventional analyses of the "materiality of the signifier"— a hackneyed formulation that supposes a split between what signifies and what is signified, between the sensuous vehicle of meaning and the meaning itself—it might have proved more useful to investigate the *materiality of the signifying*, that is, to approach signification as a mate-rial process and conversely materiality as, in fact and effect, semiologi-cal. Isn't the materiality of signifying, after all, the very historicity of statements, or enunciations, that undergirds Foucauldian critique and, ultimately, the account of biopolitics itself?

Despite my reservations, I found in Breu's book a compelling and timely effort to grapple with the political relevance and limitations of literature in the age of biopolitics. In lieu of a formal conclusion, I'd like to suggest a slightly different direction for future works. What if, instead of predicating materiality's resistance on what resembles a modern iteration of the old nature/culture divide, we imagined a cul-ture produced not just *with* but *by* bodies and matter? Isn't this the lesson of biopolitics, after all, that politics infiltrates life no less than life shapes politics? That life is not merely disciplined and controlled by some mysterious transcendent mastercodes but actively and inti-mately informs the domain of the political? Conceiving the material as extraneous to the neoliberal body politic and restricting its potency to mere resistance or insistence may paradoxically prevent us from accounting for what bodies and matter can effectively do. We may thus read *Insistence of the Material* as an invitation to ask what literature as a material and materialist practice can tell us about our biocapitalist age. To do so, we would need to correct the conclusion's second axiom, which stipulates that "language and other forms of materiality exist in necessary contradiction," precisely so that we can begin to understand why and how "literature and the arts become some of the crucial media through which we can access the material" (198).

Antoine Traisnel is assistant professor of English and comparative literature at the University of Michigan. He has published in the fields of American, French, and German literature and philosophy. He is the author of *Hawthorne: Blasted Allegories* (2015), coauthor of *Donner le change: L'impensé animal* (2016), with Thangam Ravindranathan, and translator of *Sheppard Lee* (2017).

Notes

1. While this is one of the guiding leitmotivs of the book, Breu does not identify any specific thinker or school of thought under this rubric, which indexes a general theoretical orientation more than a clearly defined philosophical movement.

2. In the opening sentence of his acknowledgments, Breu notes that "writing is, of course, a material practice" (201). This concession that reads like a confession is symptomatic of the book's constitutive and productive ambivalence toward the materiality of writing. I will come back to this point in the latter part of my essay.

3. A version of this argument can be found in Beatriz Preciado's *Testo Junkie*: "If we consider that the pharmaceutical industry (which includes the legal extension of the scientific, medical, and cosmetic industries, as well as the trafficking of drugs declared illegal), the pornography industry, and the industry of war are the load-bearing sectors of post-Fordist capitalism, we ought to be able to give a cruder name to *immaterial labor*" (39, emphasis in original). Beatriz Preciado, *Testo Junkie: Sex, Drugs, and Biopolitics in the Pharmacopornographic Era*. Trans. Bruce Benderson (New York: The Feminist Press, 2013).

4. When they discuss biopolitical production, Hardt and Negri explicitly state that it is imperative to shift perspectives from the juridical to the material if we want to understand "how the imperial machine is actually set in motion." Our analysis, they write, must "descend to the level of that materiality and investigate there the material transformation of the paradigm of rule" (*Empire*, 22). One may disagree with their conclusions or analyses, but it seems misguided to view their interpretation of immaterial labor as a move away from materiality. Hardt and Negri insist: "One of the most serious shortcomings has thus been the tendency [among thinkers of immaterial labor] to treat the new laboring practices in biopolitical society *only* in their intellectual and incorporeal aspects. The productivity of bodies and the value of affect, however, are absolutely central in this context" (ibid., 29–30, emphasis in original). Michael Hardt and Antonio Negri, *Empire* (Cambridge, Mass.: Harvard University Press, 2001).

5. Karl Marx, *Capital: A Critique of Political Economy, Volume I*. Trans. Ben Fowkes (New York: Penguin Books, 1990), 165.

6. For a detailed analysis of this phenomenon, see Saskia Sassen, *Globalization and Its Discontents: Essays on the New Mobility of People and Money* (New York: New Press, 1998).

7. See, for instance, Paul Gilroy, 1994. "'After the Love Has Gone': Biopolitics and Etho-poetics in the Black Public Sphere," *Third Text* (1994): 8.28–29, 25–46; Mbembe, Achille, "Necropolitics," *Public Culture* 15, no. 1 (2013): 11–40; Fred Moten and Stefano Harney, *The Undercommons: Fugitive Planning and Black Studies* (New York: Autonomedia, 2013); and Alexander H. Weheliye, *Habeas Viscus: Racializing Assemblages, Biopolitics, and Black Feminist Theories of the Human* (Durham: Duke University Press, 2014).

8. I want to flag here the suspect "naiveté" proclaimed by the new ontologists and speculative realists, whom Breu repeatedly invokes, for their claims to attend to objects "for" and "in themselves" may be construed, as Jordy Rosenberg has recently argued, as collusive with and perhaps even conducive to the recent financialization of capital accumulation. (Jordana Rosenberg, "The Molecularization of Sexuality: On Some Primitivisms of the Present," *Theory and Event* 17, no. 2 [2014]).

9. Even though Breu is careful to write "language and nonlinguistic forms of materiality," implying thereby that language is not immaterial, the contrast between language and these other forms of materiality unambiguously rests on a strict binarism between language and materiality.

10. Michael Foucault, *The History of Sexuality, Vol. 1*, trans. Robert Hurley (New York: Vintage, 1990), 148.

11. The slippage is explicit when Breu contrasts Derrida's pale revenants with Bellamy's "more substantial" vampires, who he claims "represent a turn toward ontology and the ineluctability of material embodiment and the flesh of being" (128). If Derrida's (and Marx's) specters escape the bounds of traditional ontology, however, they are undoubtedly material figures.

FEMINIST FILMMAKING AND
THE FUTURE OF GLOBAL FILM POLITICS

WOMEN'S CINEMA, WORLD CINEMA:
PROJECTING CONTEMPORARY FEMINISMS
BY PATRICIA WHITE
Duke University Press, 2015

Maggie Hennefeld

In an age of rising feminist activism and gendered media consumerism, how can we theorize the geopolitical aesthetics of women's filmmaking? In *Women's Cinema, World Cinema: Projecting Contemporary Feminisms*, Patricia White gives us the critical tools to understand the global formations of our contemporary feminisms. She argues, "While remappings of world cinema in the current phase of globalization are the object of growing attention in film studies, questions of gender have yet to structure such inquiry significantly" (6). White traces the complex, transnational exchange between individual examples and collectivist models of feminism, focusing on twenty-first century, feature-length festival films by non-Western women directors. White looks at films by women who: (a) came of age during the heyday of second-wave feminism, (b) whose filmmaking navigates the complexities of public space across national borders in an increasingly privatized, globalized media landscape, and (c) whose innovative aesthetics help make visible the unresolvable contradictions internal to present-day feminist film politics. Feature films by directors including Deepa Mehta, Claudia Llosa, Lucrecia Martel, Zero Chou, Nadine Labaki, Samira Makhmalbaf, Sabiha Sumar, Marjane Satrapi, Nia Dinata, Jeong Jae-eun, and others innovate new moving image paradigms for articulating the renewed centrality of women's cinema as a concept. This is precisely White's core argument: "In this book I seek to explore how feminism, a discourse that has been profoundly

Cultural Critique 99—Spring 2018—Copyright 2018 Regents of the University of Minnesota reshaped by transnational perspectives and realities in recent decades, can inform [the] geopolitical reimagination" (14) of world cinema. By helping "to define twenty-first century art house aesthetics," as White asserts (and as I will further explain), these "members of a new generation of women filmmakers are also transforming film politics" (4).

White's book, the first of its kind to establish the centrality of women's filmmaking to the geopolitics of world cinema, locates itself at the crossroads of film studies scholarship on transnational cinema and feminist theory. Recent work on world cinema has actively pursued a concept of totality—or at least a consolidated perspective from which to understand the complex vicissitudes of transnational filmmaking, distribution, and exhibition. Key texts that explore the circulation of cinema through the framework of "the world" include Natasa Ďurovičová and Kathleen Newman's edited volume *World Cinemas, Transnational Perspectives* (2009), Lúcia Nagib's *Theorizing World Cinema* (2011), and Karl Schoonover and Rosalind Galt's *Queer Cinema in the World* (2016).[1] As White argues, "World cinema has the potential to renew [the] public emphasis [of feminist politics] amid the privatization of global mass media and the screens on which we encounter it. Women have a crucial role as producers of this public social vision" (3). Cinema's capacity to project an image of the world thus becomes the stake for feminism's renewed potential to politicize the public spaces of film reception—as opposed to merely fostering the private commoditization of film consumption.

Although the proliferating concept of world cinema still remains a far cry from Fredric Jameson's bold assertion in *The Geopolitical Aesthetic* (1992),[2] that all thinking through cinema "is *also*, whatever else it is, an attempt to think the world system as such" (4), the world still seems graspable (or at least conceivable) through the lens of these alternative film totalities. For example, Hamid Naficy's notion of "accented cinema"—which theorizes diasporic and exilic filmmakers as "situated but universal figures" (10)[3]—inflects White's own attempt to place women's world cinema in relation both to transnational film geopolitics and to the histories of feminist film theory.

Since the 1990s, feminist film studies has been increasingly turning its gaze toward the local, the empirical, the fragmented archive, the forgotten microhistory, and the singular, pioneering individual. These pointedly archival and local approaches to the gender and sexual politics of film representation have vividly reshaped the field of feminist film theory. Its key texts and debates concern the cultural scope and material lack of archival evidence, the paradoxes of assigning feminist authorship in the wake of masculinist discourses of auteurism, and the affirmative value of activist sociologies. Single-director, archival studies (of female filmmakers including Lois Weber, Alice Guy-Blaché, Maya Deren, and Germaine Dulac),[4] cultural histories of gender experimentation in cinema (focused on themes such as cross-dressing, performance, and intermedial display),[5] as well as sociological explorations of industry diversity and ethnographic representation now take precedence over psychoanalytic, Marxist, or feminist semiotic theorizations of sexuality and difference.[6] From the universalized, gendered gaze exhaustively critiqued by second-wave feminist film theorists such as Laura Mulvey, Mary Ann Doane, Judith Mayne, and Teresa de Lauretis,[7] the concept of visibility in contemporary feminist film studies, instead, hinges on the recuperation of archival evidence and the attribution of political significance. The waning interest in theorizing structural models of gender and sexual difference in feminist theory has become implicated in the dissolution of public or collectivist politics of feminist activism and media representation.

White's theorization of the concept of "projection"—in a very different iteration than the complicated psychoanalytic metaphors for universal spectator desire posited by apparatus theory[8]—provides a mediating term between the local specificities of women's cinema and the expansive views fostered by scholarship on transnational film geopolitics. White's concept of projection derives neither from the libidinal unconscious nor from the ideological structures of the film apparatus. Rather, projection emphasizes process, multidirectionality, and the overdermination of gazes: between textual inscription and contingent viewer receptions, across multimedia cinematic formats, as well as between middle-class white Western feminists and non-Western, marginalized others whose perspectives they frequently assume and ventriloquize.

White's terminological flexibility, exemplified by but not limited to her versatile notion of projection, is neither a methodological flaw nor as an asset in itself: rather, it is a reflection of the state of the field. Through her close readings of recent women's films in their historical, geopolitical, and authorial contexts—alongside scrupulous attention to the exhibition and distribution networks through which these films circulate—White provides a critical account of the mutually constitutive relationship between women's cinema and world cinema. She focuses on the tensions between local stories, national representation, and international traversal in an era when so many women directors "are ambivalently recruited to [the] corrective project" of "preserv[ing] film art and national identity" (6) through the authenticating but ambiguous discourse of women's cinema. If women are often tasked with speaking on behalf of the nation-state—especially to repair the fractured cohesion and waning legitimacy of this entity—then, geopolitics, at least, offers women a stage for complicating the frameworks through which their voices and images are cinematically projected and globally consumed.

Navigating the relationship between women's cinema and world cinema in the twenty-first century marks the central challenge of this book. White's study spans films and filmmakers from Argentina, Bosnia and Herzegovina, Canada, France, India, Indonesia, Iran, Lebanon, Pakistan, Peru, Taiwan, and South Korea; elite film festivals from Cannes, Venice, and Berlin, to International Women's Film Festivals in Seoul, Chile, and Sierra Leone; and genres including romantic comedy, queer chick flick, coming-of-age road movie, auteurist meta-film, and humanitarian melodrama. Women's films—a discourse carried over from 1930s Hollywood tearjerkers, to 1970s feminist political advocacy, to 2010s cosmopolitan, neoliberal makeover movies—can (and often do) mean everything to anybody. White argues that what women need, therefore, is not representation, but a more expansively precise terminology for navigating their utter centrality to cinema's expansion through the entire surface of the globe.

WOMEN'S FILMS

For White, the terrain of the world is at least as vast and open-ended as the politics and aesthetics of women's cinema. Though published several years before the flourishing of Time's Up and #MeToo, White's book is necessary reading in our current moment of energetic feminist activism and global protest against gender inequity in the film industry. Given the obscene gender gaps in Hollywood (where women comprise only 7 percent of directors on top-grossing films)[9] and in prestigious international film festivals such as Cannes (where only one woman has ever won the Palme d'Or),[10] feminist advocates have fought the paucity of female representation by emphasizing the importance of singular examples. Exceptional women filmmakers (including Kathryn Bigelow, Sofia Coppola, and Jane Campion), whose successes belie industry and film-festival statistics, populate lists such as "The 25 Best Films Directed by Female Film Directors"[11] and "68 Films Directed by Women That You Can't Afford to Miss."[12] In the first of these two lists, Second-Wave European classics (*Jeanne Dielman* and *Seven Beauties*), recent queer coming-of-age films (*Tomboy* and *Pariah*), multinational Arab dramas (*Wadjda* and *The Square*), "postfeminist" romantic comedies (*Big* and *Lost in Translation*), and poetic war films (*The Ascent* and *The Hurt Locker*) all lead up to the big reveal: "the best film directed by a female film director" ever is *Triumph of the Will*, Leni Riefenstahl's 1935 documentary glorifying the rise of Nazi fascism in interwar Germany.[13] In other words, what do any of these examples have to do with one another—what collective values or structural insights do they share?

Refraining from the temptations of list-mania provides a starting point for White's polemic. She compares the feminist film politics of our own moment to the debates about "positive images" that formatively divided 1970s feminist film studies between celebratory affirmation and negative critique. In 1978, Diane Waldman challenged Linda Wengraf and Susan Artel's groundbreaking study, *Positive Images: Non-Sexist Films for Young People* (1976).[14] Arguing that "There's More to a Positive Image Than Meets the Eye" (1978),[15] Waldman drew a line between the valorization of "positive images" (exemplified by non-sexist films featuring strong, independent female protagonists) and the articulation of complex methodologies for theorizing the construction of sexual difference in media representation. In her book review of Wengraf and Artel's text for *Jump Cut*, Waldman poses the question pointedly: "In ascribing positive characteristics to certain depictions are we claiming a truth value for them?" The feminist celebration of positive images (as in good objects) thus gives way to the uncritical acceptance of certain valorized images as positive signs—as self-evident texts: the semiotician's worst nightmare.

White productively raises the specter of these formative, positive image debates in her analysis of how women's films today navigate the global commodification of art cinema. "Too often women's access to directing is correlated with a perceived affinity with worthy subject matter" (69). Instead of signposting stories about female aviators or political leaders (as per Wengraf and Artel's call for more nonsexist images), women's cinema simply becomes a placeholder for the transparency of ethnographic experience and ethical testimony. Humanitarian urgency, ethnographic visibility, and ethical sensitivity provide key frameworks that both mobilize and delimit "women's cinema as art cinema"—an apt reworking of Steve Neale's 1981 essay "Art Cinema as Institution."[16] The stakes of this tendency to commodify women's cinema as middlebrow, foreign-language art cinema—as universal humanism with subtitles—are more than ethical: White argues, they are avowedly political. She asserts: "Instead of being received in the context of feminisms or of collective, political, or representational debates, [these films] are recast as exemplars of expressive sensibility, risk, the human spirit, or local color" (69). White reworks Claire Johnston's foundational feminist essay, "Women's Cinema as Counter-Cinema" (1973),[17] by extending Johnston's notion of art cinema's "invasion of myth around the feminine" beyond issues of textual representation to consider practices of film exhibition and promotion.

Reawakening the capacity to imagine transnational feminist collectivities, not through false universalisms but through more precise representations of their pointed antagonisms, is really the wager of this book, and is also the immense challenge of White's project. Much more work needs to be done in this regard to situate the politics of transnational feminisms that circulate by way of women's world cinema. White's book provides many critical tools and useful examples for establishing the collectivist, public, and global stakes of women's filmmaking—beyond libidinal models of the psyche or the ideological structures of the cinematographic apparatus.

Feminist film theory of the 1970s and '80s has a tendency to universalize its collectivist polemics, even if only to critique the phallocentrism of psychoanalytic desire and Hollywood narrative spectatorship. Present day feminist film advocacy often suffers from the opposite problem: irreducible individuality. List-mania is one such symptom of the deep cynicism about projecting collectivity onto transnational feminist publics—an abiding cynicism that finds temporary relief through the somber discourse of universal humanism that so often sets the tone for women's political filmmaking (from *Suffragette* to *Forbidden Voices*).[18] White emphasizes that her book "makes no effort to be inclusive but rather explores selected cases in depth" (7). Exemplary films are chosen as much for their cultural significance as for the ways in which their geopolitical and filmmaking contexts "reveal the institutional shapes of film culture—the politics of funding and programming, protocols of reviewing and the anointing of celebrities, and various political agendas" (7). The crucial question shaping each chapter, then, becomes: *What are the key aesthetic, geopolitical, and filmmaking criteria by which women's cinema can become valorized and thereby receive critical acclaim and cultural visibility?*

These gendered categories of visibility and value include (to paraphrase): Self-Reflexive Auteurism, Art Cinema, Chick Flick Genre, Asian Networking, and Global Humanitarianism. The range encompassed by these categories is as immense as the distance between Dee Rees's *Pariah* and Leni Riefenstahl's *Triumph of the Will*. What they each have in common, then, is their profound influence shaping the global frames through which women's films circulate. Women who win awards at Cannes, or women who make sexually daring films about lesbians living under conservative religious regimes, gain special prominence through their singularity. In contrast, women who draw on the popular conventions of the chick flick, or who make art films that sentimentalize social struggle, inherit and inflect market clichés of the women's film genre. The specter of humanitarian authenticity haunts both of these entities (through melodramatic depictions of oppressed women's exceptional daring), as White argues, thereby authorizing women directors as unreflexive voices of truth in an unevenly democratized world system. Again, these are the complex geopolitical discourses that women's films must negotiate, as White outlines and constructs them. These geopolitical discourses set the terms by which marginalized and minoritarian women find their places behind the camera.

Then, given the tendency of these gendered frames of authenticity to naturalize the labor of the filmmaker herself, White begins, logically, with the gendered contradictions of feminist film authorship. Auteurism represents a sticky terrain for feminist film scholarship, given its overwhelmingly male roster of superstars (from Jean-Luc Godard and Roberto Rossellini to Wong Kar-Wai and Abbas Kiarostami), as well as its explicit basis in theories of the patriarchal symbolic.[19] Yet, how else to underscore the fact that *women DO make movies*—not to mention the archival challenges of recuperating overlooked female filmmakers from the silent era to the present day—than to assert women's existence as virtuosic film authors? White navigates this high-wire act, between affirming exceptional virtuosity and critiquing systemic inequality, with playful rigor.

She opens with a fittingly overdetermined example: Jane Campion's peculiar presence alongside thirty-four male filmmakers in the 2007 Cannes omnibus film, *Chacun son Cinéma* ("To Each His Own Cinema"). That Campion was the lone woman director (out of thirty-five!) included more than justifies the slight pronoun imprecision of this omnibus film's English title translation.

The New Zealand filmmaker Campion, who won Cannes's highest prize, the Palme d'Or, in 1993 for *The Piano*, contributed a short, satirical, metafilm, *The Lady Bug*, about a dancing female insect who is drawn into the moth light by a male janitor and then summarily stomped on. The janitor shouts, "You silly fool, I'll squash you!", a sad punchline echoed by the *Hollywood Reporter's* dismissal of the film as a byproduct of Campion's "squirrely self" (35).[20] White reads this ad hominem, sexist review as a symptom of the paradoxes of female film authorship: damned if you do, and damned if you don't. What does it mean for women to represent their gendered singularity within an overwhelmingly patriarchal canon without reifying or denying the gender politics of their marginal inclusion? As White notes, citing Alison Butler's *Contested Screens* and Catherine Grant's "Secret Agents: Feminist Theories of Woman's Film Authorship,"[21] many feminist film theorists have called for women's film discourse to move beyond auteurism. Yet, "an interrogation of auteurist discourse is essential to any study of how cinematic value is constructed" (33). Neither celebrating the transparent value of women's film authorship nor valorizing their ideology critique as ends in themselves, White's theoretical approach to the binds of women's film authorship is persuasively pragmatic.

Love it or hate it: auteurism remains a dominant framework through which individual filmmakers gain visibility and patronage, as well as funding, selection, publicity, exhibition, and distribution, to reach ever wider transnational film audiences. For White, the project of politicizing women's cinema must therefore involve an extensive interrogation of the funding, curating, and exhibition protocols that would allow women's films to circulate in the first place—as well as an adequate understanding of the cinematic hierarchies of value that exclude or tokenize women's films within certain exhibition contexts (such as Cannes). This systemic view of women's world cinema by no means excludes aesthetic critique or formal analysis; rather, it aims to situate such methodologies in relation to the geopolitical economies that shape and delimit any gendered politics of aesthetics.

GENDERED POSITIONALITIES: NATIONAL AUTHORSHIP, MIDDLEBROW TASTE, CHICK FLICK GENRE, ASIAN NETWORK, AND UNIVERSAL HUMANITARIANISM

The modes, genres, politics, and locations of women's world cinema, as White defines its formations, arguably cover a broader terrain than the world itself. They include: self-reflexive auteurism (Lucrecia Martel's *Headless Woman*, Samira Makhmalbaf's *At Five in the Afternoon*); middle-brow art-house programming (Deepa Mehta's *Water*, Marjane Satrapi's *Persepolis*, Shirin Neshat's *Women Without Men*); "postfeminist," chick flick genres (Jeong Jae-eun's *Take Care of My Cat*, Nadine Labaki's *Caramel* and *Where Do We Go Now?*); Asian feminist and LGBT film networking (Nia Dinata's *Love for Share*, Zero Chou's *Drifting Flowers* and *Spider Lilies*); and universal human rights advocacy (Sabiha Sumar's *Silent Waters*, Jasmila Zbaniç's *Grbavica*, Claudia Llosa's *Milk of Sorrow*). Other than their commonalities as feature-length, multinational, twenty-first century fiction films by emergent, non-Western women directors, the incongruities among these examples overwhelmingly outweigh their similarities, as White demonstrates.

Film auteurs at upper-crust film festivals are often made to play ambassadors for their respective nations—with the decline of national cinemas comes the rise of national film authors. *Women's Cinema, World Cinema* emphasizes the gendered crisis of boundaries that takes place when the author of the film is also identified as a woman. For her case studies, White chooses films that problematize the allegorical slippages between woman and nation—especially ones that do so also by obfuscating the relationship between woman filmmaker and female protagonist. For example, Samira and Hana Makhmalbaf's "sororal cinema" navigates its own reterritorialization as national allegory by thematizing border crossing. Samira and Hana were literally homeschooled in cinema in Tehran by their internationally famous filmmaker parents, Mohsen Makhalbaf and Marzieh Meshkini. Meshkini's films, such as *The Day I Became A Woman* (2000), overtly addresses Iranian gender politics and the hijab within the constraints of Islamic censorship laws.

Like Meshkini, the Makhmalbaf sisters find loopholes in Islamic gender laws, as White points out, by focusing on coming-of-age stories, and filming primarily in outdoor spaces to evade transgressing the codes of domestic modesty and intimacy. Samira's film *At Five in the Afternoon* (2003) thematizes geopolitics, and the gendered visual spaces of national border crossing. The film takes place largely in Afghanistan after the fall of the Taliban, focusing on the story of a displaced family of refugees from war-torn Pakistan. Makmalbhaf's protagonist, Nogreh (played by a local, nonprofessional actor, Ageleh Rezaie), dreams of becoming a political leader, and secretly attends a secular school in Kabul behind the back of her pious father. As Samira was making *At Five in the Afternoon* on location in Kabul (while her own family was exiled from Iran), her younger sister Hana filmed a documentary, *Joy of Madness* (2003), about the off-camera politics of intimacy between Samira and Rezaie, who apparently feared retribution from the Taliban for her participation in the film.

White identifies these differential power relationships—between world-class female filmmaker and local, working class, nonprofessional, female actor—through her aesthetic readings of the film: "a divide is inscribed in the form of the film. . . . Makhmalbaf foregrounds the issue of the female director as both subject and object, creator of the image and object of the gaze" (63). Precisely because Samira fails to transcend the geopolitics of her own feminist and cinematic positioning as a woman filmmaker—not that her sister Hana would ever let her forget them—White argues that her film represents a metadiscourse on its own appropriation by a Eurocentric gaze to speak on behalf of the nation (especially a nation as obsessively scrutinized and ideologically mystified as Iran has been). White's method of reading frequently ascribes the politics of women's filmmaking to the capacity of any given film to make visible the limits of its own gaze.

Again, this feminist gaze is a far cry from the universal gaze of "the other" sutured by classical Hollywood film ideology. In other words, it is more than a purely textual entity to be disrupted and dismantled by ever more rigorous methods in semiotic analysis and close reading. Yet, this gaze by no means defies interpretation—it is neither all form nor beyond form. Part and parcel of her larger project to assert the public politics of increasingly privatized film viewing spaces (and the collectivist traction of even singular, ethical, or neoliberal feminisms), White's approach to aesthetic interpretation can never become entirely autonomous. Formal analysis and close reading remain embedded in the concrete positionalities afforded by individual gazes (of filmmaker, actor, and an expanded sphere of transnational film viewers). The incommensurability of looks among women—especially as they index differential relations of power—becomes legible through White's retooled methods in feminist film interpretation.

It would be interesting to test White's approaches to close reading against less resonant examples. Explicitly, White focuses on films that manifest the overdetermination of female gazes between textual inscription, authorial framing, and their contingent contexts of exhibition and reception. *The Headless Woman* (Lucrecia Martel, Argentina, 2008) provides a key example. As White argues, this film refuses to allegorize the gendered disaffection of its female protagonist Veró. Nominated for the Palme d'Or, and famously booed at Cannes because of its slow aesthetic, confusing character relationships, and spare plot narration, *The Headless Woman* thematizes gendered blockages of vision. It depicts the visual and ethical blind spots of an Argentine bourgeois dentist, Veró, who accidentally runs over a body with her car. Unsure of whether she has hit a wild animal or a working-class child (she never looks back to check), Veró bears a cryptic and ultimately unknowable relation to Martel's own filmmaking vision. Beyond "decapitation as castration" (to invoke Hélène Cixous),[22] White's notion of headlessness, which she extracts from careful readings of Martel's aesthetics and filmmaking persona, opens onto the feminist geopolitics of ethical morality. Frequently decapitated by Martel's framing, "the headless woman" signifies more than an aesthetic motif, or even a national allegory of the willful amnesia about mass political disappearances of leftists under the 1970s Argentine dictatorship: female headlessness, White argues, springs from the ethical limits of gender and power. As White remarks, Veró has the power to act—the resources to address class stratifications in her community—but she fails to do so. Martel represents her through the willful impasses in Veró's own subjectivity. In contrast, the Makhmalbaf sisters' protagonist, Nogreh, in *At Five in the Afternoon*, possesses the vision to act, but lacks the resources.

If feminist auteurist cinema is irreducibly singular (hence White's parodic subtitle, "To Each Her Own Cinema"), feminist art cinema democratizes gendered vision under the aegis of middlebrow art culture. In "Framing Feminisms: Women's Cinema as Art Cinema," White focuses on the art-house distribution networks that valorize women's cinema by constructing feminized categories of taste. Here, White "considers how films by women directors are positioned within a humanist definition of art cinema as well as by the social organization of art house exhibition as a middlebrow and arguably feminized taste culture" (68). In a Bourdieu-ian twist, White argues that diasporan women filmmakers such as Indian-Canadian director Deepa Mehta and Iranian-French Marjane Satrapi use their cultural capital (their "privileged relation to cultural authenticity . . . to speak 'as' or 'for' their culture") into political capital (70). It is this gendered liquidity between cultural capital and political capital—which White denotes as the symbolic capital of women's art cinema—that makes this category so very interesting. Rather than simply exposing and critiquing the deceptive transparency and false authenticity of art-house films about the oppression of non-Western women of color, White examines the contradictory endpoints of their signification. After all, cultural capital legitimizes habits and tastes, fostering new imaginations of location and environment for transnational art-house spectators, while also shaping future material conditions for the next generations of women filmmakers.

This question of feminist inheritance is further crucial for situating the geopolitics of how women's films circulate outside their local production and reception contexts. White poses this as a question of connotative mobility. For example, does a woman's film, then, become a "cipher," as Alison Butler argues in her critique of Mehta's *Fire* (1996), for displaced images of nationalism and fundamentalism? Does "the invasion of myth" endemic to art cinema's depictions of female muses (this formulation of Johnston's provides a keystone for White), yet again, "naturalize women's suffering and endurance" (85)? White focuses on three carefully selected, exemplary films: Deepa Mehta's *Water* (2006), the final installment in Mehta's "Elements" trilogy, about ostracized widows in prepartition India; Marjane Satrapi's *Persepolis* (2007), an animated film adapted from Satrapi and Vincent Paronnaud's graphic novel about a girl coming of age in Revolutionary Iran; and Shirin Neshat's stylistically experimental, French-German-Austrian coproduction, *Women Without Men* (2009), about four women's experiences in Iran during the American-backed coup that reinstalled the Shah in 1953.

These three films strategically invoke a spectrum of positions: from consationalizing difference for a Western feminist gaze (as *Water* arguably does), to obfuscating difference through accented film style (again invoking Naficy's term). White persuasively demonstrates how "Satrapi and Neshat make visible, in their works' form and content, enunciation and address, feminist Iranian identities in the transnational public sphere" (101).[23] These are completely crucial distinctions to elaborate, and ones that do not get reinforced often enough. As White emphasizes, *not all representations of ethnographic difference marketed to Eurocentric audiences function exactly the same way.* Through her comparative readings of these three feminist art films, White identifies the marks of how transnational public-sphere politics might signify cinematically. For example, Mehta's *Water*, which advertised itself by flagging the Hindu protests and backlash against depiction of lesbian sexuality in *Fire*, uses melodramatic conventions to sentimentalize feminist social issues: the Hindu mistreatment of widows, child brides, and religious misogyny in rural India. In contrast, White argues, *Persepolis* and *Women Without Men*, in different ways, signpost their gendered constructions of difference with accented images.

Persepolis enlists graphic animation, black-and-white silhouettes, cartoon metamorphosis, and frequent humorous breaks to disrupt the allegorical slippage between woman and nation—between women oppressed by religious law, and the liberated Western feminist gazes solicited through the pleasures of humanitarian rescue and humanist sentiment. These tensions are aesthetically encoded, but with concrete geopolitical effects. Again invoking Naficy, "In *Persepolis*, animation is also a technique of estrangement, of deterritorialization, or accented style. . . . In a scene from the film that illustrates this particularly poignantly, the narrator recounts passage from childhood to adult femininity. . . . Satrapi identifies this moment with cultural liminality and physical monstrosity" (93). As White aptly captures this richly visual and humorously imaginative scene, "Accompanied by cartoon sound effects of stretching and rebounding, the [narrator's] self-portrait morphs through images evoking Picasso's *Guernica*, Quasimodo, and Barbie to end up as a teenager dressed in new-wave fashion" (93). More intrusively, Neshat clutters her live-action footage of women's veiling and unveiling with superimpositions of Persian script, troubling any easy referentiality associated with images of hijab.

However, rather than valorizing modernist reflexivity and dismissing humanitarian melodrama, White focuses on the productive instability of either mode. "Though both global film festivals and global feminism involve the transnational politics of the image, they bestow value in different ways—and these directors occupy that gap" (91). These are the crucial political stakes of reading women's films: to make visible the feminist geopolitics "that might seem at best indexed by the films' plots" (105), as White describes the project of her chapter on "Feminist Film in the Age of Chick Flicks." How could any book on contemporary women's cinema not touch on the chick flick?

The polemics of reclaiming women's films not as a commercial genre marketed to women, but as a feminist framework for foregrounding the identity of the director, comes full circle in this chapter. Fittingly, White opens with an analysis of a "global chick flick" from South Korea, *Take Care of My Cat* (Jeong Jae-eun, 2001), whose plot sounds uncannily like a zoomorphic precursor to Hollywood's *Sisterhood of the Traveling Pants* (Ken Kwapis, 2005). In this film, five working-class teenage girls from outside Seoul collectively share a cat: a communal pet that provides a totem of their friendship and solidarity with one another despite their very different personal struggles, stressful family situations, and divergent career aspirations.

The logic behind White's selections for her case studies itself bears further elucidation. In her other key example of the global chick flick, Nadine Labaki's *Caramel* (2007), Lebanese women overcome class, ethnic, Muslim-Christian religious, and generational differences in the homosocial space of the hair salon: "a chick flick topos par excellence and a microcosm of its concerns" (120). Rather than bracket the debased connotations of this hyper-commercial, unfailingly formulaic, and largely depoliticized genre, White inherits the chick flick's overwhelming address to women. "I argue that each of these films functions to a significant extent on the generic and affective level of the women's picture, and that this is part of their engagement with, not their retreat from, feminist geopolitics" (119). The fun of weddings and makeovers, and pathos of loss and suffering, do not resolve, but rather underscore, the gendered tensions of class, religion, age, and opportunity that these films otherwise only hint at. In other words, "*Caramel* embraces both contemporary consumerist chick flick themes and the affective energies of traditional women's genres—while steering clear of overt framing in terms of contemporary Arab feminisms" (121). As White argues, "this gendering facilitated the film's circulation and in doing so challenged masculinist discourses of the nation" (ibid.). Through their softly coded textual representations, which catalyze their tremendous global mobility, films like *Caramel* actively geopoliticize the homosocial spaces of the romantic comedy genre.

White's gesture to accent the romantic comedy machine further reveals the broader feminist stakes of her argument. Romantic comedies have repeatedly been cast out as bad objects—as emblems of "postfeminism," or of depoliticized, neoliberal, and popular feminisms—according to key feminist texts such as Angela McRobbie's *Aftermath of Feminism* and Yvonne Tasker's *Interrogating Postfeminism*.[24] By situating the homosocial spaces of the romantic comedy in relation to their geopolitical circulation and overcoded cultural contexts, White points to another way in which this quintessential women's genre might continue to produce feminist counter-readings.

Other possibilities persist as well: White's interpretations of queer coding and lesbian desire, the subject of her first book, *Uninvited: Classical Hollywood Cinema and Lesbian Representability* (1999),[25] are especially sharp here in her focus on women's genres, and again take center stage in "Network Narratives: Asian Women Directors." Given the immense, rising, global visibility of Asian cinema since the 1980s, which has fostered the international stardom of directors like Chen Kaige, Zhang Yimou, and Hou Hsiao-Hsen, White asks what kinds of transnational audiences are envisioned in films made by Asian women directors? "Indeed, neither catalogs of women's contributions to national cinemas nor auteurist studies alone can account for the creativity and impact of Asian women's filmmaking today" (133). White uses the term "network narratives" to theorize the flexible address of women's films with multiple, linked storylines to transnational queer and feminist audiences. Zero Chou's *Spider Lilies* (2007) and *Drifting Flowers* (2008), both lesbian love stories that evoke incompatible gazes, and Nia Dinata's *Love for Share* (2006), a somewhat humorous indictment of Indonesian polygamy, provide the exemplary texts for White's case studies of networked narrative form and circulation.

Again, White's analysis encompasses local geopolitics (such as Taiwanese and Indonesian gay civil rights activism), international film festival exhibition (ranging from the Seoul International Women's Film Festival to Berlin and San Francisco), and special-interest distribution networks (such as Women Make Movies and Wolfe Video). White teases out these films' conflicting modes of discourse: from sexually stylized gay advocacy, to subtler instances of lesbian coding that allow queer films to forge surprising patterns of reception and recognition—and to find their ways to unanticipated audiences. For example, Chou's films address contradictory Chinese-language, global art house, and LGBTQ special-interest groups. "With regard to national recognition, Chou can again be regarded as a flexible author. Her films signify as authentically lesbian and authentically Chinese, without being so specific that they cannot travel" (151). This idea of women's "flexible authorship" in many ways extends from White's problematized embrace of film authorship, a crucial focus of chapter 1, while adapting her consideration of authorship to account for the cultural and commercial constraints of international film markets.

To situate this link between auteurist and flexible modes of women's film authorship, White draws on alternative theories of how gender and authorship are signified in Chinese cinema. Two key references here include Rey Chow's notion of "primitive passions"[26]— the traditional forms that encode sexuality in Chinese cinema—and Lingzhen Wang's groundbreaking work on the aesthetic politics of multiple modernities in Chinese women's cinema.[27] However, what is truly new about White's analysis is her attempt to situate Asian women's films not just through their flexible address to transnational audiences, but in relation to other spaces and locations of non-Eurocentric women's filmmaking. The metaphor of the network, iconized in Chou's filmmaking, represents a visual encoding that goes beyond difference and sexuality: it links up with disparate collectivities of transcultural film production through multifarious feminist networks of film reception and distribution (such as Wolfe and WMM). White's textual interpretations of networked narrative form thereby interlock with her detailed accounts of the actual feminist networks through which these film images circulate.

If Asian women's cinema capitalizes on the flexibility and multiplicity of its unstable reception frameworks, human rights films seem to presume that "The Whole World Is Watching." White's final chapter, rhetorically titled "Is the Whole World Watching? Fictions of Women's Human Rights," traces the gendered tensions between local context and global mobility, which are made "visible with some urgency, as they concern women's human rights violations and attempt to convey the specificity of the perspectives from which they are experienced" (169). A crucial intervention of this chapter is its timely critique of the cynicism with which humanitarian appeals are often spurned by Western critics, who too easily dismiss rather than problematize the false transparency and melodramatic victimization enlisted in gendered depictions of humanitarian urgency.

White neither valorizes nor condemns women's regional filmmaking for catering to a Eurocentric gaze. Rather, she rightly and importantly emphasizes the severe limitations of cynical ideology critique as an altogether unsatisfying alternative to unproblematized ethnography. Instead, White offers imaginative new strategies in reading film, both aesthetically and geopolitically. "I want to argue that filmmakers do more than stand in for national problems . . . their works push back against objectifying funding directives and exhibition patterns" (173) and therefore must not be "taxed with resolving the contradiction between the universal and the particular" (170). In other words, the overcoded aesthetics of these films both emerge from and respond to their contradictory geopolitics. They thereby have the power to challenge the humanitarian fantasies of immediacy and of transparent identification between Western spectator and Third World Other that they might otherwise authorize.

This is further central to what White means by projection: "Projecting Contemporary Feminisms" looks beyond the defensive desires of the ego to foreground the very incommensurability of looks and address that these women's films orchestrate. White reflects on Priya Jaikumar's reading of a foundational text,[28] Gayatri Spivak's "Can the Subaltern Speak?,"[29] as a theoretical discourse on cinematic ethnography. What would it mean for a filmmaking subject to be recognized on her own terms? Instead, Jaikumar emphasizes the filmmaker's right to speak on behalf of her subject: to make a film that gives voice to the silences it represents—without overwriting them. Pakistani filmmaker Subiha Sumar's German-French coproduction *Silent Waters* (2003), according to Jaikumar and White, attempts precisely this aim: to foreground the limits of what can be articulated on another's behalf. Sumar's film depicts the patriarchal and fundamentalist violence against women that erupted during General Zia's rise to power in Pakistan in 1979. White associates Sumar's film with non-Eurocentric geneaologies of "post-Third-Worldist" (to invoke Ella Shohat's term)[30] feminist cinemas: films by women directors including Sara Gomez (Cuba), Assia Djebar (Algeria), and Sarah Maldoror (Angola) that resist allegorizing woman as nation in order to reflect upon the complexities of their transnational solicitations.

This gendered entitlement to represent another's own difference, as White emphasizes, comes with tremendous responsibility, the logistics of which must unfold over time. For example, Jasmila Zbanič's Bosnian film *Grbavica* (2006) tells the story a mother whose adolescent daughter, unbeknown to the daughter, was conceived through rape in a prisoner of war camp during the Bosnian War. This film, White argues, exemplifies the "incommensurable gazes" (181) of world cinema that women's cinema today has inherited. Zbanič herself attended Sarajevo's Academy of Performing Arts, where, during wartime, the world outside the academy was no less imaginable than the representation of cinema itself. Zbanič reflects on her film education: "'There was a war raging in the country while I was studying, and we did not have neither [sic] electricity nor cinemas for three and a half years. The studying itself was quite absurd. . . . We actually studied by imagining films'" (182). Conjuring her removed experiences of the Bosnian War through her a-cinematic education in cinema, Zbanič chases after the unrepresentability of ethnic genocide in her filmmaking by focusing on the vicissitudes of its memory one generation later: the coming-of-age of a child conceived through rape in a prisoner of war camp.

Peruvian filmmaker Claudia Llosa poses a similar dilemma, through very different cinematic strategies, in *Milk for Sorrow* (2009): an Oscar nominated musical comedy–drama, in which an indigenous Andean woman's fatal memories of Peruvian Civil War become transmittable to her daughter via breast milk. This film, in its self-conscious aesthetics and transnational address, is utterly emblematic for White's study: "Llosa's work inhabits the spaces of contemporary world cinema . . . fancifully register[ing] the effects of the recent past on the bodies of the next generation" (187). Llosa's previous film, *Madeinusa* (2006), similarly depicts the irreducibly local story of an indigenous Andean woman, Madeinusa, the film's ironically named eponym. The character's name apparently derives from a T-shirt logo that she wears, symbolizing the satirical gap between her marks of American origin and her Andean indigencity. Similarly, Madeinusa's interactions with foreign visitors during the carnivalesque festivities of Holy Week anticipate the film's own cultural visibility and vast circulation beyond its immediate Peruvian contexts and local frames of reception. *Milk for Sorrow* forges quite a path: from local Quechuan-language testimony, to fledgling Peruvian domestic industry, to prestigious international awards circuits, to universal humanitarian advocacy, to neoliberal global reception and consumption.

What Llosa playfully foregrounds, and what White teases out and theorizes, are the decentered patterns of global media transmission that go beyond mere cultural appropriation. By explaining, describing, and interpreting these complex lineages of transnational feminist mediation, White provides a helpful vocabulary and a rich array of examples for asserting the very gendered stakes of film's proliferating and accelerated transnational geopolitics.

FEMINIST GEOPOLITICS "COULD CHANGE THE WORLD"

This is a must-read book for a wide variety of audiences. White's writing, rich and densely coded, avoids overly specialized terminology: her words speak broadly to media scholars, students, activists, feminists, filmmakers, and film lovers. White has the unique ability as a writer to reformulate a different vision of her entire argument with every new idea or example, but without overwhelming the clarity of any specific point or insight. This is the rhetoric of multiplying appeals that White has been tracing across non-Western, feature-length fiction films by a new generation of women filmmakers. Reading this book feels like a comprehensive experience in learning how to read the world differently: as a gendered effect of the incommensurability of too many forms of difference to encompass within a universal structure (be it cinematic, psychosexual, linguistic, or sovereign)—yet that must nonetheless be grappled with in their provisional geopolitical and feminist totality.

In 1981, Mary Ann Doane located the project of feminist film theory at the crossroads of women's films: between their "possession" and "address."[31] The political problem stemmed from the failure of Hollywood narrative films made for women, in effect, to speak as women. If anything, now, the opposite seems to be the problem: films attempt to speak as women too much, but often by way of images explicitly not made for the women whose voices they ventriloquize. In order to confront these deep-rooted vicissitudes between possession and address—and to track them through a dauntingly expanded, global field of women's filmmaking—*Women's Cinema, World Cinema* navigates exhaustively between aesthetic inscription (address), regional cultural context (possession), and the multidirectional networks that mediate between these two entities. White eloquently and incisively lays out the agenda, through her careful and resonant case studies, her comprehensive map of feminist film theory's relation to world cinema scholarship, and her thoughtfully provocative close readings: today the world, tomorrow women's cinema.

Maggie Hennefeld is an assistant professor of cultural studies and comparative literature at the University of Minnesota, Twin Cities. She is the author of *Specters of Slapstick and Silent Film Comediennes* (2018) and coeditor of two forthcoming volumes: *The Abject Objection* and *Unwatchable*.

Notes

1. Nataša Durovicová and Kathleen E. Newman, *World Cinemas, Transnational Perspectives* (New York: Routledge, 2010); Lúcia Nagib, Chris Perriam, and Rajinder Kumar Dudrah, *Theorizing World Cinema* (London: I.B. Tauris, 2012); Karl Schoonover and Rosalind Galt, *Queer Cinema in the World* (Durham: Duke University Press, 2016).

2. Fredric Jameson, *The Geopolitical Aesthetic: Cinema and Space in the World System* (Bloomington: Indiana University Press, 1992).

3. Hamid Naficy, *An Accented Cinema: Exilic and Diasporic Filmmaking* (Princeton: Princeton University Press, 2001).

4. Although concerned primarily with twenty-first century, non-Western cinemas, White's feminist intervention into the vicissitudes of female film authorship could not be more timely. There has been a recent proliferation of excellent monographs written by women about individual female filmmakers. See Shelley Stamp, *Lois Weber in Early Hollywood* (Berkeley: University of California Press, 2015); Tami Williams, *Germaine Dulac: A Cinema of Sensations* (Urbana-Champaign: University of Illinois Press, 2015); Sarah Keller, *Maya Deren: Incomplete Control* (New York: Columbia University Press, 2015).

5. Laura Horak, *Girls Will Be Boys: Cross-Dressed Women, Lesbians, and American Cinema, 1908–1934* (New Brunswick, N.J.: Rutgers University Press, 2015); Victoria Duckett, *Seeing Sarah Bernhardt: Performance and Silent Film* (Urbana-Champaign: University of Illinois Press, 2015); Alison Griffiths *Shivers Down Your Spine: Cinema, Museums, and the Immersive View* (New York: Columbia University Press, 2008).

6. Gabrielle Kelly and Cheryl Robson, *Celluloid Ceiling: Women Film Directors Breaking Through* (Twickenham: Supernova Books, 2014); Melissa Silverstein, Elizabeth Harper, Heather McLendon, Eva Krainitzki, Laura Shields, and Emilie Spiegel, *In Her Voice: Women Directors Talk Directing* (California: Women and Hollywood, 2013).

7. Mary Ann Doane, *The Desire to Desire: The Woman's Film of the 1940s* (Bloomington: Indiana University Press, 1987); Laura Mulvey, *Visual and Other Pleasures* (Bloomington: Indiana University Press, 1989); Judith Mayne, *The Woman at the Keyhole: Feminism and Women's Cinema* (Bloomington: Indiana University Press, 1990); Teresa De Lauretis, *Alice Doesn't: Feminism, Semiotics, Cinema* (Bloomington: Indiana University Press, 1984).

8. Apparatus theory refers to a movement in film studies to interpret the ideological structures of the film apparatus in relation to the implied spectator's unconscious desires. Key texts by theorists such Jean-Louis Baudry, Jean-Luc Comolli, Christian Metz, Stephen Heath, Laura Mulvey, and Kaja Silverman draw extensively on semiotic, Marxist, and psychoanalytic theories.

9. Martha Lauzen, "The Celluloid Ceiling: Behind-the-Scenes Employment of Women on the Top 250 Films of 2014." http://womenintvfilm.sdsu.edu/files/2014_Celluloid_Ceiling_Report.pdf.

10. Jane Campion won Cannes's top prize, "The Palme d'Or" ("Golden Apple"), in 1993 for her film *The Piano*.

11. "The 25 Best Films by Female Directors," Raindance.org.

12. V. Renée, "68 Films Directed by Women That You Can't Afford to Miss," Nofilmschool.com.

13. *Seven Beauties* (Lina Wertmueller, 1976), *Tomboy* (Celine Sciamma, 2011), *Pariah* (Dee Rees, 2011), *Wadjda* (Haifaa al-Mansour, 2011), *The Square* (Jehane Noujaim, 2013), *Big* (Penny Marshall, 1988), *Lost in Translation* (Sofia Coppola, 2003), *The Ascent* (Larisa Shepitko, 1977), and *The Hurt Locker* (Kathryn Bigelow, 2009).

14. Linda Wengraf and Susan Artel, *Positive Images: Non-Sexist Films for Young People* (San Francisco: Booklegger Press, 1976).

15. Diane Waldman, "There's More to a Positive Image Than Meets the Eye." In *Jump Cut: A Review of Contemporary Media,* no. 18 (August 1978): 31–32.

16. Steve Neale, "Art Cinema as Institution," *Screen* 22, no. 1 (1981): 11–40.

17. Claire Johnston, "Women's Cinema as Counter Cinema," in *Notes on Women's Cinema,* ed. Claire Johnston (London: Society for Education on Film and Television, 1973).

18. *Suffragette* (Abi Morgan, 2015) uses melodrama to depict the fight for women's suffrage in Britain while inscribing successful campaigns for women's voting enfranchisement in a Eurocentric telos in the closing credits: from New Zealand in 1893 to Saudi Arabia, starting in 2015. *Forbidden Voices* (Barbara Miller, 2012) represents Internet blogging as a utopian feminist discourse that transcends culture or location, focusing on three female bloggers' fight for Human Rights and Freedom of Speech in Cuba, China, and Iran.

19. White historicizes the importance of auteurism in its post–World War II contexts, when directors such as Jean-Luc Godard, Roberto Rossellini, and Akira Kurosawa directly challenged the declining hegemony of the vertically integrated Hollywood studio system.

20. Kirk Honeycutt, "Review of *To Each His Own Cinema,*" *Hollywood Reporter,* May 20, 2007.

21. Alison Butler, *Women's Cinema: The Contested Screen* (London: Wallflower, 2002); Catherine Grant, "Secret Agents: Feminist Theories of Woman's Film Authorship," *Feminist Theory* 2 (April 2001): 113–30.

22. Hélène Cixous, "Castration or Decapitation?," trans. Annette Kuhn, *Signs* 7, no. 1. (Autumn 1981): 41–55.

23. White's notion of women's world cinema as a transnational public sphere is explicitly influenced by Miriam Hansen's theory of early cinema as a feminist public sphere. See Miriam Hansen, *Babel and Babylon: Spectatorship in American Silent Film* (Cambridge, Mass.: Harvard University Press, 1994).

24. Angela McRobbie, *The Aftermath of Feminism: Gender, Culture, and Social Change;* Yvonne Tasker and Diane Negra, *Interrogating Postfeminism: Gender and the Politics of Popular Culture* (Durham: Duke University Press, 2007).

25. Patricia White, *Uninvited: Classical Hollywood Cinema and Lesbian Representability* (Bloomington: Indiana University Press, 1999).

26. Rey Chow, *Primitive Passions: Vision, Sexuality, Ethnography, and Contemporary Chinese Cinema* (New York: Columbia University Press, 1995).

27. Lingzhen Wang, *Chinese Women's Cinema: Transnational Contexts* (New York: Columbia University Press, 2011).

28. Priya Jaikumar, "Translating Silences: A Cinematic Encounter with Incommensurable Difference," in *Transnational Feminism in Film and Media,* ed. Katarzyna Marciniak, Anikó Imre, and Áine O'Healy (New York: Palgrave Macmillan, 2008).

29. Gayatri Chakravorty Spivak and Rosalind C. Morris, *Can the Subaltern Speak? Reflections on the History of an Idea* (New York: Columbia University Press, 2010).

30. Ella Shohat and Robert Stam, *Unthinking Eurocentrism: Multiculturalism and the Media* (London: Routledge, 1994).

31. Mary Anne Doane, "The 'Woman's Film': Possession and Address," in *Re-Vision: Essays in Feminist Film Criticism*, ed. Mary Ann Doane, Patricia Mellencamp, and Linda Williams (Bethesda, Md.: University Publications of America, 1984).

BOOKS RECEIVED

Amin, Kadji. *Disturbing Attachments: Genet, Modern Pederasty, and Queer History*. Durham: Duke University Press, 2017.

Arnold, Gina, and Daniel Cookney, et. al., eds. *Music/Video: Histories, Aesthetics, Media*. New York: Bloomsbury Press, 2017.

Bateman, Benjamin. *The Modernist Art of Queer Survival*. New York: Oxford University Press, 2018.

Bell, Robert C., and Robert M. Ficociello. *America's Disaster Culture: The Production of Natural Disasters in Literature and Pop Culture*. New York: Bloomsbury, 2017.

Bentley, R. Alexander, and Michael J. O'Brien. *The Acceleration of Cultural Change: From Ancestors to Algorithms*. Cambridge, Mass.: MIT Press, 2017.

Borgerson, Janet, and Jonathan Schroeder. *Designed for Hi-Fi Living: The Vinyl LP in Midcentury America*. Cambridge, Mass.: MIT Press, 2017.

Botha, Marc. *A Theory of Minimalism*. New York: Bloomsbury, 2017.

Braziel, Jana Evans. *Riding with Death: Vodou Art and Urban Ecology in the Streets of Port-au-Prince*. Jackson: University of Mississippi Press, 2017.

Brettschneider, Marla, Susan Burgess, et al., eds. *LGBTQ Politics: A Critical Reader*. New York: New York University Press, 2017.

Brown, Trent, ed. *Sex and Sexuality in Modern Southern Culture*. Baton Rouge: Louisiana University Press, 2017.

Burchhardt, Martin, and Dirk Höfer. *All and Nothing: A Digital Apocalypse*. Translated by Erik Butler. Cambridge, Mass.: MIT Press, 2017.

Callaci, Emily. *Street Archives and City Life: Popular Intellectuals in Postcolonial Tanzania*. Durham: Duke University Press, 2017.

Castiglia, Christopher. *The Practices of Hope: Literary Criticism in Disenchanted Times*. New York: New York University Press, 2017.

Chaney, Anthony. *Runaway: Gregory Bateson, the Double Bind, and the Rise of Ecological Consciousness*. Chapel Hill: University of North Carolina Press, 2017.

Cheng, Eileen J., and Kirk A. Denton, eds. *Jottings Under Lamplight: Lu Xun*. Cambridge, Mass.: Harvard University Press, 2017.

Cohen, Kris. *Never Alone Except for Now: Art, Networks, Populations*. Durham: Duke University Press, 2017.

Curtis, Edward E. *The Practice of Islam in America: An Introduction*. New York: New York University Press, 2017.

Debaise, Didier. *Nature as Event: The Lure of the Possible*. Durham: Duke University Press, 2017.

De Lagasnerie, Geoffroy. *The Art of Revolt: Snowden, Assange, Manning*. Stanford: Stanford University Press, 2017.

Dittmer, Jason. *Diplomatic Material: Affect, Assemblage, and Foreign Policy*. Durham: Duke University Press, 2017.

Ellcessor, Elizabeth, and Bill Kirkpatrick, eds. *Disability Media Studies*. New York: New York University Press, 2017.

Fishman, Jessica M. *Death Makes the News: How the Media Censor and Display the Dead*. New York: New York University Press, 2017.

Flores, Tatiana, and Michelle A. Stephens. *Relational Undercurrents: Contemporary Art of the Caribbean Archipelago*. Long Beach, Calif.: Museum of Latin American Art, 2017.

Flores-González, Nilda. *Citizens But Not Americans: Race and Belonging Among Latino Millennials*. New York: New York University Press, 2017.

Foster, Laura A. *Reinventing Hoodia: Peoples, Plants, and Patents in South Africa*. Seattle: University of Washington Press, 2017.

Gago, Verónica. *Neoliberalism from Below: Popular Pragmatics and Baroque Economies*. Durham: Duke University Press, 2017.

Geller, Jay. *Bestiarium Judaicum: Unnatural Histories of the Jews*. New York: Fordham University Press, 2018.

Gómez-Barris, Macarena. *The Extractive Zone: Social Ecologies and Decolonial Perspectives*. Durham: Duke University Press, 2017.

Grewal, Inderpal. *Saving the Security State: Exceptional Citizens in Twenty-First Century America*. Durham: Duke University Press, 2017.

Greyser, Naomi. *On Sympathetic Grounds: Race, Gender, and Affective Geographies in Nineteenth-Century North America*. New York: Oxford University Press, 2018.

Grobe, Christopher. *The Art of Confession: The Performance of Self from Robert Lowell to Reality TV*. New York: New York University Press, 2017.

Han, Byung-Chul. *Shanzhai: Deconstruction in Chinese*. Boston: MIT Press, 2017.

Harol, Corrinne, and Mark Simpson, eds. *Literary/Liberal Entanglements: Toward a Literary History for the Twenty-First Century*. Toronto: University of Toronto Press, 2017.

Herrstrom, David S. *Light as Experience and Imagination from Paleolithic to Roman Times*. Lanham, Md.: Fairleigh Dickinson University Press, 2017.

Highmore, Ben, ed. *The Everyday Life Reader*. New York: Routledge, 2002.

Hoffman, Danny. *Monrovia Modern: Urban Form and Political Imagination in Liberia*. Durham: Duke University Press, 2017.

Hough-Snee, Dexter Zavalza, and Alexander Sotelo Eastman, eds. *The Critical Surf Studies Reader*. Durham: Duke University Press, 2017.

Jarczok, Anita. *Writing an Icon: Celebrity Culture and the Invention of Anaïs Nin*. Athens, Ohio: Swallow Press, 2017.

Josiffe, Christopher. *Gef! The Strange Tale of an Extra-Special Talking Mongoose*. London: Strange Attractor Press, 2017.

Kelley Jr., Bill, and Grant H. Kester, eds. *Collective Situations: Readings in Contemporary Latin American Art, 1995–2010*. Durham: Duke University Press, 2017.

Kelly, Caleb. *Gallery Sound*. New York: Bloomsbury, 2017.

Karatani, Kojin. *Isonomia and the Origins of Philosophy*. Durham: Duke University Press, 2017.

Kent, Eddy, and Terri Tomsky, eds. *Negative Cosmopolitanism: Cultures and Politics of World Citizenship after Globalization*. Montreal: McGill-Queen's University Press, 2017.

Kordela, A. Kiarina. *Epistemontology in Spinoza-Marx-Freud-Lacan: The (Bio)Power of Structure*. New York: Routledge, 2018.

Krouk, Dean. *Fascism and Modernist Literature in Norway*. Seattle: University of Washington Press, 2017.

Lange, Hartmut. *Positive Nihilism: My Confrontation with Heidegger*. Translated by Adrian Nathan West. Boston: MIT Press, 2017.

Lauro, Sarah Juliet. *Zombie Theory: A Reader*. Minneapolis: University of Minnesota Press, 2017.

Lause, Mark. *The Great Cowboy Strike: Bullets, Ballots, and Class Conflicts in the American West*. New York: Verso, 2017.

Lewis, Nathaniel, and Stephen Tatum. *Morta Las Vegas: CSI and the Problem of the West*. Lincoln: University of Nebraska Press, 2017.

Lifschitz, Avi, and Michael Squire, eds. *Rethinking Lessing's Laocoon: Antiquity, Enlightenment, and the 'Limits' of Painting and Poetry*. New York: Oxford University Press, 2017.

Lowney, John. *Jazz Internationalism: Literary Afro-Modernism and the Cultural Politics of Black Music*. Urbana: University of Illinois Press, 2017.

Mangharam, Mukti Lakhi. *Literatures of Liberation: Non-European Universalisms and Democratic Progress*. Columbus: Ohio State University Press, 2017.

McGuire, Elizabeth. *Red at Heart: How Chinese Communists Fell in Love with the Russian Revolution*. New York: Oxford University Press, 2018.

Menely, Tobias, and Jesse Oak Taylor, eds. *Anthropocene Reading: Literary History in Geologic Times*. University Park: Pennsylvania State University Press, 2017.

Miller, Daniel. *The Comfort of People*. Medford, Mass.: Polity Press, 2017.

Miller, Ruth A. *The Biopolitics of Embryos and Alphabets: A Reproductive History of the Nonhuman*. New York: Oxford University Press, 2017.

Moten, Fred. *Black and Blur*. Durham: Duke University Press, 2017.

Nguyen, Viet Thanh. *Nothing Ever Dies: Vietnam and the Memory of War*. Cambridge, Mass.: Harvard University Press, 2016.

O'Gorman, Francis. *Forgetfulness: Making the Modern Culture of Amnesia*. New York: Bloomsbury, 2017.

Parks, Lisa, and Caren Kaplan, eds. *Life in the Age of Drone Warfare*. Durham: Duke University Press, 2017.

Patel, Geeta. *Risky Bodies and Techno-Intimacy: Reflections on Sexuality, Media, Science, Finance*. Seattle: University of Washington Press, 2016.

Pilsch, Andrew. *Transhumanism: Evolutionary Futurism and the Human Technologies of Utopia*. Minneapolis: University of Minnesota Press, 2017.

Price, Brian. *A Theory of Regret*. Durham: Duke University Press, 2017.

Puar, Jasbir K. *The Right to Maim: Debility, Capacity, Disability*. Durham: Duke University Press, 2017.

Rabinow, Paul. *Unconsolable Contemporary: Observing Gerhard Richter*. Durham: Duke University Press, 2017.

Ryersson, Scot D., and Michael Orlando Yaccarino. *Infinite Variety: The Life and Legend of Marchesa Casati*. Minneapolis: University of Minnesota Press, 2017.

Sahlins, Peter. *1668: The Year of the Animal in France*. New York: Zone Books, 2017.

Schaberg, Christopher. *Airportness: The Nature of Flight*. New York: Bloomsbury, 2017.

Schaefer, William. *Shadow Modernism: Photography, Writing, and Space in Shanghai, 1925–1937*. Durham: Duke University Press, 2017.

Schrimshaw, Will. *Immanence and Immersion: On the Acoustic Condition in Contemporary Art*. New York: Bloomsbury, 2017.

See, Sarita Echavez. *The Filipino Primitive: Accumulation and Resistance in the American Museum*. New York: New York University Press, 2017.

Shepherd, Philip. *Radical Wholeness: The Embodied Present and the Ordinary Grace of Being*. Berkeley: North Atlantic Books, 2017.

Simpson, Leanne Betasamosake. *As We Have Always Done: Indigenous Freedom through Radical Resistance*. Minneapolis: University of Minnesota Press, 2017.

Smith, Angela M. *Hideous Progeny: Disability, Eugenics, and Classic Horror Cinema*. New York: Columbia University Press, 2011.

Squier, Susan Merrill. *Epigentic Landscapes: Drawing as Metaphor*. Durham: Duke University Press, 2017.

Stearns, Peter N. *Shame: A Brief History*. Chicago: University of Illinois Press, 2017.

Steinweg, Marcus. *Inconsistencies*. Translated by Amanda Demarco. Cambridge, Mass.: MIT Press, 2017.

Strathausen, Carsten. *Bioaesthetics: Making Sense of Life in Science and the Arts*. Minneapolis: University of Minnesota Press, 2017.

Terry, Jennifer. *Attachments to War: Biomedical Logics and Violence in Twenty-First Century America*. Durham: Duke University Press, 2017.

Ungureanu, Delia. *From Paris to Tlön: Surrealism as World Literature*. New York: Bloomsbury, 2018.

Vargas, Deborah R., et al., eds. *Keywords for Latina/o Studies*. New York: New York University Press, 2017.

Walworth, Catherine. *Soviet Salvage: Imperial Debris, Revolutionary Reuse, and Russian Constructivism*. University Park: Pennsylvania State University Press, 2017.

Wang, Ban, ed. *Chinese Visions of World Order: Tianxia, Culture, and World Politics*. Durham: Duke University Press, 2017.

Zahlten, Alexander. *The End of Japanese Cinema: Industrial Genres, National Times, and Media Ecologies*. Durham: Duke University Press, 2017.

Žižek, Slavoj. *Incontinence of the Void: Economico-Philosophical Spandrels*. Boston: MIT Press, 2017.

Zupančič, Alenka. *What Is Sex?* Cambridge, Mass.: MIT Press, 2017.

NEW FROM MINNESOTA